MARCUS CALDWELL

Battles of the Ages: World War II 1940

Contents

The War Escalates

As the first light of 1940 dawned, the world was already caught in the throes of a conflict that would irrevocably alter the course of history. This year, a pivotal chapter in the narrative of the Second World War, was characterized by battles that not only redefined the nature of modern warfare but also left an indelible mark on the human saga. This introduction takes you through the tumultuous events of 1940, a year where strategy, heroism, and tragedy were intimately entwined on the global stage.

1940 was not merely another year; it was the crucible of conflict, testing the resilience of the human spirit. The battles of this year transcended geographical boundaries, impacting the lives of millions. From the frigid expanses of Scandinavia to the arid deserts of North Africa, from the aerial battlegrounds over Britain to the war-torn streets of France, the war touched every corner of the Earth.

The year commenced with the world in a state of apprehensive calm. Following the dramatic events of 1939, including the invasion of Poland and the subsequent declarations of war by Britain and France against Germany, a significant escalation seemed inevitable. Yet, the early months of 1940 were deceptively tranquil, a period often referred to as the "Phoney War," as the primary combatants amassed their forces in anticipation of the decisive moment to strike.

This deceptive peace was a time of intense strategic planning. Allied forces, mainly comprising British and French troops, fortified their positions along the Maginot Line, bracing for a repeat of the trench warfare that had characterized the First World War. Meanwhile, Germany, under Adolf Hitler's regime, was perfecting Blitzkrieg, a revolutionary form of warfare aiming for swift victories through a combination of rapid infantry movements, armored advances, and air support.

The facade of peace was shattered in the spring of 1940 when the German Wehrmacht unleashed its Blitzkrieg campaign. Denmark and Norway fell in April, followed by the astonishingly quick defeat of Belgium, the Netherlands, and Luxembourg in May. However, the Battle of France was the centerpiece of Germany's 1940 campaign, a stunning display of military prowess and strategic ingenuity.

Defying conventional military logic, Germany bypassed the heavily fortified Maginot Line, instead sweeping through the Ardennes Forest, deemed impassable by most military experts. This audacious strategy caught the Allies off guard, culminating in the encirclement and subsequent evacuation of hundreds of thousands of Allied soldiers from Dunkirk - an operation that became a beacon of hope and resistance.

1940's warfare wasn't confined to land. The Battle of Britain, a significant aerial conflict between the Royal Air Force and the German Luftwaffe, marked Hitler's first major defeat and showcased air power as a decisive factor in modern combat. Concurrently, the Battle of the Atlantic was underway, with Allied navies striving to protect crucial supply routes against relentless German U-boat assaults. This maritime struggle was a testament to endurance, innovation, and strategic intelligence.

Amid these strategic maneuvers and military victories, the human toll was staggering. Cities lay in ruins, civilians were uprooted, and societies were torn asunder. The year 1940 revealed the extremes of human nature, from extraordinary bravery and sacrifice to unspeakable cruelty and destruction.

The events of 1940 are a reminder of the complexities of human conflict, ambition, and power. These battles were more than isolated incidents; they were part of a larger narrative that continues to resonate. They underscore the importance of strategic foresight, the impact of technological innovation in warfare, and the enduring resilience of the human spirit.

As we delve into the events of this pivotal year, we are reminded that history is not just a collection of dates and battle names. It's a tapestry woven from the complexities of human nature and the forces that propel us toward conflict. The year 1940, with its darkness and glimmers of hope, courage, and determination, is a chapter in our collective history that demands to be remembered, analyzed, and understood, offering lessons as relevant today as they were over eight decades ago.

Operation Weserübung

In the tense prelude to World War II, the British Admiralty, aware of the brewing storm, eyed Scandinavia in 1939 as a pivotal battleground against Germany. Seeking to avoid the bloody trenches of the previous war, Britain mulled a cunning blockade strategy to indirectly cripple Germany's iron-reliant industry. The crux of this plan hinged on the strategic Norwegian port of Narvik, a vital artery for Swedish iron ore exports during winter.

Meanwhile, sensing a threat, Grand Admiral Erich Raeder of the German Kriegsmarine warned Hitler in October 1939 of the peril posed by potential British bases in Norway. He argued that controlling Norway was key to dominating the surrounding seas and launching crippling submarine assaults on the UK. However, this naval strategy initially found little enthusiasm among other German military branches, with Hitler favoring a land offensive through the Low Countries.

As winter approached, the narrative took a dramatic turn with Winston Churchill, newly inducted into the British War Cabinet, proposing a bold move: Operation Wilfred. By mining Norwegian waters, Churchill aimed to reroute German ore shipments into the vulnerable expanses of the North Sea, right into the clutches of the Royal Navy. He anticipated a German counter-move in Norway, setting the stage for the Allies' Plan R 4 to seize Norwegian territories. However, fearing international backlash from neutrals like the USA, Neville Chamberlain and Lord Halifax initially shelved the plan. The situation evolved with the onset of the Soviet–Finnish Winter War, prompting Churchill to push his mining strategy again, only to be rebuffed once more.

In a strategic shift, by December 1939, Britain and France devised a plan to aid Finland, envisioning a daring landing at Narvik to cut off the iron ore lifeline and seize control of the vital railway to Sweden. This plan, intriguingly, also presented an opportunity to occupy the rich Swedish mines. Chamberlain and Halifax supported this, banking on Norwegian cooperation to sidestep legal quandaries. However, Germany's stern warnings to Norway and Sweden sparked vehement objections from both, complicating the Allied designs. The expedition continued to be planned in the shadows, but its raison d'être faded with the signing of the Moscow Peace Treaty in March 1940, ending the Winter War.

After a pivotal discussion with Norwegian Vidkun Quisling on December 14, Hitler's focus shifted dramatically towards Scandinavia. Alarmed by the Allied threat to Germany's crucial iron ore supplies, Hitler directed the Oberkommando der Wehrmacht to commence initial planning for a Norwegian invasion. This early strategy, dubbed Studie Nord, ambitiously envisaged employing just one army division.

From January 14 to 19, the Kriegsmarine refined this plan, prioritizing two critical elements: the element of surprise to minimize Norwegian resistance and British interference, and the use of swift German warships over slower merchant vessels for troop deployment. This approach aimed for a simultaneous occupation of all targets. The revised plan was more ambitious, calling for a complete army corps including specialized units like a mountain division, an airborne division, a motorized rifle brigade, and two infantry divisions. This force aimed to seize key Norwegian cities: Oslo, Bergen, Narvik, Tromsø, Trondheim, Kristiansand, and Stavanger, with a strategic move to quickly capture the Danish and Norwegian kings, hoping for an expedited capitulation.

By February 21, 1940, General Nikolaus von Falkenhorst was appointed to lead the operation. A veteran of Arctic warfare from World War I, he was, however, limited to commanding ground forces, diverging from Hitler's preference for unified command.

The operation, now code-named "Operation Weserübung," was finalized on January 27, 1940. It involved the XXI Army Corps, including the 3rd Mountain Division and five infantry divisions, many untested in battle. The initial assault phase would deploy three divisions, with the rest following. Also, three companies of paratroopers were allocated to capture airfields. Later, the 2nd Mountain Division was added to the plan.

The operation necessitated a significant shift in U-boat activities; virtually all Atlantic U-boat operations were halted to support the operation. Submarines, including training units, were mobilized for Operation Hartmut to back Operation Weserübung.

Originally, the plan was to invade Norway and diplomatically secure Danish airfields. However, on March 1, at the Luftwaffe's behest, Hitler amended the directive to invade both Norway and Denmark, aiming to seize fighter bases and air warning stations. The XXXI Corps, formed specifically for the Danish invasion, comprised two infantry divisions and the 11th motorized brigade. The entire operation would be bolstered by the X Air Corps, deploying around 1,000 aircraft of various types.

In a bold move that escalated tensions, the Royal Navy's HMS Cossack boarded the German transport Altmark in Norwegian waters in February, a clear breach of Norway's neutrality. The Altmark, holding British prisoners of war, also violated Norwegian neutrality by not releasing them upon entering neutral territory. Hitler saw the British response to Germany's disregard for Norwegian neutrality as a sign that the Allies were equally willing to overstep boundaries, further fueling his determination to invade Norway.

On March 12, as the Winter War neared its end, the United Kingdom resolved to deploy an expeditionary force to Norway. The force began embarking on March 13, but the operation was swiftly aborted due to the Winter War's conclusion. Instead, the British Cabinet greenlit a plan to mine Norwegian waters, setting the stage for subsequent troop landings.

Operation Wilfred, long in the planning stages, was finally initiated on April 5, 1940. The Royal Navy, spearheaded by the battlecruiser HMS Renown, departed from Scapa Flow to lay mines in Norwegian waters. German forces, meanwhile, embarked on their invasion, setting sail on April 7 at 3:00 a.m. By the early hours of April 8, the Royal Navy had successfully mined Vestfjorden. Although Operation Wilfred concluded, the destroyer HMS Glowworm, which had detached on April 7 to search for a man overboard, was tragically lost in a confrontation with the German cruiser Admiral Hipper and two destroyers from the invading German fleet.

On April 9, the German invasion kicked into full gear, prompting the immediate initiation of Plan R 4 by the Allies.

Invasion of Denmark

On the eve of battle, the Danish army found itself in a precarious position. Despite forewarnings of a German onslaught, the Danish government, wary of provoking their formidable adversary, forbade any form of military deployment or defensive preparations. Thus, when the moment of truth arrived, only a handful of troops from the frontier guard and the Jutland division stood ready to face the invaders.

As dawn broke on April 9, the Germans made their move. Penetrating the Danish border at Sæd, Rens, Padborg, and Krusaa at 04:15, they simultaneously launched a maritime assault at Lillebælt. This pincer move effectively isolated Danish forces at the border. The alarm blared at 04:17, and by 04:35, Danish troops were frantically mobilizing to confront the enemy.

The first fiery encounter erupted at Lundtoftbjerg. Here, a Danish anti-tank unit, armed with two 20mm cannons and a light machine gun, lay in wait. As the German column appeared at 04:50, the Danish guns roared to life, blasting at the armored cars and motorcyclists. A barn caught fire in the melee, its smoke clouding the battlefield and slowing the German advance. Despite their valiant efforts, the Danes were compelled to fall back to Aabenraa. A few kilometers to the north, Danish bicyclists braced to defend a railway bridge but were quickly overwhelmed by armored assaults and strafing fighter planes, leading to heavy casualties and captures. The Germans, however, weren't unscathed, losing two armored cars and three motorcycles.

The drama continued at Hokkerup, where, at 05:30, another German column ran into a hastily erected roadblock by 34 Danish soldiers. The Danes valiantly disabled the leading German armored cars, but the tide turned when the Germans brought in a 37mm gun. It managed only a single shot before being silenced by the Danes' 20mm gun. In the ensuing close-quarter combat, casualties mounted on both sides. Ultimately, with air support, the German forces encircled and captured the outnumbered Danish defenders.

At the crack of dawn, about seven kilometers north of Lundtoftbjerg, a tense scene unfolded in Bjergskov around 05:00. Lieutenant Colonel S.E. Clausen led his motorcycle and two bicycle platoons into position. The motorcyclists quickly erected a roadblock, armed with two 20 mm guns, while their comrades dispersed into the surrounding woods. But at 06:30, a German column thundered in. Their tanks bulldozed through the roadblock and unleashed a hail of fire. One Danish gun heroically fired back until it was crushed under a tank. Its gunner, fleeing for the woods, fell under the strafing fire of a German aircraft. The second gun jammed, leaving the Danes vulnerable. In a desperate bid for escape, they revved their motorcycles, but the Germans, in a swift encircling maneuver with armored vehicles, ensnared them. This encounter left four Danish soldiers wounded and one German armored car damaged.

Meanwhile, in Bredevad, 10 kilometers north of the border, a fierce clash erupted. The Danish forces arrived at 6:30 AM, scrambling for cover in a garden without enough time to set up a roadblock. Armed with a machine gun and a 20 mm cannon, the Danish platoon fired warning shots at the approaching German vanguard of four armored cars. Ignored, they unleashed a barrage from 300 meters away, taking out the lead German vehicle and its driver. A heated skirmish ensued, with the Danes valiantly disabling three more armored cars but suffering four casualties. At 07:15, the situation escalated as a German motorized column from Tinglev arrived, cutting off the Danes and forcing their surrender, adding two more Danish fatalities and five wounded to the day's grim tally.

In Rabsted, a cyclist platoon from Korskro arrived at 6:45. Lying in ambush, they managed a small victory, capturing two German dispatch riders. However, upon learning of Bredevad's fall, they swiftly retreated northeastward along secondary roads, narrowly evading the tightening grip of the German advance.

In a flurry of action, the Danish troops at Søgaard army camp were hastily retreating north to Vejle, where the heart of the Jutland Division was bracing for a major confrontation. Amidst this retreat, a skirmish erupted at Aabenraa. The anti-tank platoon from Lundtoftbjerg, not yet ready to relinquish their ground, boldly engaged around 15 German vehicles in hot pursuit. After knocking out a German tank, they withdrew to Knivsberg, joining forces with a battered bicycle platoon from Stubbæk Skov, which had already faced the wrath of German aircraft, losing one soldier and suffering three wounded. The Danish Commanding Officer promptly redirected them towards northern Haderslev, adjusting to the rapidly evolving battlefield.

Haderslev was a scene of grim determination. Here, 225 men of the Jutland Division, led by Colonel A. Hartz, stood guard, defending the barracks and the town's approach. At 07:00, spurred into action by police loudspeaker announcements, the town's troops mobilized. Reinforced by retreating units, about 400 Danes fortified Haderslev, hastily erecting three roadblocks from whatever materials they could muster.

The battle reached a fever pitch around 07:50 at the southern edge of Haderslev. A Danish 37 mm anti-tank gun, manned by a crew of five, confronted the advancing German armor. Two German tanks, side by side, unleashed a barrage. The Danish gunners, with remarkable precision, landed all three shots, crippling one tank, but at a tragic cost – two gunners were killed, and the others wounded. The remaining tank ruthlessly crushed the Danish gun.

Further along Sønderbro Street, a desperate standoff ensued at the wagon roadblock. Two 20 mm cannons and a machine gun, manned by determined Danes, held the line against a torrent of German fire. The skirmish, fierce but brief, saw one Danish soldier fall and two wounded, yet they managed to pin down the German advance.

But as the clock ticked towards 08:15, the battle took a sudden turn. A surrender order from Copenhagen reached the troops, halting the fighting. The Germans cautiously advanced into Haderslev, unaware that the Danish garrison in the barracks hadn't yet received the surrender directive. As two German tanks and a motorcycle approached, the anti-tank unit from Lundtoftbjerg, lying in wait, sprung their ambush. A motorcyclist fell, and a tank was blasted off its tracks, crashing into a nearby house. But the resistance was fleeting. The order to surrender permeated the ranks, and by 08:15, the Danish defense at the barracks ceased. In this final stand, one Danish soldier and three civilians paid the ultimate price, their lives lost in the crossfire of a town caught in the tumult of war.

In the early hours of conflict in Western Jutland, the stage was set for a fierce standoff. The Tønder garrison, dispatched to Abild and Sølsted, was about to face the advancing German 11th Motorized Regiment. In Abild, a Danish 20 mm gun crew displayed remarkable prowess, disabling two

German armored cars before strategically withdrawing. The scene at Sølsted was equally intense: a Danish anti-tank unit, less than 50 strong, braced for impact. As the first German armored car rolled into their crosshairs, they unleashed a devastating strike, sending it tumbling into a ditch. The following vehicle pressed on, exchanging fire with the Danes, but had to retreat after sustaining damage. The German infantry's attempts to flank the Danish positions were met with a wall of resistance, their advances stymied by relentless Danish gunfire.

But the tide turned as the German regimental commander called for aerial backup. Soon, three German Henschel Hs 126 aircraft swooped in, raining bombs and gunfire on the Danish defenders. Despite the ferocity of this airborne onslaught, the Danes miraculously reported no casualties. Forced to fall back to Bredebro, they soon received the sobering news of the order to capitulate, bringing an abrupt end to their valiant stand.

Meanwhile, at approximately 05:00, history witnessed its first-ever paratrooper attack. 96 Fallschirmjäger, Germany's elite paratroopers, descended from nine Junkers Ju 52 planes, aiming to seize control of the strategic Storstrøm Bridge and the Masnedø island fortress. Contrary to their expectations of fierce resistance, they found the fortress minimally guarded, much to their astonishment.

Two hours later, another chapter unfolded in Aalborg, northern Jutland's principal city. Here, paratroopers from the 4th battalion of Fallschirmjäger Regiment I landed to secure a critical objective for Operation Weserübung Süd: the Aalborg airfield. This key location was to be a vital launchpad for the invasion of Norway. Remarkably, they met no resistance, and within an hour, the airfield was bustling with German aircraft. Over 200 landings and takeoffs were recorded on that first day alone, a flurry of activity facilitating the transport of troops and supplies to Norway's Fornebu Airport.

In a solitary act of defiance, a 75mm anti-aircraft gun in Esbjerg scored a hit on a German aircraft, a small but symbolic blow against the overwhelming might of the German war machine.

In a strategic move to sever the crucial links between Jutland and Zealand (Sjælland), the Kriegsmarine launched a swift operation. Troops from the 198th Infantry Division poured onto the shores of Funen, quickly gaining control of this vital landmass.

Simultaneously, a more dramatic scene unfolded as troops, bolstered by the imposing presence of the battleship Schleswig-Holstein, landed in Korsør and Nyborg. This bold maneuver effectively cut off any connection between Funen and Zealand. Encountering no resistance, the troops in Korsør marched unopposed towards Copenhagen, reaching the capital by noon.

Just hours before, at 03:55, Gedser - Denmark's southernmost city - woke up to a startling surprise attack. The Germans ingeniously used a local ferry from Warnemünde, packing it with soldiers. This unexpected invasion force swiftly disembarked, severing communication lines and pouring into the city with armor and motorcycles. In a rapid advance, they joined forces with the paratroopers at the Storstrøm Bridge, effectively capturing this strategic crossing.

The capture of Copenhagen was pivotal for ensuring Denmark's quick capitulation. At 04:20, the German minelayer Hansestadt Danzig, flanked by the icebreaker Stettin and two patrol boats, boldly entered Copenhagen harbor with battle flags unfurled. The harbor was under the watchful eye of the coastal artillery at Fort Middelgrund. In a turn of events, the Danish commander, freshly appointed and overseeing green recruits, ordered a warning shot. However, the inexperienced soldiers struggled to operate the gun. By 05:18, the Germans had landed a battalion of the 198th Infantry and swiftly overran the 70-strong garrison at Kastellet, the Danish Army headquarters, without firing a shot. Their next objective was Amalienborg Palace, the residence of the Danish royal family, marking another critical step in their rapid conquest of Denmark.

As the German infantry approached Amalienborg, the seat of Danish royalty, they were met with a ferocious defense by the King's Royal Guard. The initial German assault was fiercely repelled, leading to casualties on both sides - three Danish Guardsmen and four Germans wounded. This intense standoff intensified as Danish reinforcements, armed with Madsen machine guns, rushed from Rosenborg Barracks. The ensuing street battles, particularly brutal in Bredgade, effectively stalled the German advance.

This resolute stand by the Royal Guard bought precious time for King Christian X and his ministers to deliberate with General Prior, the Danish commander-in-chief. Amidst these crucial talks, the skies above Copenhagen thundered with the menacing drone of Heinkel He 111 and Dornier Do 17 bombers from Kampfgeschwader 4, dropping ominous OPROP! leaflets. The looming threat of a Luftwaffe bombardment on civilian areas tilted the scale overwhelmingly towards surrender, despite General Prior's opposition. The argument was stark: Denmark, with its small landmass, limited population, and flat terrain, stood little chance against the German war machine. Unlike Norway's rugged mountains offering resistance strongholds, Denmark's geography offered no such advantage. Though the country had significant water barriers, a long coastline, and a formidable navy potentially backed by British and French support, the military reality was grim.

Complicating matters was the personal dilemma of the royal family. The option of government-in-exile, like the Czechoslovakian government, was dismissed, primarily because the Crown Princess, in the final stages of her pregnancy, could not be evacuated. Faced with these dire circumstances, the Danish government ordered a ceasefire at 06:00 and formally surrendered at 08:34, retaining some semblance of autonomy in domestic affairs.

The decision to disarm the Royal Guard was met with deep frustration and anger among its ranks. Believing firmly in their ability to repel the Germans, the Guardsmen were incensed. Tensions reached a boiling point as they attempted to rearm and mount an assault on Kastellet, where the Germans had established their temporary headquarters. However, their officers, weighing the inevitable arrival of overwhelming German reinforcements against the slim chance of a successful expulsion, counseled restraint. After heated debates, the Guardsmen reluctantly ceased their resistance.

On the morning of the invasion, Denmark's entire Army Air Service, consisting of four squadrons, was stationed at Værløse, near Copenhagen. Plans had been made to scatter these squadrons to various airfields across the country in the event of a German attack, but time ran out. At 05:25, the ominous hum of Luftwaffe planes filled the sky above Værløse. In a desperate attempt to respond, a Fokker C.V-E reconnaissance plane managed to get airborne, only to be swiftly shot down by a Messerschmitt Bf 110, piloted by Hauptmann Wolfgang Falck. Tragically, both Danish crew members perished at just 50 meters in the air.

The German Bf 110s then unleashed a relentless strafing assault on the airbase, braving heavy anti-aircraft fire. In a devastating blow, they destroyed 11 Danish aircraft and severely damaged 14 others, effectively annihilating most of the Danish Army Air Service in one fell swoop. Meanwhile, the Danish Navy Air Service, stationed elsewhere, narrowly avoided this fate and remained intact.

In a remarkable act of defiance amidst widespread capitulation, the 1st company of the 11th battalion, led by Colonel Helge Bennike of the 4th Regiment in Roskilde, stood its ground. Bennike, convinced that the surrender order was a German ruse and believing that Sweden, too, had been attacked, led his unit in a daring escape to Sweden aboard a ferry from Elsinore. This brave decision to seek exile was based on a misunderstanding, but it had significant repercussions. Although the confusion was later resolved, most of these Danish soldiers chose to stay in Sweden, eventually becoming the backbone of the Danish Brigade there in 1943, a testament to their unwavering commitment to their nation's cause.

In a strategic twist of narrative, the German High Command endeavored to recast the invasion of Denmark as a tranquil occupation, painting a picture of Denmark yielding without resistance. This portrayal was aimed squarely at the propaganda machine, to foster the illusion of a seamless and unopposed expansion of German power.

Against this backdrop of manipulated narratives, author Kay Søren Nielsen unearthed intriguing details in his first monograph. Diving into the archives of DISA, a Danish weapons manufacturer, he found a report suggesting that as many as 203 German soldiers met their end in the skirmishes across Jutland (Jylland). The credibility of this figure gains heft from its collaboration with the German Waffenamt, a significant endorsement considering the source.

This account finds further support in the recollections of veterans and eyewitnesses. Among them is Frode Jensen, a veteran who recounted that, post-battle, the Germans themselves admitted to losing 18 men in an engagement where his own unit suffered only two casualties.

Yet, in the complex tapestry of wartime accounts, this figure of 203 German fatalities is met with skepticism by many historians. They regard it as an overstatement, perhaps a counter-narrative to the German portrayal of a bloodless conquest. The true extent of the losses remains a subject of debate, underlining the often-blurred lines between propaganda and reality in the fog of war.

Invasion of Norway

As the Winter War drew to a close, the Allies faced a strategic conundrum. Occupying Norway or Sweden risked pushing these neutral nations into Germany's arms. Yet, the new French Prime Minister, Paul Reynaud, emboldened by a more assertive foreign policy, was itching for a direct confrontation with Germany. In this high-stakes geopolitical chess game, Winston Churchill emerged as a key proponent of action in Scandinavia. His ambitious goal: sever Germany's iron lifeline from Sweden and sway the Scandinavian nations towards an alliance with the United Kingdom.

Churchill's strategic vision initially contemplated a bold naval foray into the Baltic in 1939. However, the plan soon evolved into a more nuanced strategy involving the mining of Norwegian waters to disrupt iron ore shipments from Narvik, goading Germany into a Norwegian engagement where the Royal Navy could flex its might.

Thus, Operation Wilfred was born. Churchill's brainchild aimed to force German transport ships out of the safety of the Leads and into the open waters, setting them up for a Royal Navy ambush. But this was just part of a larger tapestry. Plan R 4, an audacious allied operation, would be triggered by the anticipated German retaliation to Operation Wilfred. The Allies planned to swiftly occupy strategic Norwegian cities such as Narvik, Trondheim, Bergen, and Stavanger, hoping to execute this without inciting armed Norwegian resistance.

Meanwhile, a debate brewed over Operation Royal Marine, which proposed mining the Rhine River. The British were enthusiastic, but the French, wary of their reliance on the Rhine and fearing German air reprisals, stalled approval for three months. This delay pushed back Operation Wilfred, initially slated for April 5, to April 8, as the British resolved to decouple Norwegian operations from continental maneuvers.

Concurrently, the German military juggernaut, already contemplating Operation Weserübung, found renewed impetus following the Altmark incident. The invasion, designed as a 'protection' of Norway's neutrality, aimed to secure Narvik and the Leads for ore transport and establish control to thwart any Allied collaboration. A critical element of German strategy hinged on Denmark's fate. Essential for air and naval dominance in the region,

Denmark's occupation was hotly debated. Eventually, the Germans opted for a forceful takeover, deeming it less risky than mere political pressure.

Another layer of complexity was added by Fall Gelb, the impending invasion of northern France and the Low Countries. Juggling resources for both Weserübung and Gelb was a strategic headache. With spring approaching and nights shortening – crucial for concealing naval operations – the Germans had to act swiftly. The invasion date was set for April 9 (Wesertag), with the landings scheduled at 04:15 Norwegian time (Weserzeit).

In Norway, the German assault was meticulously planned. Six primary cities - Oslo, Kristiansand, Egersund, Bergen, Trondheim, and Narvik - were targeted for amphibious landings. Supporting Fallschirmjäger units were poised to seize strategic points like the Fornebu and Sola airfields near Oslo and Stavanger, respectively. The German strategy was to blitz through Norwegian defenses, swiftly occupying key locations before any organized resistance could take shape.

Battles of Narvik

The day following the German invasion, the Royal Navy seized a critical opportunity to strike a blow against the Kriegsmarine. In the dim light of early morning, the 2nd Destroyer Flotilla, led by Commodore Bernard Warburton-Lee, advanced up the fjord. This formidable flotilla, comprising the H-class destroyers HMS Hardy (flagship), Hotspur, Havock, Hunter, and Hostile, executed a surprise attack.

At 04:30, the German destroyers Hermann Künne and Hans Lüdemann, anchored alongside the tanker Jan Wellem for refueling, were caught off guard by the British offensive. The German picket ship Diether von Roeder, which could have alerted the Germans, had fortuitously left its post for refueling. As the British vessels neared Narvik, they encountered and swiftly engaged a German force at the harbor entrance. The ferocious attack resulted in the sinking of the German destroyers Wilhelm Heidkamp (claiming the life of Commodore Bonte) and Anton Schmitt, significant damage to Diether von Roeder, and lighter damage to two other vessels. Despite exchanging fire with German troops onshore, the British lacked a landing force and decided to withdraw. But not before HMS Hostile unleashed a barrage of torpedoes at the merchant vessels in the harbor, resulting in the sinking of eleven ships, including German, British, Swedish, and Norwegian vessels.

The retreat of the British flotilla triggered a counterattack from three additional German destroyers - Wolfgang Zenker, Erich Koellner, and Erich Giese, led by Commander Erich Bey. Shortly thereafter, two more destroyers, Georg Thiele and Bernd von Arnim under Commander Fritz Berger, joined the fray from Ballangen Bay. In this heated battle, the British suffered significant losses with HMS Hardy, engulfed in flames, being beached, and HMS Hunter torpedoed and sunk. HMS Hotspur also sustained severe damage. Despite these losses, the remaining British destroyers managed to inflict damage on the German destroyer Georg Thiele during their withdrawal. The German forces, hampered by depleted fuel and ammunition, didn't give chase, allowing the British to sink the ammunition supply ship Rauenfels as they exited the fjord.

The situation escalated as British reinforcements, including the cruiser HMS Penelope, blockaded the German naval forces in Narvik. During the night of April 11-12, two German destroyers, Erich Koellner and Wolfgang Zenker, ran aground in Narvik harbor. Wolfgang Zenker damaged her propellers, limiting her speed, while Erich Koellner sustained more severe damage. Plans were made to repurpose Erich Koellner as a stationary defense battery, similar to Diether von Roeder.

As the British destroyers retreated from Vestfjorden outside Narvik, they encountered a new threat: German submarines U-25 and U-51 launched torpedo attacks. However, due to issues with the magnetic detonators of the German torpedoes, possibly exacerbated by the high northern latitude, the attacks failed spectacularly.

The battle claimed the lives of commanders on both sides: the German naval commander Kommodore Friedrich Bonte aboard Wilhelm Heidkamp, and the British commander Captain Bernard Warburton-Lee on HMS Hardy. In a posthumous recognition of their bravery and leadership, Warburton-Lee was awarded the Victoria Cross and Bonte the Knight's Cross of the Iron Cross.

The Royal Navy, recognizing the critical importance of a victory in Narvik for both morale and strategic reasons, dispatched a formidable task force. Vice Admiral William Whitworth led this fleet, comprising the mighty battleship HMS Warspite and an impressive array of nine destroyers. The Tribal-class destroyers - HMS Bedouin, Cossack, Punjabi, and Eskimo - were joined by HMS Kimberley, Hero, Icarus, Forester, and Foxhound. Supplementing this naval might was air support from HMS Furious. Upon arriving at Ofotfjord on April 13, they found the eight stranded German destroyers, commanded by Fregattenkapitän Erich Bey, hamstrung by fuel shortages and depleted ammunition.

Prior to the engagement, HMS Warspite deployed its Fairey Swordfish, a seaplane equipped for reconnaissance and bombing. The crew was tasked with locating German ships and bombing viable targets. Remarkably, the Swordfish crew located and attacked U-boat U-64, anchored in Herjangsfjord near Bjerkvik. Their daring assault with two 100 lb anti-submarine bombs resulted in the U-boat's sinking, marking the first U-boat destruction by an aircraft in the war, and notably, the only instance of a U-boat being sunk by an aircraft launched from a battleship. Although the U-boat was destroyed, most of its crew survived, later rescued by German mountain troops.

The naval battle that ensued was decisively in favor of the British. Warspite and her escorts managed to sink three of the German destroyers, while the remaining five were scuttled by their crews, driven to desperation by the lack of fuel and ammunition. The first to fall was Erich Koellner, which attempted an ambush but was detected by Warspite's Swordfish. After a combined assault from the battleship and accompanying destroyers, its commander, Alfred Schulze-Hinrichs, and the surviving crew were captured by Norwegian forces. The other German destroyers - Wolfgang Zenker, Bernd von Arnim, Hans Ludemann, and Hermann Künne - engaged the British, managing only minor damage to HMS Bedouin while failing to land a successful torpedo strike on Warspite.

The British intensified their assault with a squadron of ten Swordfish from HMS Furious, armed with 250lb bombs, targeting the German destroyers. Despite their valiant efforts, they failed to secure direct hits, and two of the aircraft were shot down. One crew was lost to the sea, while the other, after a forced landing on the shore, was rescued by HMS Punjabi. This fierce engagement not only demonstrated the Royal Navy's dominance at sea but also underscored the perilous nature of naval warfare in the fjords of Norway.

As the battle in Narvik reached its climax, the German destroyers, running low on ammunition, began to withdraw. However, one ship, Hermann Künne, missed the retreat order. Unscathed but out of ammunition, the crew of Hermann Künne made the decision to scuttle their ship in the shallow waters of Trollvika in Herjangsfjord. As they prepared the ship for scuttling, setting demolition depth charges, HMS Eskimo, in relentless pursuit, launched a torpedo strike. The torpedo ignited Hermann Künne, leading to a fierce explosion. The exact cause of the explosion, whether the ship's own depth charges or the torpedo from Eskimo, remains a matter of debate.

The engagement continued with HMS Eskimo facing an ambush by the German destroyers Georg Thiele and Hans Ludemann. Eskimo suffered significant damage, losing her bow, but remarkably managed to stay afloat. Meanwhile, Diether von Roeder and Erich Giese, hampered by engine troubles, remained docked yet still managed to inflict damage on HMS Punjabi and Cossack before they were ultimately sunk. This marked the end of the German counter-offensive.

the port of Bodø and alleviate the pressure on the elite Gebirgsjäger units engaged in the fierce battles near Narvik.

Following the Battle of Gratangen, the Germans were compelled to abandon Gratangsbotn and retreat from strategic positions at Lapphaugen and Gratangsdalen due to escalating Norwegian attacks and logistical challenges in supplying their forward troops.

In response, the Norwegians commenced a southward push towards Narvik. As plans for a major Allied invasion of Narvik crystallized by mid-May, the Norwegian advance redirected towards Bjørnfjell. The British forces, arriving first, established their headquarters in Harstad on April 14. Subsequently, they deployed three battalions across key locations like Sjøvegan, Skånland, and Bogen, with a naval base set up at Skånland. These forces later moved to positions south of Ofotfjord, in Ballangen and Håkvik.

On April 28, the British were bolstered by a French expeditionary force, the Corps expéditionnaire français en Scandinavie (CEFS), commanded by General Antoine Béthouart. This contingent, comprising mountain troops including Alpine battalions and units from the 13th Demi-Brigade of the Foreign Legion, initially deployed around Ofotfjord, with later operations focusing mainly to the north of the fjord. The arrival of four Polish battalions on May 9 further strengthened the Allied presence. Initially positioned north of Ofotfjord, these units, later reorganized into the Polish Podhale Independent Highland Brigade under General Zygmunt Bohusz-Szyszko, shifted to the southern sector and became part of CEFS.

Despite these reinforcements, the Allies grappled with the strategic challenge of recapturing Narvik and the vital iron ore railway. A lack of unified command complicated the situation, with Norwegian and Allied forces operating under separate leadership and experiencing coordination difficulties. Within the British ranks, disagreements between Army commander Major-General Pierse J. Mackesy and Navy commander Admiral of the Fleet William Boyle,

Lord Cork, further hindered operational harmony. Cork favored a direct, maritime assault, while Mackesy preferred a more cautious, multi-front approach. This discord led to Lord Cork being appointed as the supreme commander of all Allied forces on April 21.

By mid-May, significant developments occurred on the Narvik front. The Norwegians, advancing east of Gratangseidet, and French alpine troops, pushing up the Laberg valley with Norwegian ski troops support, made considerable headway. However, Allied efforts in the south showed limited success, and progress was stalled to the north of Ofotfjord. The Norwegian mountain campaign continued its effective push, culminating in mid-May with pivotal Allied victories. Pressure from Paris and London over the slow progress in Narvik spurred the French commander Béthouart to advocate for more decisive action.

The Allies, shifting from their initial cautious approach on land, orchestrated a bold amphibious assault just before midnight on May 12. This offensive, aimed at Bjerkvik, commenced with a formidable naval bombardment from British warships stationed in Herjangsfjord. Following this, landing crafts deployed French Foreign Legionnaires, backed by a contingent of five French Hotchkiss H39 light tanks from the 342e CACC (Independent Tank Company). This force made a successful incursion into Bjerkvik, stormed the Elvegårdsmoen army camp, and pushed northeast to intercept retreating German forces and also advanced south along the east side of Herjangsfjord.

Simultaneously, Polish troops were tasked with advancing towards Bjerkvik from the west side of the fjord. However, challenging terrain impeded their progress, causing a delay that meant they did not arrive until after Bjerkvik had fallen to the Allies. The original plan also included a northward advance by French and Norwegian troops to encircle the Germans. However, coordination issues between Norwegian and French commanders resulted in a gap that allowed German forces to escape. Nonetheless, this victory opened a direct route for the Allies north of Narvik, setting the stage for a subsequent attack across Rombaksfjord.

Recognizing the need for more centralized command as troop numbers in Narvik increased, London anticipated the establishment of a corps headquarters. Lieutenant-General Claude Auchinleck arrived in Narvik on May 11 and assumed command of the Allied land and air forces under Lord Cork's overall leadership on May 13, overseeing what was now termed the North-Western Expeditionary Force.

The Allies understood that securing Narvik was contingent on controlling Bodø to the south in Nordland, which was on the German advance route from Trondheim. Consequently, Auchinleck refocused all British efforts towards this southern objective. French Brigadier-General Béthouart, with expertise in mountain and winter warfare, was appointed to lead French and Polish troops in Narvik, coordinating with Norwegian forces.

The planned attack was momentarily delayed as the Allies awaited full establishment of air support from Bardufoss. At 23:40 on May 27, a naval bombardment initiated the offensive from the north. Two French and one Norwegian battalion were ferried across Rombaksfjord to approach Narvik from the north, while Polish battalions advanced towards Ankenes and inner Beisfjord in the south. The initial landing force, limited to 290 men per wave and with a 45-minute reinforcement interval, managed to secure a foothold on Ornes. Subsequently, French troops advanced west towards the city and east along the railway, while Norwegian forces headed towards Taraldsvik mountain, encircling and descending towards Narvik. Faced with this multifaceted assault, the German commander opted for evacuation before 07:00, retreating along Beisfjord.

Battle of Drøbak Sound

In the midst of political turmoil, 64-year-old Oberst (Colonel) Birger Eriksen found himself at a crucial juncture. Without definitive orders and uncertain of the approaching warships' allegiance – German or Allied – Eriksen was poised on a knife-edge. Norway's official stance of neutrality was overshadowed by a leaning towards the British, should Norway be drawn directly into the war.

The fortress Eriksen commanded was a hive of activity with fresh-faced recruits, inducted just a week earlier on April 2nd. These 450 new soldiers, mostly untrained and inexperienced, resulted in the naval mines of the fortress remaining undeployed on April 9th. Their training schedule included laying these mines, but that was planned for the coming days.

The torpedo battery at Oscarsborg was in a state of transition. Its usual commander had been on sick leave since March 1940. In his stead, the retired Kommandørkaptein (Commander Senior Grade) Andreas Anderssen, a resident of nearby Drøbak, was called upon. With the looming threat of an unidentified flotilla breaching the southern outer fortifications of the Oslofjord on the night of April 8th, Eriksen urgently summoned Anderssen. Donning his old uniform and crossing the fjord by boat, Anderssen arrived at the torpedo battery, a place he knew intimately from his service starting in 1909. Despite being a pensioner for 13 years, having retired in 1927, Anderssen was no stranger to the aging torpedoes of the battery. Equipped with three torpedo tunnels capable of firing six torpedoes without the need for reloading, and nine torpedoes ready to launch, the stage was set for an unexpected but pivotal confrontation.

In 1940, under unique circumstances, Oberst (Colonel) Birger Eriksen, commander of Oscarsborg fortress, chose to command from a backup station situated on the eastern side of South Kaholmen's Main Battery, rather than the usual combat station on Håøya island, northwest of the location.

On the early morning of April 9th, at 04:21, Eriksen made a decisive move against an unidentified fleet advancing towards Oslo. He ordered the Main Battery to open fire on the lead ship. Faced with skepticism, Eriksen famously declared, "Either I will be decorated or I will be court-martialed. Fire!" This bold command led to the firing of two 28 cm Krupp guns, Moses and Aron, at the German cruiser Blücher. The guns, loaded with live 255 kg high-explosive shells, breached the pre-war Norwegian rules of engagement, which typically required warning shots. Eriksen justified his decision by citing the German naval force's prior disregard for warning shots from other fortresses down the fjord.

The first shell struck the Blücher near the aft mast, igniting a fire that spread from the midship to the foremast. A second round hit one of the ship's forward gun turrets, causing extensive damage and further fires. Limited by a slow reload time and manned primarily by 30 untrained recruits, the Main Battery managed only these two shots. Even cooks were pressed into service alongside a single crew of actual artillerymen, with no opportunity to reload or to use the third gun, Josva, which remained loaded but unmanned.

The impact of these two rounds was catastrophic for the Blücher. The first shell penetrated the ship and exploded inside a magazine storing oil, smoke dispensers, incendiary bombs, and other ordnance, leading to intense fires and structural damage. The second shell disabled the ship's electrical central, rendering the main guns inoperable and preventing any return fire.

Amidst the chaos, the Norwegian coastal batteries unleashed a barrage of firepower on the blazing Blücher. From the modest 57 mm guns at Husvik, tasked with defending the absent mine barrier, to the formidable 15 cm guns of the Kopås Battery on the fjord's eastern flank, the assault was relentless. The larger guns inflicted severe damage, while the smaller 57 mm guns targeted the cruiser's superstructure and anti-aircraft armaments. Despite the fierce counter from Blücher's light AA guns, which forced the abandonment of the Husvik battery, the Norwegian forces suffered no casualties.

The Norwegian salvo was unrelenting, landing thirteen 15 cm rounds and about thirty 57 mm shells on the German cruiser. One critical hit from Kopås disabled Blücher's steering, compelling the crew to maneuver with the engines to avoid grounding. The cruiser's fire-fighting systems were also ravaged, exacerbating the challenge of controlling the fires and aiding the wounded.

Amidst the din of battle, the identity of the intruders became clear. Echoing over the tumult, the voices of Blücher's crew rang out, singing "Deutschland, Deutschland über alles," revealing to the fortress defenders their adversary's nationality. Confirmation of the ships' German origin came at 04:35, though communication delays hindered its timely delivery to Oberst Eriksen at Oscarsborg.

Blücher's return fire was largely ineffective. Her light artillery was mis-aligned, and the damage inflicted by Oscarsborg's Main Battery rendered her main guns inoperable. The exchange of fire, lasting merely five to seven minutes, ended in an eerie silence, with no movement detectable on the crippled cruiser.

In this dire moment for Blücher, Kommandørkaptein Anderssen prepared to launch the torpedoes. Positioned at the torpedo battery, he eyed the burning cruiser, now within 500 meters. The torpedoes, vintage Austro-Hungarian Whitehead weapons, were of uncertain reliability, having been used only in practice. Anderssen initiated the launch at approximately 04:30. The first torpedo, slightly misjudged, inflicted minor damage. But the second, with corrected aim, struck with devastating effect, hitting the cruiser amidships, in the same area as the initial 28 cm shell. This blow was catastrophic, breaching multiple bulkheads and flooding the decks, while flames engulfed the vessel. A third torpedo remained ready, anticipating further targets, while the others were reloaded for any subsequent threats.

After sustaining critical damage from the second torpedo strike, the crippled cruiser Blücher anchored near the Askholmene islets, just north of Oscarsborg Fortress's firing range. Desperate to control the escalating onboard fires, the crew fired their torpedoes at land to prevent accidental detonation. Despite their efforts, at around 5:30 AM, the situation took a dire turn when an ammunition hold for the cruiser's 10.5 cm Flak guns exploded, tearing a gaping hole in the ship's side and igniting further fires.

At 6:22 AM, Blücher's fate was sealed. She sank bow first into the Oslofjord's icy depths, tilting onto her port side, capsizing, and finally vanishing beneath the waves. In a tragic aftermath, oil leaking from the sunken ship spread across the water, igniting and engulfing many of the nearly 2,000 German soldiers and sailors struggling to survive in the frigid fjord, resulting in hundreds more casualties.

The disaster claimed the lives of 650–800 German personnel. Meanwhile, onshore, approximately 550 of the 1,400 survivors, shivering and drenched, were taken into custody by the Norwegian Royal Guards under Captain A. J. T. Petersson. While the intention was to capture all the Germans, the guardsmen prioritized aiding the numerous wounded and dying. Approximately 1,000 Germans, including high-ranking officers Generalmajor Erwin Engelbrecht and Admiral Oskar Kummetz, were lightly guarded at a nearby farm, with no interrogations conducted.

By evening, the Norwegian soldiers had withdrawn, leaving the Germans behind. Engelbrecht and Kummetz then made their way to Oslo, arriving at the Hotel Continental by 10 PM, though without the majority of their intended occupying force.

In a parallel effort, many of the German wounded were initially taken to the Åsgården summer hotel in Åsgårdstrand, which served as an improvised medical facility for the Royal Norwegian Navy Hospital, previously evacuated from Horten.

As Blücher sank, the rest of the German fleet destined for Oslo had already retreated. Mistaking the explosions on Blücher for mines, the commander of the cruiser Lützow (formerly the pocket battleship Deutschland) ordered a retreat at 04:40, fearing similar fates. The swift assault on Oslo was abandoned in favor of a more cautious land advance along the Oslofjord.

Despite the retreat, the fortress's firepower left its mark. The Kopås battery's 15 cm guns scored three hits on Lützow, disabling its forward 28 cm turret. The battery continued its assault until the ships vanished into the mist, and later, Lützow responded with long-range bombardment from a safer distance.

Meanwhile, another casualty of the battle was mistakenly identified. The Norwegian defenders at Oscarsborg initially thought they had sunk another German warship. However, it was the Norwegian cargo cutter Sørland, caught in the crossfire while transporting paper from Moss to Oslo. Mistaking the conflict for a military drill, Sørland continued its journey until it was set ablaze by German minesweepers and sank, marking the first civilian Norwegian ship lost in the invasion.

The fortress endured heavy Luftwaffe bombing later that day. Despite limited anti-aircraft defenses, the fortress miraculously suffered no casualties. The air attack lasted nearly nine hours, with around five hundred bombs dropped on Oscarsborg, including a strike by twenty-two Junkers Ju 87R "Stuka" dive bombers.

Despite Oscarsborg's valiant defense, Oslo fell to German forces later that day. Colonel Eriksen, realizing the futility of further resistance without adequate support, agreed to a ceasefire that evening. The fortress was surrendered intact the following morning.

The German forces treated the captured soldiers differently based on their location in the fortress. Those from the main battery and Håøya were released a week later, while the officers were held longer, with reserve officers released by mid-May and full-time officers released from Grini prison camp by the end of May.

The battle at Oscarsborg was remarkable for its David versus Goliath nature: an ancient fortress, manned largely by untrained recruits and retirees, with outdated weaponry, managed to sink a state-of-the-art German cruiser. This victory delayed the German occupation, allowing key Norwegian figures and assets, including the King, the cabinet, and the national gold reserve, to escape. The Norwegian government managed to continue its operations until its eventual exile in the United Kingdom, demonstrating the significant, albeit temporary, impact of Oscarsborg's defense.

Battle of Dombås

In the grip of harsh weather, with hail and sleet clouding the skies, a daring military operation unfolded on the afternoon of April 14th. Fifteen Junkers Ju 52 transport planes roared off from Fornebu Airport near Oslo, embarking on a treacherous journey despite the poor visibility. An hour before, a lone Ju 52 had scouted the drop zone at Dombås but failed to penetrate the dense cloud cover.

Compelled by a direct command from Adolf Hitler, the mission's officers reluctantly proceeded despite the menacing weather. This mission marked a historic moment in warfare: the second-ever opposed paratroop attack, following the first just five days earlier at the Norwegian airbase of Sola near Stavanger.

As the German planes neared Dombås, gaps in the clouds sporadically appeared, allowing most of the Ju 52s to release their paratroopers. However, the inclement weather scattered the Germans across a vast expanse, spanning from Lesja in the west to Vålåsjø in the north-east, and even southwards into the Gudbrandsdal valley.

Unbeknownst to the Germans, their target area was also the temporary base of the Norwegian Army's 2nd Battalion of Infantry Regiment 11, recently mobilized and stationed at Dombås. Prepared for a major operation to retake Trondheim, the battalion had improvised air defenses, mounting Colt M/29 heavy machine guns for anti-aircraft purposes.

The sudden appearance of the German aircraft caught the Norwegian forces off guard, but they quickly responded with a barrage of fire from all available weapons. The Ju 52s, flying perilously close to the treetops, returned fire. Chaos ensued as paratroopers descended into a hail of bullets. The fierce ground fire devastated the German transport aircraft, with only five making it back to Fornebu and two to Værnes Airbase, all bearing the scars of battle. The rest were either shot down or forced to land.

In Sweden, one stricken Ju 52 made an emergency landing on Lake Vänern near Mariestad, later retrieved and returned to the Luftwaffe by Swedish authorities.

Of the initial 185-strong force, Oberleutnant Schmidt could only rally 63 men, the rest lost to the battle or dispersed over the terrain. Determined, Schmidt and his diminished force set about their mission to disrupt Norwegian communications and transport. They blocked the main road, severed telephone lines, and commandeered a Norwegian taxicab. Packed with his men, Schmidt drove north toward Dombås, pausing intermittently for reconnaissance, in a bold attempt to fulfill their daunting objective amidst the chaos and uncertainty.

In a dramatic turn of events, the German paratrooper force, traveling by taxi, encountered a formidable challenge near the Li farmstead on their way to Dombås. There, they clashed with soldiers from the No. 5 Company of the Norwegian Infantry Regiment 11, loaded in two trucks. The encounter, initially marked by confusion, quickly escalated into a fierce skirmish. The Germans, armed with submachine guns and hand grenades, charged into battle, but the Norwegians retaliated forcefully. During the intense firefight, Oberleutnant Schmidt suffered severe wounds, and the Norwegians managed to repel the attackers.

Despite Schmidt's critical condition, with injuries to his hip and stomach, he maintained command. The German force withdrew to the Ulekleiv and Hagevolden farms, establishing a formidable hedgehog defense that covered all directions and dominated the terrain. Even in his gravely wounded state, Schmidt demonstrated resourcefulness by ordering his men to write messages in the snow using sand, signaling to the Luftwaffe for essential supplies of provisions and ammunition. Unfortunately for them, their calls for aid went unseen, and no supplies were dropped at their position.

The German attack at Dombås inadvertently accelerated the Norwegian response in protecting their national assets. The Norwegian Central Bank, upon hearing of the paratrooper landings, hastened the evacuation of the country's 50-ton gold reserve. Initially moved from Oslo on April 9th to a vault in Lillehammer, the gold was swiftly relocated to Åndalsnes by train, from where it was further evacuated through a combined effort of British cruisers and Norwegian fishing boats.

The attack also had significant implications for Norway's royal family. King Haakon VII and his son, Crown Prince Olav, were in Dovre, perilously close to the drop zone and merely 30 minutes from the nearest paratrooper groups when the attack unfolded. In a swift and crucial move, members of the Dovreskogen Rifle Club escorted the King and Crown Prince out of the danger zone, ensuring their safety during this critical phase of the invasion.

April 15th marked a critical juncture for the German Fallschirmjäger unit at Dombås, as the final stragglers rejoined, with no further reinforcements arriving. That morning, they managed to disrupt the railway line at three points, partially fulfilling their mission. However, their success was short-lived as Norwegian crews swiftly repaired the damage, allowing train services to resume the next day.

Norwegian forces, meanwhile, had been mobilized with the objective of halting the German advance in the Dombås region. With limited intelligence on the Fallschirmjägers' strength and location, Norwegian commanders faced a challenging situation. Under the direction of government minister Trygve Lie, a bold assault was launched by a group led by Kaptein Eiliv Austlid, aiming to secure a safe passage for the Norwegian royal family and cabinet. This assault, however, turned tragic as Austlid and his team, advancing across a snow-laden field under heavy machine-gun cover, were ambushed. Austlid was fatally wounded, leading to the capture of 28 Norwegian soldiers and the escape of five others.

The situation escalated on April 16th with the arrival of No. 1 Company, IR 5, led by Kaptein Botheim. They attacked the German positions from the south, while II/IR 11 launched an assault from the north, supported by mortars and machine guns. However, the firefight was briefly paused when the Germans used a captured Norwegian soldier to convey a surrender ultimatum, misinterpreted as a threat to execute prisoners. The Norwegians, in turn, sent a captured German Feldwebel back with a demand for German surrender, which was refused.

As negotiations stalled, Oberleutnant Schmidt planned a strategic retreat. With ammunition supplies dwindling and tactical dynamics changed by Norwegian mortars, Schmidt aimed to relocate to a more defensible position. He prolonged negotiations to buy time for his troops to escape under the cover of darkness, hoping for reinforcement from German forces believed to be nearby. However, unbeknownst to Schmidt, these forces were far south, stuck near Minnesund.

The deadlock ended when the Norwegians resumed their attack, but a sudden ground blizzard obscured their vision, enabling the Germans to launch a counterattack and escape the encirclement. The Norwegian forces in the north, caught off guard, retreated to Dombås. That night, Schmidt's unit disengaged and started moving south towards Dovre.

April 16th also witnessed continued efforts by Norwegian units to neutralize German forces in the area. They successfully captured 22 Germans near Kolstad at Lesja and another 23 at Bottheim train station, detaining them in the Ulekleiv Hotel in Dombås.

On the early morning of April 17th, the German Fallschirmjäger, bolstered by heavy machine guns seized from Norwegian forces, began a tactical withdrawal from their positions. They formed a combat column with grenadiers leading, followed by the wounded and POWs on trucks, and a rear guard to cover their escape.

Their retreat led to a confrontation at Landheim road bridge, where a small Norwegian force of 25 men attempted to block their path. However, the Germans, using a surprise night attack with hand grenades, quickly overpowered the Norwegians, pushing them back to Dovre Church. The German unit then established temporary positions at Einbugga road bridge, strategically located between Toftemo and Dovre.

By dawn, the Germans sought a new stronghold and found it at the North and South Lindse Farms, strategically positioned on a hillside overlooking both the railway line and the main road. The North Lindse, with its stone barn, became the central defense point, while the South Lindse housed Norwegian prisoners. The farms were quickly fortified, and the injured Oberleutnant Schmidt was carried there on a door by Norwegian POWs.

The next morning, Norwegian forces, led by Major Alv Kjøs and No. 1 Company, walked into German ambushes near Lindse. Kjøs was captured, along with the vanguard of No. 1 Company. The remainder of the company managed to retreat to Dovre Church by 10:00 AM. Unaware that the Germans had relocated to Lindse, the Norwegians spent the day regrouping and receiving reinforcements, including a machine gun platoon from the Norwegian Army Air Service's Jagevingen unit.

On the night of April 17th to 18th, the situation intensified with the arrival of a 40 mm anti-aircraft gun, enhancing the Norwegian firepower.

April 18th proved pivotal. The Germans, now encircled by Norwegian forces, faced relentless attacks. Despite their fortified position, dwindling ammunition supplies left them in a dire situation. In a stroke of luck, a Junkers Ju 52 air-dropped crucial supplies, momentarily boosting their morale. However, continued bombardment from a Norwegian 40 mm AA gun, positioned at Dovre Train Station, battered their defenses.

By the dawn of April 19th, the Germans were completely encircled by well-armed Norwegian troops, including a rail-mounted howitzer manned by Royal Marines. The howitzer began firing at 06:00 AM, further tightening the noose. A Ju 52 transport plane attempted to resupply the Germans but turned back after receiving a surrender message from Schmidt.

Negotiations ensued, with Leutnant Ernst Mössinger, the German second-in-command, seeking favorable surrender terms. However, Norwegian commander Major Arne Sunde demanded unconditional surrender, threatening renewed bombardment. With time running out, the Germans fired three signal flares at 11:30 AM, signaling their surrender.

Forty-five Fallschirmjäger, including six wounded, were captured at Lindse Farms. After being fed at the municipal building in Dovre, they were transported by train to Dombås, marking the end of a grueling and intense confrontation.

Invasion of the Netherlands

In 1939, the United Kingdom and France, responding to Germany's aggressive invasion of Poland, declared war, yet the initial months witnessed a deceptive calm. This period, known as the Phoney War, saw no significant military action in Western Europe. During this deceptive lull, the Allies bolstered their forces, bracing for a prolonged conflict, while Germany, in a sinister alliance with the Soviet Union, completed its domination of Poland.

Meanwhile, the Dutch found themselves in a precarious position. Despite the escalating threats, their military preparations lagged behind their neighbors. The Dutch government, cautious not to provoke Germany, their crucial trade partner, remained reticent, even suppressing criticism of Nazi policies. The conservative governments, hamstrung by the crushing impact of the Great Depression, struggled to allocate adequate funds for defense. This hesitance was epitomized by Prime Minister Hendrikus Colijn, who firmly believed in the sanctity of Dutch neutrality, a conviction that permeated the military establishment.

As the 1930s drew to a close, international tensions surged. Germany's expansionist moves—the occupation of the Rhineland, the annexation of Austria and Czechoslovakia, and Italy's conquest of Albania—rattled the Dutch government. Although these developments prompted a partial mobilization of Dutch forces, the response was measured, reflecting a deep seated desire to maintain neutrality.

With the outbreak of World War II following Germany's invasion of Poland, the Netherlands clung to its neutral stance, hoping to replicate its non-engagement from the First World War. The Dutch military was mobilized and fortified, and substantial funds were poured into defense. However, the exigencies of war and reliance on German supplies for military equipment hampered these efforts. Additionally, significant resources were diverted to the Dutch East Indies, reflecting the colonial priorities of the era.

The Low Countries, strategically nestled between France and Germany, were crucial to the military strategies of both sides during World War II. Their position, adjacent to the fortification lines of the major powers, made them a prime target for a potential offensive. In a bold attempt to sway the tides of war, Winston Churchill, in a radio address on January 20, 1940, urged the Low Countries to abandon their stance of neutrality and join the Anglo-French alliance. Despite this plea, and even in the face of the alarming Mechelen Incident, where German attack plans were inadvertently revealed, both Belgium and the Netherlands steadfastly refused to align with either side.

The French military leadership toyed with the idea of preemptively breaching the neutrality of these countries if they did not join the Anglo-French coalition, especially in light of the anticipated large-scale Entente offensive planned for the summer of 1941. However, the French government, wary of public backlash, quashed these plans. Still, contingency plans lingered, including a potential invasion if Germany attacked the Netherlands alone, or if the Dutch inadvertently aided the Germans by allowing them passage into Belgium. This complex web of scenarios was known as the hypothèse Hollande.

Within the Dutch government, there was no unified stance on how to react in the event of such contingencies. While the majority leaned towards resistance, a minority, along with Queen Wilhelmina, adamantly refused any alliance with Germany under any circumstances. Amidst these tensions, the

Dutch sought to mediate peace between the Entente and Germany.

However, the landscape of war shifted dramatically with Germany's invasion of Norway and Denmark. Coupled with a stark warning from Japanese naval attaché Captain Tadashi Maeda, the Dutch military realized that remaining neutral might no longer be feasible. Preparations for war intensified, both in terms of mindset and military readiness. Dutch border troops heightened their vigilance, and measures were taken to protect airfields and ports from potential attacks, spurred by fears of internal betrayal by a 'fifth column'.

Despite these preparations, many civilians clung to the hope that their nation would be spared from conflict, a sentiment later characterized as a state of denial. The Dutch hoped for a repeat of the restrained policies of the major powers from World War I, eager to avoid the devastating human toll of another major conflict. Even when Britain and France renewed their request for Dutch participation on April 10, the Netherlands held firm in their refusal, maintaining their perilous position on the brink of a world at war.

Battle for The Hague

On the fateful morning of May 10th, as the skies over the Netherlands darkened with the ominous presence of the Luftwaffe, the citizens of The Hague were jolted awake, not by deception, but by a stark realization of imminent danger. German aircraft, with ruthless precision, launched a devastating bombardment on The Hague's New Alexander Army Barracks and the neighboring Waalsdorp Army Camp, claiming the lives of scores of soldiers. Simultaneously, another contingent of German planes set their sights on the Ypenburg airfield. As dawn broke around 04:15, these aircraft unleashed their fury, paving the way for a wave of paratroopers to descend upon the area.

The Dutch defenders, undeterred, responded with a hail of machine gun fire, inflicting significant casualties and disrupting the German landings.

Their fierce resistance resulted in numerous damaged or destroyed German planes, effectively blocking subsequent arrivals. Although German troops managed to seize the main building of the airfield and unfurl the German flag in a premature declaration of victory, the Dutch stymied their advance, preventing them from penetrating further into The Hague.

Meanwhile, at the Ockenburg airstrip, a similar scenario unfolded. German paratroopers met stubborn resistance from the Dutch, who, though initially overwhelmed, bought crucial time for reinforcements to arrive. These additional Dutch forces effectively forestalled a German advance into The Hague. Recognizing the strategic importance of the Ockenburg airstrip, the Dutch resorted to bombing it themselves to deny its further use to the enemy.

The Valkenburg airstrip, still under construction, became yet another battleground. German forces bombarded it before dispatching their troops. The Dutch defenders suffered heavy losses, and despite inflicting severe casualties on successive waves of German paratroopers, they could not prevent the airstrip from falling into enemy hands. However, the incomplete state of Valkenburg airstrip thwarted the Germans' ability to use it for further landings. Many of their aircraft were forced to land on nearby beaches, where they were decimated by Dutch aircraft and the artillery fire of the Dutch destroyer HNLMS Van Galen.

In the ensuing chaos, German forces succeeded in occupying the village of Valkenburg and established control over several key points in Katwijk, along the Old Rhine. These intense skirmishes marked a crucial phase in the German invasion, showcasing the resilience and determination of the Dutch even in the face of overwhelming odds.

Despite the initial success of German troops in seizing three key airfields, their larger strategic goals—to capture The Hague and compel the Dutch to surrender—remained unfulfilled. In response, the Dutch Army launched a vigorous counter-offensive from the Ypenburg airfield. The Dutch Grenadier

Guards, though outnumbered and using captured ammunition, fought valiantly to position themselves for an effective artillery assault on the airstrip. This attack inflicted severe damage, forcing the Germans to abandon their fortified positions in the burning buildings. In the ensuing skirmishes, the Dutch not only reclaimed the airstrip but also captured numerous German soldiers.

Simultaneously, at the Ockenburg airstrip, the Dutch delivered a significant blow to the Germans. Four Dutch Fokker T.V aircraft bombed the site, decimating idle German Junkers Ju 52s. Ground troops then launched an assault, pushing the Germans into retreat and capturing several prisoners-of-war. However, a contingent of German forces managed to regroup in nearby woods, repelling further Dutch attacks and ultimately making their way towards Rotterdam.

Near Valkenburg, the Dutch forces, having secured key areas including Leiden and Wassenaar, regained control of an important bridge. With reinforcements bolstering their ranks, they intensified their attacks on German positions on the ground. Dutch bombers played a crucial role, destroying German transport planes on the ground. Despite stiff resistance, the German defenses eventually crumbled under the weight of concentrated Dutch fire, leading to their retreat by late afternoon.

Throughout the day, numerous small-scale engagements unfolded, with both sides fighting for control over various positions. The Dutch, supported by artillery fire from the nearby village of Oegstgeest, which suffered significant damage as a consequence, made strategic gains.

By day's end, the Dutch had reclaimed the airfields, marking a significant, albeit brief, tactical victory. However, this success was overshadowed just days later, on May 14th, when the Luftwaffe's devastating bombing of Rotterdam led General Winkelman to capitulate.

Battle of Rotterdam

On the dawn of May 10th, a daring German operation commenced on the Nieuwe Maas river, marking a pivotal moment in the Battle for Rotterdam. Twelve Heinkel He 59 seaplanes executed a stealthy landing on the river, deploying rubber dinghies to transport approximately 80 German soldiers. These troops, equipped for combat, swiftly landed on the riverbanks and a nearby island. Capitalizing on the element of surprise, they quickly overran several unguarded bridges, facing only minimal resistance from a few Dutch policemen.

The strategic initiative shifted to Oberstleutnant Dietrich von Choltitz, commander of the 3rd Battalion of the 16th Air Landing Regiment, who had established his base at Waalhaven Air Force Base. Von Choltitz immediately set about organizing his forces, directing them towards the critical bridges in Rotterdam. The Dutch military presence in the southern part of the city was sparse, comprising a makeshift unit of about 90 infantrymen, supplemented by local butchers, bakers, and riflemen who had retreated from the airfield. These Dutch defenders took up positions in houses along the Germans' route to the bridges, where they mounted a spirited ambush.

The ensuing clash was intense and wrought casualties on both sides. The Germans, reinforcing their assault with a PaK anti-tank gun, steadily increased the pressure on the Dutch defenders, who were eventually compelled to withdraw. This allowed the German forces, notably the 9th Company of the 16th Air Landing Regiment, to advance towards the bridges.

In another part of the city, the 3rd Battalion's staff encountered Dutch resistance in a square. A fierce engagement ensued, during which von Choltitz's adjutant led a charge but was fatally wounded. The Germans, seeking an alternate route to the bridges, exploited a gap created by their vanguard along the quays, making contact with the bridge defenders around 09:00.

The Dutch company in the south of the city, though heavily outnumbered, managed to hold its position until the afternoon. Their resilience was eventually overcome by the arrival of the 10th Company of the 16th Air Landing Regiment, bolstered by mortar fire. Faced with overwhelming odds and depleted ammunition, the Dutch troops were left with no choice but to surrender.

As the battle for Rotterdam intensified, Dutch forces in the northern part of the city sprang into action, spurred by the ominous sound of German planes overhead. With only a Captain at the helm, the garrison headquarters quickly mobilized troops and distributed ammunition. Multiple small units were dispatched to key locations: bridges, nearby railway stations, and areas along the Nieuwe Maas where German landings were reported. The Germans, noticing the Dutch mobilization, were forced to consolidate their forces around the bridges.

The initial Dutch response was led by a small contingent of Marines and an incomplete army engineers company. They strategically positioned themselves around the German-held area north of the bridges and set up machine guns at various strategic points. This led to the first intense exchanges of fire between the invading German forces and regular Dutch army units. The Dutch gradually pushed the Germans back, confining them to a shrinking perimeter around the traffic bridge, with both sides suffering significant casualties.

The Dutch then intensified their efforts to squeeze the German troops at the bridgehead into an increasingly tight pocket. Civilians watched the unfolding battle with apprehension. In a crucial move, the Dutch Navy deployed two vessels – an outdated gunboat and a motor torpedo boat (Z 5 and TM51) – to support the defense at the bridges. These ships launched two attacks on the Germans at the traffic bridge. Despite unleashing a barrage of shells, they had little impact on the entrenched enemy. A Luftwaffe bombing run inflicted considerable damage on the motor torpedo boat, forcing both navy vessels to withdraw after sustaining casualties.

On the German side, reinforcements arrived, including 37 mm PaK 36 anti-tank guns and light infantry guns. They fortified their positions with heavy machine guns and mortars on the Noordereiland, a strategic island in the river. The fierce battle for control of the northern riverbank culminated in the Germans taking shelter in the large National Life Insurance Company building, a position difficult for the Dutch to assail due to poor firing angles. Continuous mortar fire forced the Dutch troops in nearby houses to retreat, leading to a stalemate that lasted until the surrender of the Netherlands on May 14th.

Colonel Scharroo, recognizing the gravity of the German assault, urgently requested reinforcements from The Hague. These reinforcements, drawn from reserves behind the Grebbe Line and the eastern front of Fortress Holland, were soon dispatched, bolstering the Dutch defense in a city under siege.

Colonel Scharroo, the garrison commander, received vital reinforcements from the northern sector of Fortress Holland during the night and early morning. He immediately set about reorganizing his defenses, deploying troops along the river and on the western, northern, and eastern approaches to the city. This strategic decision was driven by Scharroo's concern over potential German attacks from these directions. Amidst this heightened state of alert, his staff was inundated with reports of phantom landings and supposed treachery among civilians. This flurry of activity left little room for devising organized countermeasures against the entrenched German forces for May 11th.

At 04:00, hostilities around the bridgehead flared up again. The German contingent, numbering around 40 to 50 men, had fortified themselves in the National Life Insurance building north of the traffic bridge. Isolated due to Dutch advancements on May 10th, both sides were locked in a stalemate:

Dutch forces couldn't seize the building, and German attempts to resupply or reinforce their position failed. Any Germans attempting to cross the bridge by vehicle were either shot or repelled. The bridge had effectively become a deadly impasse, controlled by machine gun fire from both sides.

The Royal Netherlands Air Force joined the fray in support of the ground forces, following a request from Scharroo. Dutch bombers targeted the bridges, and although their primary objectives were missed, stray bombs succeeded in destroying several German machine gun positions near the bridge. However, a subsequent air raid by the Dutch attracted the attention of 12 patrolling Messerschmitt Bf 110s from the Luftwaffe. In the ensuing aerial battle, the Dutch lost three aircraft compared to the Germans' five, a significant loss for the smaller Dutch air force.

On the ground, the Germans had strategically positioned machine guns on the SS Statendam, a Holland America Line ship. This move, however, drew intense Dutch fire. Mortar and machine gun assaults targeted the German positions on the ship and its surroundings. The intense engagement led to multiple fires, eventually engulfing the ship itself. The Germans were forced to evacuate the burning vessel, which continued to smolder well beyond the Dutch capitulation on May 14th.

On May 12th, the Dutch forces, though unable to reclaim control of the city, mounted relentless assaults against the German positions. This unyielding pressure led to escalating casualties on both sides, causing growing concern within the German command about the precarious situation of their 500 troops entrenched in the heart of Rotterdam. Oberstleutnant von Choltitz, under the strain of this intense combat, received permission from Generalleutnant Kurt Student to withdraw his men from the northern pocket if he deemed it necessary for operational survival.

Meanwhile, to the northwest of Rotterdam, in the village of Overschie, a gathering of German forces was taking shape. These troops, initially involved in the air landings at Ockenburg and Ypenburg, had regrouped under General Graf von Sponeck. Having moved the remainder of his force from Ockenburg, von Sponeck skillfully navigated his troops through Dutch-held territories. However, upon reaching the village of Wateringen, the Germans encountered resistance. A confrontation with a Dutch guard squad at a command post, and the sudden arrival of two armored Dutch cars, forced the Germans to retreat and seek an alternate route.

Despite this setback, the bulk of von Sponeck's group successfully reached Overschie, where they joined forces with the surviving German troops from the battle of Ypenburg.

On the evening of May 12th, Colonel Scharroo, in charge of the Dutch forces in Rotterdam, received a critical directive from the General Headquarters. He was ordered to concentrate all efforts on eliminating the German resistance at the northern approaches to the city's bridges, and, if necessary, to destroy these vital crossings. This strategic shift was a direct response to the arrival of the 9th Panzer Division at the Moerdijk bridges, posing a significant threat to the Dutch defense of Fortress Holland.

Colonel Von Frijtag Drabbe, commander of the local marines, was tasked with a daunting mission: eradicate all German pockets of resistance on the north end and secure the northern approach to the bridge, prepping it for potential demolition. He assembled a robust force for this operation, comprising over 100 of his most seasoned marines, backed by a similar-sized company of navy auxiliary troops. This task force was further reinforced with two batteries of 105 mm howitzers, two armored cars, and a company of six 81 mm mortars.

As the marines advanced, they encountered intense German machine gun fire from the south. Despite initial artillery support, the rounds proved ineffective, falling short or overshooting their targets, leading to a cessation of artillery fire. The armored cars also faced severe challenges; one was crippled by German anti-tank fire, and the other remained at a safe distance, unable to effectively engage the enemy. The planned assault on the eastern side of the bridgehead was ultimately abandoned.

Simultaneously, a platoon of marines advanced along the Nieuwe Maas from the northwest, reaching the northern headland unchallenged by the Germans. However, their attempt to cross the bridge was met with a deadly ambush from German forces entrenched in the insurance building. The marines, caught in a lethal crossfire, suffered heavy casualties and were forced to retreat, with some finding temporary shelter under the bridge.

Faced with the failure of the bridge assault, Dutch commanders in Rotterdam pivoted their strategy to fortify the northern river bank. Seven infantry companies were deployed to form a defensive line along the river, and artillery units were positioned for potential barrages on the bridge headlands.

Meanwhile, the arrival of German tanks in Rotterdam's southern outskirts signaled a shift in the German approach. General Schmidt, leading the XXXIX Armeekorps, hesitated to order a tank assault across the bridges, wary of the strong Dutch defenses, including artillery and anti-tank guns. The Germans, recalling their recent losses in similar situations, concluded that only a tactical aerial bombardment could weaken the Dutch resistance.

At this juncture, the German high command intervened. Hermann Göring advocated for a comprehensive aerial bombardment of Rotterdam's city center. However, both Schmidt and Student were opposed to such a drastic measure, favoring a more targeted approach. General Georg von Küchler, overseeing operations in the Dutch area, instructed Schmidt to present an ultimatum to the Dutch on the morning of May 14th, demanding the unconditional surrender of the city.

On the morning of May 14th, a crucial moment unfolded in the Battle of Rotterdam. General Schmidt, the German commander, drafted an ultimatum for the Dutch forces, demanding the cessation of resistance or else face the destruction of Rotterdam. This note, written in Dutch, was carried to the Maas bridges by three German negotiators under a flag of truce. The Dutch, wary and vigilant, disarmed the negotiators and blindfolded them before escorting them to Colonel Scharroo's command post in the city.

Upon receiving the ultimatum, Scharroo contacted General Headquarters for guidance. General Winkelman instructed that any ultimatum must be formally signed, including the name and rank of the issuing officer, to be considered valid by the Dutch. Colonel Scharroo dispatched Captain J. D. Backer with this response to the Germans.

Meanwhile, unaware of these diplomatic exchanges, the German air force, on Göring's orders, prepared for a bombing raid over Rotterdam. The 90 Heinkel He 111 bombers of Kampfgeshewader 54 (KG 54), commanded by Oberst Walter Lackner and Oberstleutnant Friedrich Höhne, set off towards the city.

The Germans promptly revised their ultimatum in line with Dutch demands, extending the deadline to 16:20. However, as Captain Backer returned with the response, German bombers were already approaching Rotterdam. General Schmidt, witnessing the bombers' arrival, realized the impending disaster.

On the ground, German soldiers in the city, unaware of the high-level negotiations, panicked at the sight of their own air force overhead. Von Choltitz ordered the launching of red flares as a signal, but the smoke from the initial bombings obscured them. The following bombers, seeing the situation, aborted their attack.

However, the larger formation from the northeast, led by Oberst Lackner, proceeded with the bombardment. Due to the smoke, the bombers flew lower, missing the signals entirely, and devastatingly unloaded their payload over Rotterdam's city center. The tragic result was the loss of 800 to 900 lives, the displacement of over 80,000 people, and the destruction of more than 25,000 buildings.

Remarkably, the Dutch defenses remained largely intact despite the raid. However, the ensuing fires threatened their positions, forcing a withdrawal. Isolated and facing the overwhelming catastrophe, Colonel Scharroo, under pressure from local officials and realizing the broader implications for the Netherlands, made the grave decision to capitulate. General Winkelman, through his representative, concurred with this decision.

Colonel Scharroo, accompanied by his adjutant and a Sergeant Major, formally presented Rotterdam's capitulation at the bridges to General Schmidt. Expressing his deep resentment over the events, Scharroo was met with a sympathetic response from Schmidt, who was himself taken aback by the Luftwaffe's actions.

By 18:00, German troops began moving through the devastated city. The Dutch forces, following their commander's orders, ceased resistance and laid down their arms. A final, tragic skirmish occurred in Overschie, resulting in the death of an SS soldier, marking the end of hostilities in a city ravaged by war and tragedy.

Battle of Zeeland

On May 10th, the first day of the conflict was relatively calm in terms of ground combat. The German forces were waiting for additional reinforcements, while the Dutch were strengthening their defenses and anticipating the arrival of French troops. The main activity of the day involved German planes repeatedly strafing Dutch positions.

The situation escalated on May 11th with the arrival of the first companies of a French detachment, consisting of five infantry regiments and forming part of the 68th Infantry Division. Additionally, two French mail-boats, escorted by

French and British naval ships, arrived at Vlissingen. Despite being attacked by German bombers, the convoy was protected effectively by anti-aircraft guns. British Hurricanes were also active in the skies, engaging in multiple encounters with the Luftwaffe, resulting in the loss of six British planes but also shooting down three German aircraft. On the ground, the Dutch army in the south managed to reestablish their positions near Bergen op Zoom after retreating from the Peel-Raamline.

May 12th saw further aggression, particularly at the port of Vlissingen, which was targeted by German bombers. This raid caused substantial damage to the harbor and surrounding infrastructure, resulting in civilian casualties. Allied ships and anti-aircraft defenses responded vigorously, but the harbor suffered significant destruction. This day also marked a realization for the French supreme command that their operational plans for the 7th Army were no longer feasible due to the German advance and the retreat of the Belgian army.

By May 13th, the German forces had almost reached Zeeland, and the soldiers stationed at the Bathline could hear the distant sound of heavy artillery, indicating the approach of the German army. Dutch troops were ordered to destroy railway tracks to impede the German advance, tracks they had only recently repaired. A false alarm of a German infiltration in Vlissingen caused widespread panic among the Dutch forces. The Luftwaffe's activity in Zeeland decreased as their focus shifted to supporting the fierce battle around the island of Dordrecht and aiding the 9th Tank Division. The morale of the Dutch troops was severely impacted by the continued retreat from the east and the departure of Queen Wilhelmina to Britain.

On May 14th, the Dutch faced a challenging situation in Bergen op Zoom, where their units were encircled by SS battalions. Concurrently, the French, retreating from Woensdrecht, abandoned their Dutch allies, leaving behind tanks and supplies. A Dutch force of about 200 men, initially controlling a forest south of Bergen op Zoom, had to retreat due to the French withdrawal.

The French counter-attack at Huijbergen, involving armored cars and light tanks, resulted in the loss of equipment and the capture of 200 men. This led to a continued German advance, resulting in the capture of more French and Dutch prisoners.

Despite these setbacks, the Dutch casement occupants at the Bathline resisted valiantly and managed to hold their positions against German patrols, countering with heavy machine gun fire. However, by the evening, most of the Bathline was deserted, save for a few central sections and the casement crews. At 19:00, the Dutch army officially capitulated, except for the forces in Zeeland. The formal surrender agreement was signed the following day.

On May 15th, the Germans prepared an assault on the remaining sections of the Bathline, planning to use a negotiator to demand an immediate surrender. This move was more of a bluff, as the Germans lacked the resources for a massive assault. However, they found the line already abandoned as the Dutch had withdrawn overnight.

The focus then shifted to the Zanddijkline in Zeeland. The German advance triggered minefields, causing casualties among their ranks. After clearing the mines, they resumed the assault with air and artillery support. Despite resistance from Dutch naval artillery, the Dutch troops eventually evacuated the northern sector of the line. The southern part of the line was also evacuated after a few hours.

Meanwhile, on the island of Tholen, Dutch forces effectively repelled a German patrol with machine-gun fire. A subsequent German bombardment inflicted little damage. When the German infantry advanced, the Dutch defenders unleashed mortar and machine gun fire, causing heavy German casualties and forcing a retreat. Despite their success, the Dutch forces, recognizing their unsustainable position, retreated further into the island during the night.

On May 14th, SS units halted at the canal through Zuid-Beveland after breaching two defense lines. During the night, German soldiers managed to cross the canal using rafts. The French, tasked with defending the canal, were significantly outnumbered and faced a challenging 9 km front. Despite the canal's width forming a formidable barrier, the Luftwaffe's persistent attacks demoralized many French soldiers, forcing them to abandon their positions.

As the French defenses at the canal crumbled, a hurried retreat ensued. The Germans, having repaired a river crossing to the north, pushed forward with light armored vehicles, chasing the retreating French. By evening, they had reached the Sloedam but avoided direct engagement. Meanwhile, most Dutch units near Goes had managed to evacuate, but many French units were left stranded as the Luftwaffe dominated the skies.

In Tholen, German negotiators failed twice to secure a Dutch surrender. Following their refusal, German artillery bombarded Dutch positions. Despite this, the Dutch battalion commander received orders to evacuate the island and reinforce Schouwen-Duiveland. However, Schouwen-Duiveland soon fell to the Germans after a brief resistance, leaving the Dutch coastline vulnerable.

May 17th saw critical developments at the Sloedam on Walcheren island. The French, contemplating reinforcement, ultimately decided against it, deeming the defense of the Sloedam crucial to cover their northern flank. The day began with heavy German artillery fire, but the joint French and Allied naval response was formidable, causing the Germans to falter for the first time in the campaign. However, a massive German assault by day's end left Walcheren exposed.

The focus then shifted to Vlissingen, where the advancing Germans met little resistance until the outskirts. French General Deslaurens, attempting a last stand, was killed in action, the only general to die on Dutch soil that

May. Overnight, the remaining pockets of resistance were systematically eliminated by the Germans.

Simultaneously, Middelburg experienced a devastating bombing on May 17th, resulting in widespread destruction and homelessness. This attack, reported by the now Nazified Dutch press, caused massive fires that raged until controlled the next evening.

By late afternoon on May 17th, it became evident that the Germans had effectively conquered Zeeland, except for Zeelandic Flanders. Discussions about capitulation emerged among the Dutch forces in Walcheren. Despite reluctance from Commander Van der Stad, who wanted to support the still-fighting French, a surrender was eventually broadcast. Lieutenant-Colonel Karel officially surrendered the Dutch forces on Walcheren and Zuid-Beveland to the SS Regiment commander.

Noord-Beveland, initially not included in the armistice, also surrendered on May 18th after being informed of the wider Dutch capitulation. These days marked the end of significant Dutch resistance in the region, signifying a crucial phase in the German occupation of the Netherlands.

Battle of the Grebbeberg

Germany's Army Group B, led by the formidable 207th Infantry Division under Karl von Tiedemann, launched a surprise invasion into the Netherlands. Their mission was clear yet daunting: seize control of the strategic Grebbeberg within a single day. As part of the 18th Army, this division, bolstered by the formidable SS-brigade Der Führer, faced unexpected fierce resistance at the IJssel Line near Westervoort. The ensuing battle was intense and prolonged, stretching into the evening before the Germans could claim Wageningen, a key city east of the Grebbeberg. Preparations were swiftly made for an all-out assault on the hill the following day.

May 11 dawned with a crucial phase of the invasion: the Germans needed to penetrate the heavily fortified outpost line guarding Grebbeberg. Spanning 3 km, this line, not submerged by floodwaters, was manned by the resilient Dutch forces of the 8th Infantry Regiment. However, German artillery, with a devastating barrage, crippled the Dutch communication lines, leaving them without crucial artillery support. In a tactical masterstroke, the SS brigade launched a full-frontal attack at dawn. The Dutch defenses, though valiant, were primarily makeshift - sandbags and wooden barricades. The Germans, using coordinated teams of machine gunners, systematically dismantled these positions, exploiting their lack of overlapping fields of fire.

The northern sector of the line witnessed intense skirmishes. The Dutch 19th Infantry Regiment, due to coordination challenges, succumbed to the German onslaught, retreating and inadvertently opening a flank. This allowed the Germans to encircle and overpower the southern Dutch positions. Near the Rhine, the Germans ingeniously used a dike for a rear attack, going undetected through orchards that masked their advance. By 18:00, the line of outposts was overwhelmed, and the Germans stood victorious.

However, the Dutch were not defeated yet. In a bold move, they launched a counterattack that evening. German armored cars, aiming for the hill, were thwarted by a fierce Dutch anti-tank gun. In a controversial and tragic twist, Chris Meijer, an artillery sergeant, faced a court-martial and execution for desertion, a decision later scrutinized for its legality. General Harberts of the 2nd Corps, driven by rumors of a massive rout, ordered the 19th Infantry Regiment to recapture the outposts under the veil of night. However, the Dutch battalion, expecting to face a mere hundred Germans, walked into a trap of 3,000 SS troops. A tragic miscommunication with other Dutch forces led to friendly fire, sowing chaos and ultimately halting the counterattack by dawn. Despite the setback, the Dutch artillery managed to deter a planned German night assault.

The day after the German forces captured the outposts, they shifted their focus to the Frontline along the Grebbeberg's eastern slope. Karl von Tiedemann, leading the German forces, understood that a direct assault like the previous day's would be ineffective against the well-armed Dutch defenses. The Frontline was strongly held by Dutch forces, including two companies from the 8th Infantry Regiment, a machine gun company, and an anti-tank unit. Von Tiedemann ordered a prolonged morning artillery barrage, aiming to weaken the morale of the mostly conscript Dutch troops, rather than destroy their fortifications.

As the German artillery ceased at 12:40, the SS brigade moved to seize the Hoornwerk, an 18th-century fortification critical to their strategy. The Dutch defenders, already low on ammunition due to earlier skirmishes, began to falter by early afternoon. After a brief but intense fight, the Germans captured the Hoornwerk and surged up the hill. Despite their strong position, the Dutch troops were outflanked by the Germans, leading to a fierce battle on the wooded slopes.

By 16:00, German forces reached the Stopline atop the Grebbeberg, clashing with the Dutch defenders. Major Johan Henri Azon Jacometti of the Dutch forces led a valiant but ultimately unsuccessful counterattack, falling in the attempt. The Dutch unit II-19 RI, previously thwarted in a counterattack, was called again but mistakenly fired upon by their compatriots, leading to their withdrawal.

The concentrated SS brigade, while advancing, became vulnerable to Dutch artillery. However, the Dutch artillery, cautious not to hit their own troops, limited their fire mainly to pre-planned targets, with only some commanders taking initiative against the German concentration.

As the day progressed, the SS brigade methodically cleared the area between the Stopline and the Frontline. By 20:00, they had made limited but significant progress. Obersturmbannführer Hilmar Wäckerle, dissatisfied with the slow advance, impulsively moved two companies into the Stopline, breaching it near the Rhenen-Wageningen road. However, this rapid advance left his forces isolated deep in enemy territory.

Simultaneously, Dutch reinforcements began to arrive. The Royal Marechaussee, under Captain G.J.W. Gelderman, valiantly defended the railway viaduct, a crucial access point to Rhenen, even containing Wäckerle's advancing SS company in a nearby factory.

The Dutch Field Army commander, Baron van Voorst tot Voorst, sent reinforcements and drew up a new attack plan. This plan involved reinforcing the Grebbeberg, Stopline, and final line, with a flanking attack from Achterberg to recapture the Frontline and stabilize the local situation. As night fell, the Dutch, though severely challenged, still held onto a section of the Frontline, a testament to their resilience in the face of overwhelming odds.

On the morning of May 13, Von Tiedemann faced a challenging situation on the Grebbeberg. He had lost contact with Wäckerle, and the conditions on the hill were unclear. Believing that the Dutch were bolstering their forces on the hill, he decided to initiate a secondary attack. This time, the 207th Infantry Division would engage directly on the Grebbeberg, aiming to reinforce the German position and clear the Stopline. Meanwhile, the two remaining battalions of the SS brigade, weary from continuous combat, were tasked with confronting the Dutch troops north of the hill. Concurrently, the Dutch were gearing up for an offensive in the same area.

Both sides supported their ground operations with indirect fire. The Dutch sought air assistance from the British Royal Air Force, but, preoccupied with the battle in France, the RAF could not comply. Instead, the Royal Netherlands Air Force deployed its remaining resources: four Fokker C.X light bombers, escorted by the last operational fighters. These aircraft relentlessly bombed and strafed German positions along the Rhenen-Wageningen road. The Dutch also employed artillery, though cautiously to avoid friendly fire. The Germans, preparing for their assault, planned a similar use of artillery later in the morning.

The planned Dutch counterattack near Achterberg, originally scheduled for 04:30, was delayed until 08:00. Brigade B, which had arrived the previous evening, contributed four battalions, including middle-aged men who had not undergone recent training and lacked a strong sense of camaraderie. This lack of cohesion would later prove detrimental.

Initially, the Dutch advanced with little resistance, reclaiming positions at the Stopline. However, as they moved beyond the Stopline, they encountered a German artillery barrage, signaling an impending SS attack. Ideally, the Dutch should have switched to a defensive stance, but unaware of German intentions, their command ordered the advance to continue. This decision led to heavy casualties from both German artillery and friendly fire. By noon, disorganized and leaderless, many Dutch troops began retreating back to the Stopline. A subsequent attack wave also failed, and parts of the Stopline were abandoned.

The situation worsened at 14:00 when 27 Junkers Ju 87 Stuka dive bombers targeted the Grebbeberg. Although Brigade B was not the primary target, the attack triggered a panic among the retreating battalions, leading to a general disorderly retreat.

The Dutch counterattack's success hinged critically on the endurance of the Stopline on the Grebbeberg. If the Stopline fell, the chances of a successful defense would vanish. To bolster the Stopline, fresh troops were needed, but communication was hampered by the presence of Wäckerle's isolated SS unit. The day prior, many trenches south of the Rhenen-Wageningen road had been hastily vacated by Dutch forces. Fièvez, with a limited understanding of the situation near the Stopline, had designated the final line near the Rhenen railway as the primary defense, leading to an undermanned Stopline. Furthermore, the final line was more of a rallying point than a defensive stronghold, and it was too late to reinforce the critical Stopline when these oversights were realized.

The failure to clear wooded areas near the Stopline now played against the Dutch defenders, who struggled to repel the Germans concealed by the trees. The Stopline, the last substantial line of defense, lacked depth, making its breach a critical threat to the Grebbe Line. After a short artillery attack, the Germans launched their first assault. Although initially unsuccessful, some German troops managed to infiltrate the line. A subsequent, more organized attack by a second wave of German forces finally overwhelmed the Stopline after midday, leading to intense combat in the woods.

Dutch command posts, located behind the Stopline, came under direct assault. One notable instance was the heroic defense by Major Willem Pieter Landzaat of I-8 RI, who urged his men to fight to the last bullet. After running out of ammunition, Landzaat's body was later found by his wife, and he was posthumously awarded the Netherlands' highest military honor. The area between the Stopline and the railway was not fully cleared of Dutch soldiers until 17:00, and by then, Dutch morale had plummeted, making a German assault on the final line unnecessary.

Meanwhile, scattered Dutch forces in Rhenen struggled with coordination and exhaustion due to continuous bombardment. Jonkheer De Marees van Swinderen, commanding the 4th Hussar Regiment, had no clear picture of the situation at the Grebbeberg and didn't send reinforcements. Instead, he ordered some troops to form a reserve in Elst, further weakening the Dutch position in Rhenen.

In the factory where they were stranded, Wäckerle's SS company made two desperate attempts to breach the final line, violating the laws of war. They first used Dutch prisoners as human shields, and then disguised themselves in Dutch uniforms. Both attempts were foiled by the vigilant Royal Marechaussee unit led by Captain Gelderman. Wäckerle was badly wounded and later evacuated.

The same air attack that had demoralized Brigade B also impacted the final line, causing a mass retreat among the Dutch troops. By 16:00, Captain Gelderman found himself with only 15 men, having expected to feed 600. Realizing the gravity of their defeat, the Dutch 4th Division began a retreat to preserve their remaining forces. Despite a late effort by the 11th Border Battalion to recapture the railway station, their action was in vain, and they too retreated as Rhenen succumbed to flames.

Dutch Surrender

Despite the capitulation of Rotterdam and the potential for German forces to advance into the heart of Fortress Holland, General Winkelman initially intended to continue the fight. The Dutch had anticipated the possibility of terror bombings and had prepared for government continuity even amid widespread urban destruction. The defense perimeter around The Hague could still potentially repel an armored attack, and the New Holland Water Line, despite its vulnerabilities, provided some defensive capability.

However, Winkelman's resolve was challenged when he received a message from Colonel Cuno Eduard Willem baron van Voorst tot Voorst, the commander of Utrecht. The Germans demanded the city's surrender, threatening it with the same fate as Warsaw. Winkelman interpreted this as a German policy to obliterate any city that resisted. Considering his mandate to minimize suffering and the bleak military situation, Winkelman decided to surrender. At 16:50, he informed higher-level army units of his decision via telex, instructing them to destroy their weapons before surrendering to German forces. By 17:20, the German envoy in The Hague was notified, and Winkelman publicly announced the surrender around 19:00 through a radio speech, which was also how the German command learned of the Dutch capitulation. This implied a ceasefire from both sides.

Winkelman, serving as both the Dutch Army commander and the highest executive authority, created an ambiguous situation. Vice-Admiral Johannes

Furstner, the commander of the Royal Dutch Navy, had already left to continue the fight elsewhere, and Dutch naval vessels were generally not included in the surrender. Several ships had departed, some were scuttled, and others sailed for England. Rear-Admiral Hoyte Jolles initially intended to resist with the naval base at Den Helder but eventually complied with Winkelman's surrender order. Many army units, especially those less engaged in combat, were hesitant to accept the surrender.

On May 15th, Winkelman met with General von Küchler in Rijsoord to negotiate the surrender terms. They quickly agreed on most conditions, with Winkelman surrendering the army, navy, and air forces, but he refused to treat pilots fighting with the Allies as irregular combatants. This clarified that only the homeland forces, excluding Zealand, would capitulate, not the Netherlands as a nation. The capitulation document was signed at 10:15.

Following this, Queen Wilhelmina established a government-in-exile in Britain. The German occupation officially began on May 17, 1940, marking the start of a five-year period before the entire country was liberated. During this time, the Netherlands suffered heavily, with over 210,000 war victims, including 104,000 Jews and other minorities targeted in genocide, and possibly 70,000 more deaths due to indirect consequences of the occupation.

Invasion of Belgium

Belgium's defensive strategy against potential German aggression in the 1930s was a complex chess game of politics and military tactics. Facing the threat of German invasion, Belgium grappled with a critical decision: should they fortify their border with Germany, mimicking France's Maginot Line, or seek a different approach? The direct border defense seemed risky, leaving Belgium open to a surprise attack through the Netherlands.

Politically, Belgium was in a quandary. Their alliance with France was under strain. Marshal Philippe Pétain's proposals in the early 1930s for a French strike on Germany's Ruhr region, using Belgium as a launchpad, had heightened Belgian fears of being dragged into a war. The 1935 Franco-Soviet pact only added to these anxieties. Furthermore, the Franco-Belgian agreement was ambiguous about Belgium's obligations in case of a German invasion of Poland, leaving them uncertain about their response.

Belgium found the idea of an alliance with the United Kingdom more appealing. The British had stood by Belgium during the First World War, particularly in response to the German violation of Belgian neutrality. The Belgian Channel ports, crucial in the previous war, could again become strategic assets, potentially for German naval and aerial operations against the UK. However, the British government's lack of engagement with Belgian concerns, especially evident in their indifference to the remilitarisation of the Rhineland, was disheartening for Belgium. This perceived apathy led

Belgium to distance itself from the Western Alliance.

Ultimately, Belgium was left to ponder its fate. The lack of a robust response from France and Britain to the remilitarisation of the Rhineland was seen as a sign of their reluctance to defend strategic interests, including those of Belgium. Faced with this reality, the Belgian General Staff prepared to defend their nation's interests independently, if need be.

The German military strategy unfolded with a clever but risky plan. At its heart, Army Group B, with its limited armored units, was to push into central Belgium, luring the Allied First Army Group into a precarious position. Meanwhile, the real surprise would come from Army Group A, which would launch a stealthy assault through the dense Ardennes forest. Belgium, thus, was not the primary target but a diversion.

The success of this operation hinged on rapid advances in Belgium, creating a vice-like trap for the Allies. However, formidable obstacles stood in their way: the defenses of Fort Eben-Emael and the Albert Canal. The bridges at Veldwezelt, Vroenhoven, Kanne, and Maastricht were crucial for the speedy advance of Army Group B. Should these bridges fall, Walter von Reichenau's 6th Army could find itself trapped and vulnerable.

In a twist of fate, Adolf Hitler called upon Lieutenant-General Kurt Student and his 7th Air Division for an audacious plan to seize these strategic points. Initial plans for a parachute assault were scrapped due to the slow, vulnerable Junkers Ju 52 transports and unpredictable weather. Instead, Hitler, spotting a weakness in the fort's defenses, proposed a bold glider landing on the fort's flat, unprotected roofs. This would deploy a small force of 80-90 elite paratroopers directly onto the target.

The operation's linchpin was the introduction of the Hohlladungwaffe, a 50-kilogram explosive device, capable of decimating the Belgian gun emplacements. This marked the beginning of the first major strategic airborne operation in history.

Battle of Fort Ében-Émael

In a clandestine operation leading up to a crucial moment in World War II, Sturmabteilung Koch, a specialized German assault unit, was scattered across the Rhineland, awaiting the signal to strike against Fort Ében-Émael and its critical bridges. On May 9th, they received the initial call to gather at a predetermined location, and soon after, a second directive confirmed the commencement of Operation Fall Gelb at 05:25 on May 10th.

Under the cover of darkness and to the stirring sounds of Richard Wagner's "Ride of the Valkyries," the elite Fallschirmjäger troops assembled on a dimly lit tarmac at 03:00. By 04:30, a fleet of forty-two gliders, carrying 493 airborne soldiers, took off from Cologne, heading south towards Belgium in utter silence. The absence of radio communication compelled the pilots to navigate using a series of signal fires and also meant they were unaware of two critical mishaps: one glider's tow-rope had snapped, landing it inside Germany, and another released its tow-rope too early, failing to reach its intended target. These incidents significantly weakened Group Granite, leaving it undermanned and under the command of Oberfeldwebel Helmut Wenzel, as their leader, Oberleutnant Witzig, was aboard one of the affected gliders.

The remaining gliders were released 20 miles from their targets at an altitude of 7,000 feet, a height calculated to enable a precise landing near the bridges and atop the fort, while also allowing for a steep descent to ensure accuracy. As the Ju 52 transport planes began their retreat after releasing the gliders, Belgian anti-aircraft guns spotted them and opened fire, alerting the defenses to the impending airborne invasion.

Group Steel, comprising nine gliders, executed a precise landing near the Veldwezelt bridge at 05:20. Their arrival was dramatic, with barbed wire on their skids abruptly halting their momentum. Tragically, one glider landed too far from the bridge, and another right in front of a Belgian pillbox, sparking an immediate firefight. Despite this, the airborne troops quickly neutralized the pillbox with grenades and explosive charges, clearing the path for further action. Meanwhile, Lieutenant Altmann and his men ingeniously disabled demolition charges on the bridge, thwarting Belgian efforts to destroy this crucial crossing. Although German reinforcements later arrived to push back the Belgian defenders, Group Steel struggled against two field guns until air support from Junkers Ju 87 Stukas turned the tide. The fierce fighting left eight of the airborne soldiers dead and thirty wounded, and they weren't relieved until 21:30 due to persistent Belgian resistance.

Simultaneously, Group Concrete faced their own harrowing challenges at the Vroenhoven bridge. Ten of their eleven gliders landed successfully at 05:15, with one unfortunately hit by anti-aircraft fire and forced down in Dutch territory. Amidst heavy fire, one glider tragically stalled and crashed, injuring three soldiers. Despite these setbacks, the airborne troops swiftly overran a fortification, disabling the bridge's detonators and saving it from destruction. Repeated Belgian counterattacks were repelled, assisted by machine guns dropped by parachute. This group sustained seven fatalities and twenty-four injuries before being relieved at 21:40.

Meanwhile, Group Iron's mission at the Kanne bridge was marked by misfortune. Nine of their ten gliders navigated through intense anti-aircraft fire, but the bridge was already demolished by Belgian defenders who had been forewarned by the early arrival of German mechanized reinforcements. As the gliders landed, one was struck by anti-aircraft fire and crashed, causing significant casualties. However, the surviving airborne troops bravely overcame the defenders and secured the area, including the nearby village of Kanne. They endured several fierce counterattacks throughout the night, necessitating air support from Stuka dive bombers. Group Iron suffered the highest casualties: twenty-two killed and twenty-six wounded. In a dramatic twist, one of their captured soldiers was later liberated by

German forces from a British POW camp at Dunkirk.

Group Granite successfully executed a daring airborne assault on Fort Ében-Émael. Using nine gliders equipped with arrester-parachutes, they landed on the fort's roof at a critical moment. Under the impromptu command of Oberfeldwebel Helmut Wenzel, the troops swiftly emerged and began their mission: disabling the fort's artillery, which threatened the recently captured bridges.

The assault was marked by precision and urgency. In the southern part of the fort, they first incapacitated an artillery observation casemate, then moved to destroy a traversing turret and another turret housing 75mm guns. Despite an initial setback where one of the guns remained operational, the troops relentlessly re-engaged and neutralized it. In another section, they faced larger turrets with heavy-caliber guns. Despite the challenge, they managed to damage them using primitive shaped charges, though complete destruction eluded them.

In the fort's northern section, the airborne troops employed similar tactics against machine-gun casemates and observation cupolas, even using a flamethrower in one instance. They encountered unexpected resistance from a retractable cupola, which necessitated air support from a Stuka squadron. Although the bombing didn't destroy the cupola, it effectively neutralized it for the remainder of the battle.

As the group focused on secondary targets, including anti-aircraft weapons and machine-guns, Oberleutnant Rudolf Witzig remarkably joined the fray. After an initial mislanding in German territory, he managed to arrive with a second glider, boosting the morale and strength of the group.

Despite continuous Belgian counter-attacks, the airborne troops held their ground effectively. The Belgian infantry, lacking coordinated artillery support, couldn't breach the fort's defenses. The Germans maintained control, sealing off the fort's entrances and exits and using patrols to contain the garrison. Any potential counter-attack was thwarted by the fort's design, with a single spiral staircase being the only viable route for a Belgian assault.

Originally, Group Granite was to be relieved within hours, but due to heavy resistance and logistical challenges, relief didn't arrive until the morning of May 11th. When the 51st Engineer Battalion finally arrived, they joined forces with an infantry regiment to mount an attack on the fort's main entrance. This led to the surrender of the garrison, with the Germans capturing over a thousand Belgian soldiers. Group Granite's bold and effective operation resulted in six fatalities and nineteen injuries, significantly impacting the course of the war.

Battle of Hannut

General Billotte faced a critical decision: whether to deploy his armored forces to bolster the beleaguered Belgian Army or to take a more cautious approach. His subordinate, General Prioux, harbored deep reservations about the Belgian defense capabilities and was wary of exposing his forces to the formidable Luftwaffe. Prioux's strategy was to form a layered defense, positioning his dragoons and support units in fortified strongholds, with tanks strategically placed behind for swift counterattacks against any breaches by enemy forces. Billotte, recognizing the urgency of the situation, concurred with Prioux's plan. He underscored the necessity of rapid movement for the First Army Group, insisting they advance both day and night towards Gembloux, undeterred by the looming threat of enemy aircraft, to stall the relentless advance of the Panzers until the dawn of May 14th.

Meanwhile, at 11:00 A.M. on May 11th, Billotte made a pivotal move to ensure the safety of his advancing forces by redirecting the majority of the French 23rd Fighter Group to provide critical air cover. This decision, however, left the cavalry with minimal air support as more fighters were allocated for bomber escort missions. The Allied bombers focused their efforts on slowing the menacing advance of Hoepner's Panzers. As the enemy's armored units advanced, Prioux's reconnaissance units gradually retreated towards the main cavalry force, which was entrenched in a series of robust positions along a 40-kilometer front.

The battlefield chosen by Prioux was a strategically advantageous plateau, interspersed with woods, a dense road network, and isolated large farms, providing a complex terrain for the impending clash. The Mehaigne and Petite Gette streams, with their deep, rocky beds, offered not only natural barriers but also concealed routes for potential infiltrators. The pivotal terrain feature, however, was the ridge running from Hannut through Crehen and Merdorp, presenting a natural corridor for mechanized forces.

Prioux's deployment of the 3rd Light Mechanized Division over a 17-kilometer front stretched the limits of French military doctrine. The 1939 French cavalry manual, partly authored by General Langlois who now commanded the 3e DLM, advised on decentralized command in such scenarios. It suggested positioning combined-arms forces on each flank of potential breaches, with mobile artillery and reserves maintaining a continuous line of fire. However, this defense would transform into a strategic retreat if the enemy launched a full-frontal assault. The manual emphasized that in the face of overwhelming odds, particularly on open terrain against superior armored forces, the units should concentrate their forces rather than spread them thinly. Yet, Prioux chose to deviate from these guidelines.

On May 11th, the French command structured its cavalry front. The 3e DLM, under General Langlois, was divided into northern and southern sectors. The northern sector, led by Colonel Dodart des Loges, comprised various units strategically positioned along the Petite Gette, backed by a formidable array of Hotchkiss tanks and artillery support. The southern sector, under General de Lafont, guarded the open terrain near Hannut with dragoon battalions fortified in key locations, supported by both artillery and SOMUA tank squadrons. South of Crehen, the 2nd Light Mechanized Division formed a defensive line along the Mehaigne creek, extending to Huy on the Meuse river, preparing to face the impending German onslaught.

On the 12th of May, the German 4th Panzer Division, part of General Hoepner's command, rapidly advanced towards Hannut, their initial target, arriving in the vicinity that morning. Hoepner had instructed both the 3rd and 4th Panzer Divisions to focus their efforts on capturing Hannut, a move critical for securing the 6th Army's flank. Major-General Stever of the 4th Pz. Div., facing challenges such as a lack of fuel and the delayed arrival of artillery and infantry support, requested an emergency air-drop of fuel. Despite these setbacks and believing he was up against a single French battalion, Stever boldly initiated an engagement against the French defenses.

That morning, the 4th Pz. Div. encountered a French armored force comprising approximately 25 tanks. In a significant show of strength, the 4th Pz. Div. managed to destroy seven French tanks without sustaining any losses themselves.

Meanwhile, Allied air forces intensified their focus on Stever's unit, potentially complicating his mission. The RAF deployed 38 bombers, losing 22 in the process. The French Air Force launched two major bombing raids, including one with 18 of its new Breguet 693 bombers, resulting in the loss of eight aircraft. The German Jagdgeschwader 27, equipped with 85 Messerschmitt 109s, flew 340 sorties that day, claiming 26 Allied aircraft for the loss of only four of their fighters. German anti-aircraft artillery also claimed 25 enemy aircraft. However, that afternoon, General Georges redirected air support priorities from the Belgian plain to the more vulnerable central front near Sedan, significantly reducing air cover for Prioux's cavalry formations.

Prioux, having relinquished the initiative and with only limited air reconnaissance capabilities, found himself in a position of waiting to discern the Panzers' focus. He anchored his right flank on the Meuse, defending Huy with two battalions of motorized heavy infantry, along with some dragoons and artillery. His left flank was in coordination with British light cavalry and elements of the Belgian Cavalry Corps, which were delaying enemy advances along the St. Trond-Tirlemont axis. That afternoon, German armored cars and infantry units made probing moves towards Tirlemont, leading the French Cavalry Corps to dispatch a squadron of tanks and one of its divisional reconnaissance groups to the area, supported by arriving British reinforcements. This German effort mainly served as reconnaissance and a diversion.

On the battlefield, the German 35th Panzer Regiment, part of Stever's division advancing towards Hannut, encountered strong resistance from well-positioned French armor, which launched several counterattacks. Eventually, the French forces withdrew from Hannut without a direct confrontation. Unaware of this retreat, German forces attempted to encircle the town. In an unexpected encounter, about 50 German light Panzers clashed with a French strongpoint at Crehen, defended by 21 Hotchkiss tanks of the 2nd Cuirassiers and elements of the 76th Artillery Regiment, with additional support from the nearby 2nd Light Mechanized Division (2d DLM). The dragoons suffered heavy losses, but the Hotchkiss tanks played a crucial role in the defense, even after losing their commander. As German medium tanks tried to pin down the French forces, their light tanks attempted to flank the position. However, the main French force fell back to Merdorp. The encircled 2nd Cuirassiers were eventually rescued by a counterattack from the 2d DLM, using SOMUA S35 tanks to break through the German lines. This breakout resulted in significant French casualties, leaving the right flank of the 4th Pz. Div. in a vulnerable position.

Swiftly mobilizing from Oreye, approximately 11 kilometers northeast of Hannut, the German 3rd Panzer Division was dispatched to counter the emerging threat. By 4:30 P.M., the German 6th Army, keen on understanding the battlefield dynamics, called for air reconnaissance. The Luftwaffe's report revealed the presence of French armored units at Orp and motorized forces at Gembloux. In response, Reichenau, the commander of the German 6th Army, directed Hoepner to advance the XVI Corps towards Gembloux, aiming to thwart any French efforts to establish a defensive line. However, Hoepner remained concerned about his stretched supply lines and, notably, his vulnerable flanks. While the IV Corps was engaged in the St. Trond area, moving towards Tirlemont and keeping Prioux on edge, the XXVII Corps was delayed north of Liège, about 38 kilometers east of Hannut, leaving a significant gap on Hoepner's southern flank.

To address this, the Germans formulated a plan to create a vanguard comprising a Panzer battalion, a rifle battalion, and two artillery groups. This unit was to advance to Perwez, situated 18 kilometers southwest of Hannut. Stever, however, instructed that if they encountered substantial resistance, the attack should be halted. Under robust air and artillery support, the German force approached the French strongpoint at Thisnes, while disregarding the French counterattack at Crehen. In Thisnes, barricaded streets and intense French artillery fire halted the leading tank company. The rest of the German unit tried to flank the French position, but poor visibility complicated their maneuver. Reaching the western edge of Thisnes, they faced fierce artillery fire from another French strongpoint at Wansin. Ordered to regroup and establish a defensive perimeter, their efforts were disrupted by a counterattack from French SOMUA tanks, resulting in the destruction of the Panzer Regiment commander's vehicle. After intense combat, both French and German tanks withdrew under the cover of darkness, occasionally encountering each other. The French pulled back to Merdorp, while the Germans retreated to the Hannut area.

At 8:00 P.M., Stever reported to Hoepner, expressing his belief that they were facing two French mechanized divisions, one positioned in front of them and the other behind the Mehaigne river. They concurred on launching a major offensive the following day, with the 4th Pz. Div. focusing on the right side of Gembloux, coordinating with the 3rd Panzer Division, which would receive support from Fliegerkorps VIII.

That night, the Germans tested the French defenses with an attack. The French strongpoint at Wansin engaged in an all-night battle against German infantry, eventually withdrawing in the early hours of May 13th. The front held by the 3rd Light Mechanized Division remained intact, maintaining positions near Tienen, Jandrenouille, and Merdorp. Similarly, the 2nd Light Mechanized Division kept its original front. The only breach occurred at Winson, where the 2nd and 3rd DLMs converged. Ultimately, Hoepner's objective remained unfulfilled, and as the day concluded, French armor, contrary to German reports, had decidedly prevailed.

In a pivotal moment southeast of the plain, German forces initiated their main offensive across the Meuse River. Meanwhile, to the north, General Hoepner engaged in diversionary attacks, effectively pinning down the robust French First Army to prevent it from intervening. Hoepner mistakenly assumed that the newly arrived 3rd Panzer Division (3rd Pz. Div.) faced only feeble enemy forces, while he believed the 4th Panzer Division (4th Pz. Div.) was up against formidable French mechanized units at Hannut and Thisnes — areas the French had already vacated — and potentially another French mechanized division south of the Mehaigne. Late in the morning, the Luftwaffe launched strikes to weaken the enemy's defenses. The 3rd Pz. Div. advanced towards Thorembais, while the 4th Panzer aimed at Perwez, expecting to encounter strong Belgian anti-tank defenses. Consequently, the XVI Army Corps adjusted its strategy, pressing forward towards Gembloux as directed by the 6th Army.

In the face of German infantry and armored vehicle assaults, the French 12th Cuirassiers and the 3rd Battalion of the 11th Dragoons valiantly repelled wave after wave. Despite their efforts, the German 18th Infantry Division managed to break through their lines. French plans for a counter-attack with tanks from the 1st Cuirassiers to reestablish their positions were aborted due to developments across the broader front of the 3rd Light Mechanized Division (3rd DLM). By the afternoon, a French command retreat was ordered, with the Allied forces managing to evade pursuit due to the slow advance of the German infantry. Positioned just south of Hoepner's intended attack path, the 2nd Light Mechanized Division (2nd DLM) deployed about 30 SOMUA S-35 tanks from the Mehaigne to the Merdorp-Crehen line, aiming to alleviate pressure on the 3rd DLM. However, this move was met with intense enemy tank and anti-tank fire near Crehen, resulting in severe losses.

General Bougrain, leading the 2nd DLM, reported enemy infiltrations and armored car assaults across the Mehaigne river at Moha and Wanze, north of Huy. These attacks posed a significant threat to the large Belgian garrison in Huy. Bougrain redirected his tank reserves to address this crisis. By 3:00 P.M., a French reconnaissance aircraft spotted large German armor formations southeast of Crehen, leaving the 2nd DLM without any available reserves for intervention.

Bougrain's forces, comprising Dragoons and motorized infantry, were dispersed across isolated strongpoints, making them susceptible to enemy infiltration. Despite an offer from the retreating Belgian III Corps to bolster his troops along the Mehaigne river, Bougrain declined. This decision, coupled with Prioux's disregard for centralized French defensive doctrine, led to a fragmented command structure, adversely affecting French operational performance and compromising their defensive efforts.

On the German side, concerns about the potential interference of the 2nd DLM with their primary attack prompted the reallocation of infantry units between the XVI and XXVII Corps. They mobilized four units from the 35th, 61st, and 269th Infantry Divisions, supported by air and armored car units, to infiltrate between French strongpoints north of Huy. This maneuver successfully engaged Bougrain's armor, allowing Hoepner to focus on Prioux's front west of Hannut. Had Bougrain concentrated his armor for a north or northeast advance, he could have significantly disrupted the German plan, but no such directive was given by Prioux.

The critical action on May 13th unfolded west of Hannut. Hoepner received orders from the 6th Army not only to breach through to Gembloux but also to pursue the enemy west of that location. Hoepner amassed his Corps's Panzer and rifle battalions, including around 560 operational tanks, on a 12-kilometer front. This force was complemented on the right by the 18th Infantry Division of the IV Corps. The 3rd Panzer, facing Marilles and Orp to the north, and the 4th Panzer, facing Thisnes and Merdorp, initiated their offensive around 11:30 A.M. The 3rd Panzer Brigade, with its 5th and 6th Panzer Regiments, led the charge. By noon, they engaged in intense combat in the barricaded and mined towns along the Petite Gette river. After about 90 minutes, both regiments managed to push back elements of the French defense across the stream. Most of the 6th Regiment then pivoted south towards Jandrain and Jandrenouille to support the 4th Panzer Division in more favorable terrain. Encountering French armor inthe Orp area, they faced further French assaults but ultimately combined to repel these attacks.

In the heat of the afternoon, the German forces launched their assault. The 3rd Panzer Division was positioned to the north, facing Marilles and Orp, while the 4th Panzer Division was oriented towards Thisnes and Merdorp. Both the 5th and 6th Panzer Brigades of the 3rd Pz. Div. encountered aggressive French armor, leading to a fierce confrontation with both sides on the offensive. The German Panzers, with their numerical advantage, moved in large formations compared to the smaller, slower-firing groups of the French. From 3:00 to 3:48 P.M., the 3rd Panzer Brigade urgently requested anti-tank support and air assistance from the Luftwaffe to counteract the French tanks. During this time, the 2nd Battalion of the 5th Panzer Regiment, near Marilles, found itself unexpectedly flanked and attacked by superior French armored forces. A critical 15-minute period was noted in the 3rd Panzer Brigade's war diary, during which the 2nd Battalion was isolated. However, the 1st Battalion of the 5th Panzer Regiment, observing a breakthrough on their left, reinforced their right flank, turning the tide at

Marilles around 4:00 P.M. Concurrently, as the German infantry secured Orp, there was an urgent demand for 37mm and 75mm ammunition.

Earlier that day, the 2nd Battalion of the 11th Dragoons, part of the French defense, sustained heavy losses due to air and artillery bombardment. German motorcyclists and armored cars probed for weak points in their lines. Around 11:30 A.M., the 3rd Light Mechanized Division (3rd DLM) reported encountering approximately 80 German tanks near Marilles and about 100 near Orp. The Dragoons, supported by their Hotchkiss tanks, valiantly defended their positions, but their resistance began to falter around 1:30 P.M., overwhelmed by German numbers and a depletion of munitions.

Colonel Dodart des Loges, commanding the northern sector of the 3rd DLM, ordered a retreat. During the withdrawal, the remaining Dragoons, along with two Hotchkiss squadrons from the 1st Cuirassiers, counter-attacked, pushing the German armor back towards the stream. The losses were roughly equal on both sides, with the French claiming to have destroyed six German tanks at the cost of four of their own. Colonel de Vernejoul, leading the 1st Cuirassiers, dispatched 36 SOMUA S-35 tanks to stop German armor advancing from Orp towards Jandrain. However, the French forces were caught off guard by a German attack from concealed positions, leading to the defeat of the French counter-offensive.

This engagement was the main effort by the 3rd DLM to halt the advance of the 3rd Pz. Div. Meanwhile, the 2nd Light Mechanized Division conducted raids against the vulnerable flanks of the 4th Pz. Div. Although some French tank groups managed to break through, they were swiftly countered by the German 654th Anti-tank Battalion, attached to the 4th Pz. Div. Other than these sporadic raids, the 2nd DLM did not undertake any further significant attacks on the flank of the 4th Pz. Div.

As the sun reached its zenith, the 4th Panzer Division launched a daring assault on the strategic town of Medorp. Amidst a thunderous symphony of

French and German artillery, a dramatic chess game unfolded. The French, with a cunning maneuver, redeployed their armored units into Medorp, turning the deserted streets into a treacherous battlefield. The German tanks, initially stymied by the elusive French positions, made a bold decision to flank the town. This move, however, left their infantry vulnerable, sparking a fierce clash as French armor pressed their advantage.

The battle's tide turned when the Germans executed a rapid about-face, confronting the French in an open-field showdown. Utilizing their famed "schwerpunkt" tactics, the Germans concentrated their might against the French's superior firepower. Amidst the chaos, small bands of French infantry launched daring rear assaults, only to be repelled by the tenacious German infantry.

Meanwhile, the 3rd Panzer Division, in concert with the 4th, advanced towards Jandrain. There, a ferocious tank battle erupted, echoing across the countryside. The German Panzers, outnumbering their adversaries, claimed a decisive victory, leaving 22 French SOMUA S-35 tanks in ruins. The German juggernaut rolled on, capturing the town and 400 prisoners, along with numerous enemy tanks.

As night fell, the French 2nd and 3rd Light Mechanized Divisions commenced a strategic withdrawal, leaving the Panzer Divisions free to chase down the retreating forces. The 3rd Panzer Brigade tallied an impressive score of 54 French tanks destroyed, a testament to their armored prowess. Despite suffering some losses, the German forces quickly repaired their disabled tanks, maintaining their formidable presence on the battlefield.

As dawn broke, the remnants of the 3rd Light Mechanized Division held a defensive line stretching from Beauvechain to Perwez, while the 2nd Division regrouped south of Perwez.

On the morning of May 14th, a dramatic showdown unfolded as German forces launched an ambitious attack on Perwez. General Stumpff, leading the 3rd Panzer Division, was tasked with confronting the Allied defenses near Gembloux, while General Stever, at the helm of the 4th Panzer Division, aimed to penetrate the center at Perwez. Despite Hoepner's bold decision to initiate the assault without infantry support, the German forces found themselves unable to breach the staunch French positions.

In the dense woods surrounding Perwez, the 4th Panzer Division encountered fierce resistance from French armored units. It was a grueling battle, but eventually, with the arrival of German infantry reinforcements, the French defenses crumbled. The French First Army, having dispersed its tank battalions behind infantry lines, faced a dire situation. Isolated and outnumbered, these battalions succumbed to the overwhelming might of the German combined arms teams.

Meanwhile, the 3rd Panzer Division met with stubborn opposition from the 2nd Light Mechanized Division. Intense and bitter combat ensued, with the emergence of numerous French tanks sending ripples of panic through the German Command, mistakenly believing a major counterattack was underway. In reality, these were merely rearguard actions. Both sides endured heavy losses in their armored ranks.

As dusk settled, the 2nd Light Mechanized Division ceased its rearguard actions, allowing the German Command to regroup and regain its strategic poise.

Battle of Gembloux

On May 14th, the German Panzer divisions embarked on a bold mission to breach the Dyle defensive line. Until the early morning, aerial reconnaissance had led them to believe the area was undefended. However, by 09:20, the reality of a well-fortified position became apparent. General Hoepner, accompanying the 4th Panzer Division, urged a swift breakthrough near

Ernage, not waiting for the 3rd Panzer Division to join. Flanking these Panzer units were the 35th Infantry and 20th Motorized Divisions, ready to support from the right and left.

The 4th Panzer Division, combining the efforts of its Panzer and Rifle Brigades, initiated an aggressive push forward. Their left flank was shielded by a reconnaissance battalion, a machine-gun battalion, and a large contingent of an anti-tank battalion. However, at 11:30, the Eighth Company of the 35th Panzer Regiment, with around 30 tanks, faced a staunch resistance near Ernage. The enemy's artillery fire was devastating, resulting in the loss of nine tanks and forcing a retreat. The 6th Company, hindered by intense defensive fire, could not provide assistance.

By 13:30, the 4th Panzer Brigade encountered entrenched enemy forces between the railway line and the Wavre-Gembloux highway. It was clear now that the Dyle position was actively defended. The activities of the 3rd Panzer Division that day were less documented. In the morning, the 3rd Panzer Brigade, following the 4th Division, crossed the Belgian anti-tank barrier with the 5th Panzer Regiment on the right and the 6th on the left. Colonel Kuhn, leading the 6th Panzer Regiment, found himself embroiled in fierce battles in Ernage and along the Wavre-Gembloux road, facing heavy artillery and anti-tank fire. Kuhn opted to wait for infantry reinforcements.

Meanwhile, the German 6th Army mobilized its infantry corps, advancing them to secure the flanks of the embattled Panzer divisions, which had inadvertently run headlong into a robust French defensive line.

On May 14th, Schwedler's IV Corps, tasked with safeguarding the right flank of the Panzer divisions as it did against the French cavalry at Hannut the previous day, made significant headway. Encountering minimal resistance, advance units of the 31st, 7th, and 18th Infantry Divisions reached the Dyle position by afternoon and evening. At 21:50, the 6th Army's Chief of Staff ordered the infantry to bolster the 3rd Panzer Division, which was engaged in intense combat at Walhain and Ernage. By day's end, the divisions confirmed that the Dyle position was manned. However, the approach was hindered by demolitions and mines.

As the German forces advanced, the French First Army was beleaguered by Luftwaffe attacks. French aerial reconnaissance efforts, hampered by losses, were limited, providing only sporadic updates on the enemy's progression. The retreating Cavalry Corps relayed information about the Panzer movements north of Ernage (near the 3rd Light Mechanized Division) and around Grand Leez (near the 2nd Light Mechanized Division). Following their withdrawal, Blanchard ordered the cavalry's tanks to remain in reserve, while the German offensive continued southward.

That evening, Billotte's headquarters signaled a potential retreat for the First Army, a directive unknown to the troops in the field. The 1st Motorized Infantry Division, already unsettled by the retreat of the cavalry and Belgian forces and the influx of refugees, faced its first Stuka attack, leaving a profound impact. Misinformation about parachutists led to friendly fire incidents, resulting in casualties among the artillerymen. By evening, de La Laurencie's III Corps, along with British and Belgian units on the Dyle line and near Namur, engaged with German patrols.

Despite Hoepner's realization that the Dyle position was fortified, higher commands insisted he pursue the "defeated" enemy until late afternoon. The 3rd Panzer Division found itself embroiled in combat on its right flank. At 14:00, the XVI Corps directed the 35th Infantry Division towards this conflict, while the 20th Motorized Division was ordered to the opposite flank. The arrival of the 269th Infantry Division from the XVII Corps alleviated concerns to the north of Namur. At 14:05, General Stever of the 4th Panzer Division commanded the 5th Panzer Brigade, supported by a rifle battalion, to launch a narrow-front assault south of Ernage, aiming for the hills east of St. Gery. The divisional artillery was set to counter flanking fire from Ernage and Gembloux. However, the attack was postponed at 16:00 for the 3rd

Panzer Division to prepare. By 16:50, Stumpff radioed that he would signal when ready, but commenced an attack in the Ernage area independently. After 18:00, XVI Corps urged its divisions to advance, yet the density of French defensive barrages led to a false poison gas alert, halting the attacks. Finally, at 20:50, Hoepner instructed his division commanders to cease their offensive until the following morning.

During that afternoon, the 4th Panzer Division found itself beleaguered not only by the resilient French defense but also by internal command confusion. General Stever, seeking to reassess the situation, met with Colonel Breith, leader of the 5th Panzer Brigade, and Boyneburg, commander of the 4th Rifle Brigade. Both officers agreed that a coordinated attack was no longer feasible for the day. The French artillery, operating from Baudeset, unleashed a barrage that was devastatingly precise. This shelling claimed the lives of two unnamed rifle battalion commanders and struck numerous German tanks with unerring accuracy. The harassing artillery fire persisted throughout the night, compelling tank crews to seek shelter by digging in beneath their tanks.

The actions of the 3rd Panzer Division on May 14th remain somewhat ambiguous. The division's 6th Panzer Regiment, positioned on the left flank, did engage in an assault in the Ernage area during the afternoon but was halted by defensive fire. The anticipated support from riflemen never materialized, leaving the 3rd Panzer Brigade exposed and reportedly under enemy aerial surveillance after 19:00. Concurrently, intense clashes were reported with tanks (likely from the 3rd Light Mechanized Division) in the Walhain and St. Paul regions. French tanks also emerged at Ernage, leading the Panzer Brigade to erroneously conclude that they faced a critical situation. They believed that enemy armor, effectively challenged only by the 75 mm guns of their Panzer IVs, was attempting a breakthrough with artillery support coordinated by spotter aircraft. This assessment, though mistaken, reflected the psychological toll on the command of the 3rd Panzer Brigade.

As night fell, the battlefield quieted. The long-awaited infantry finally arrived, spurred on by urgent orders issued earlier. Advancing in darkness, they mistakenly came under fire from their own tanks. Despite this, one battalion nearly reached the French main position, only to find itself isolated near Ernage and Perbais without radio contact with its division as dawn approached.

General Hoepner, faced with a robust French defense, made the critical decision to deploy his tanks, bolstered by available artillery and air support, immediately rather than delay for a day to gather his two infantry divisions for a stronger coordinated attack. Influenced by encouragement from his superiors and the principles of German military doctrine emphasizing swift action to preempt enemy preparations, he resolved around 20:00 on May 14th not to wait.

Despite intelligence from the 6th Army suggesting that the Allies were in retreat and erroneously claiming that German tanks had already breached west of Gembloux, Hoepner remained committed to his plan. At 22:45, the XVI Corps ordered a combined assault by the 3rd and 4th Panzer Divisions for 08:00 on May 15th, targeting the railway line around Tilly, well ahead of the French defenses at Gembloux. The attack would be supported by the Fliegerkorps VIII and available artillery, focusing on a front less than 6 kilometers wide on both sides of Ernage. Engineering units were assigned to repair the bridges and crossroads demolished by the retreating Allies, crucial for maintaining logistical flow.

General Stever of the 4th Panzer Division arranged for his 4th Rifle Brigade to form a line extending from Gembloux to Ernage, with a staggered formation on their left flank. The plan included air support and a 30-minute artillery bombardment on the French main position, followed by smoke cover over Gembloux. Then, his artillery units, alongside a heavy battalion, would focus on counter-battery fire and areas impenetrable to armor. Anti-aircraft guns were designated to neutralize enemy bunkers, although there were none.

When the infantry crossed the railroad line, signaling with white starshell, the 5th Panzer Brigade would emerge and attack in unison with the riflemen, followed by a pursuit towards Nivelles.

Stumpff's strategy for the 3rd Panzer Division was less detailed but involved placing infantry ahead of the tanks with support from Stuka dive-bombers and artillery. He ordered a few tank units to reinforce the infantry, aiming to secure two hills west of the Chastre-Noirmont line, keeping most of the armor in reserve to counter enemy tanks or exploit any breakthrough.

On the right flank of the Panzer Divisions, the IV Corps was set for intense combat on the morning of May 15th. By 09:20, it alerted its divisions to a "decisive battle" forming on the Dyle and called for a focused attack in the Ottignies region, at the junction of the 7th and 18th Infantry Divisions. An exploitation group was prepared to advance post-breakthrough. Concurrently, the Luftwaffe, though reduced in many units to 30-50% strength, received reinforcements from Fliegerkorps I of Luftflotte 3, reflecting the high command's prioritization of the 6th Army's efforts to overpower the Allied forces.

First Battle of Perbais

On this sweltering day, French artillery had pounded the battlefield throughout the night, setting the stage for a tense morning. Despite this, the German Stuka dive-bombers and artillery commenced their preparatory barrage at 07:30. At 08:00, the infantry of the 4th Panzer Division began their advance, initially unhampered by enemy fire. By 08:10, riflemen signaled with white starshell that they had crossed the railroad line, but soon after, at 08:20, they came under intense French artillery fire. As the German tanks moved forward, they found themselves effectively immobilized by the barrage.

By 09:30, the situation was dire for the 36th Panzer Regiment, sustaining heavy losses at the frontline obstacle, with the 35th Panzer Regiment facing a similar plight by 09:45. Communication from the 5th Panzer Brigade headquarters revealed a grim assessment of the infantry's progress: "attack hopeless." By 10:00, II Battalion of the 12th Rifle Regiment had managed to reach the railway line at Gembloux with one company, but the advance was slow, costly, and came to a standstill by 11:00. Radio contact with the 5th Panzer Brigade was lost, leaving the tanks in disarray and vulnerable to being systematically destroyed.

Simultaneously, the infantry of the 3rd Panzer Division launched an attack from Walhain-St. Paul towards Perbais at 09:15. However, like their counterparts, they were bogged down by 11:00. The war diarist of the XVI Corps lamented that the tanks of the 4th Panzer Division had engaged prematurely, before the anti-tank obstacles were cleared. The corps operations officer, Chales de Beaulieu, of French descent, criticized the 3rd Panzer Division for its failure to adequately support its infantry, leaving the tanks in reserve while the infantry struggled.

The efforts of the Ju 87s and artillery to neutralize the French guns proved futile. Intelligence on French battery positions was too vague to be effective, and one reconnaissance aircraft was thwarted by enemy fighters. By 10:30, even the heavy German artillery battalion had to retreat from the French counter-battery fire. By 11:18, the intensity of the French shelling on the German approach routes and positions led the corps artillery commander to conclude that maintaining their gains and bringing in reinforcements were severely jeopardized.

Reports indicated that the German assault was effectively stalled on the Wavre-Gembloux road, with only a single battalion initially reaching the railway. This was quickly followed by a supposed French tank and infantry counterattack, against which the German anti-tank guns were largely ineffective. Some German anti-tank gun crews reportedly abandoned their positions without firing a shot. However, there are no French records confirming the presence of their tanks in the battle at this juncture.

On a day marked by fierce combat, Colonel Breith, leading the 5th Panzer Brigade in his command tank with the 35th Panzer Regiment, witnessed his attack stalling. In an attempt to rally the troops, Breith ordered some of his officers to leave their vehicles and encourage the riflemen to engage the anti-tank guns. Amid the chaos, they noticed anti-tank mines scattered unburied on the battlefield. As some French and Moroccan soldiers began to surrender and an infantry support gun joined the fray, Breith's command tank sustained two hits, though it remained unbreached. Suddenly, a bright flash struck the vehicle, lightly wounding Breith and forcing the crew to abandon the tank. A subsequent rescue attempt by a light tank failed as it too was hit, leaving the crew to seek refuge in shell holes. Nearby, Captain Jungenfeld observed the destruction of all heavy vehicles of the Fourth Company, including the tank of Lieutenant Colonel Eberbach, who declared, "further advance is simply impossible. Our tanks sit and before the obstacles the defence fire strikes us mercilessly."

As the tanks began retreating, the 12th Rifle Regiment's I. Battalion also fell back against orders, leading staff officers to intervene to stop the retreat. An effort by the 36th Panzer Regiment to exploit a gap near Lonzee against the 15th Motorized Infantry Division was instantly thwarted by French fire, halting the 4th Panzer Division.

The 3rd Panzer Division's battle unfolded differently, as it had held back its tank brigade. At dawn on May 15th, the 3rd Rifle Regiment's Third Battalion was northeast of Ernage, but its I and II Battalions had inadvertently created a gap between the 3rd and 4th Panzer Divisions. Consequently, the 3rd Panzer Division found itself more engaged against the French 110th Infantry Regiment at Perbais. Despite intense German air and artillery bombardment, the I Battalion's initial attack on Ernage was repelled by infantry fire. Following further bombardment, the II Battalion's advance towards Perbais also failed. The commanders of both battalions coordinated for a renewed effort, supported by the 75th Artillery Regiment's observed fire. This, along with a Ju 87 attack, enabled the riflemen to capture Perbais and reach the railway line, albeit with heavy losses.

Overall, the morning was detrimental for the XVI Corps. The Luftwaffe's intense efforts left a significant impact on the French side, where only minimal air support was provided by the Armée de l'Air. Reconnaissance efforts by the French First Army and IV Corps were hindered by enemy flak and fighters, ensuring German air superiority.

IV Corps bore the brunt of the Panzer assault. Reports of approximately 300 enemy tanks and successive waves of Ju 87 attacks since dawn overwhelmed the French positions. The enemy breached the railway in the 2nd Moroccan Regiment's sector, and reports of Perbais and Chastre falling raised alarms about the IV Corps' left flank. Aymes, in response, distributed his reserve infantry and called for a counterattack by the 3rd Light Mechanized Division's tank brigade. However, a command miscommunication led to General La Font of the 3rd DLM being informed that de La Laurencie of the III Corps had already commandeered the armor, unbeknownst to Aymes.

On this day, the Moroccan Division faced an overwhelming onslaught from roughly one and a third Panzer Divisions. The 7th Moroccan Regiment in Ernage, alongside the 110th Regiment in Perbais, fought valiantly before being forced to yield ground. Despite being encircled, a mixed post between these two regiments held out until 15:00. The 2nd Moroccan Regiment, positioned on exposed terrain, suffered heavy losses by noon, with seven of their front-line platoons nearly annihilated. However, their support units maintained their positions. The 1st Moroccan Regiment in Gembloux was pushed back into the town but managed to hold its ground, even as the enemy infiltrated westward along the Gembloux-Nivelles railway.

General Mellier, surveying his front on a motorcycle, assessed his center and right at Gembloux as secure but recognized the pressing threats at Ernage and along the Gembloux-Nivelles railroad. He planned to reestablish contact with the 1st Motorized Infantry Division near Cortil-Noirmont and retake the main position using the corps reserve and La Font's tank brigade. To stabilize his right-center, he intended to deploy the divisional reserve and the 35th Tank Battalion.

French artillery played a crucial role in the battle. Anticipating a reduced tank threat, forward-positioned batteries returned to their units. From dawn, the Ju 87s targeted the DM's artillery, causing chaos and overturning some guns, although they later rejoined the action. A reservist battalion panicked, and a 105mm gun battalion, not yet integrated into the fire plan, suffered casualties. When these guns fired at maximum rate against suspected German tank positions, they drew heavy air attacks.

The infantry and support weapons were hit hard, with significant losses among junior officers, crucial for leading colonial troops. The 1st Battalion of the 2nd Moroccan Regiment, positioned on the railroad line, suffered heavy casualties, including the deaths and wounding of several company commanders. Despite initial shock, the troops adapted to the Ju 87 attacks, learning to disperse and take cover only when necessary. French anti-aircraft and automatic weapons inflicted damage on their attackers.

By this stage, ammunition shortages among the French forces slowed their rate of fire. This allowed some German tanks to maneuver around their flank, but they were quickly spotted and seven tanks were destroyed. The 110th Regiment grappled with the northern wing of the Panzer attack, retreating under heavy bombardment and enemy infiltration, exposing vulnerabilities in their front.

To the northwest, the IV Corps engaged in a parallel battle. Attempts to cross the Dyle were thwarted, and the infantry divisions organized coordinated attacks, pushing French outposts back towards Ottignies around 10:00. The 7th Infantry Division prepared an attack at Limal, while the 31st Infantry Division regrouped for an engagement with the British north of Wavre. Thus, the French III Corps found itself embroiled in intense combat on the morning of May 15th, with the 110th Regiment being the only unit directly facing enemy tanks. Despite efforts from the 2nd North African Infantry Division's artillery, enemy infiltrations could not be entirely halted. By noon, the defenders were forced to retreat to Ottignies.

Second Battle of Perbais

General Hoepner, determined to break through the French defenses, coordinated a new Stuka dive-bomber attack for 12:00, instructing his divisions to capitalize on this to penetrate enemy lines. However, the relentless French artillery fire continued, and by 12:30, Lieutenant Colonel Eberbach, commanding the 35th Panzer Regiment, refused to recommence the attack after losing half his tanks, including his own. General Stever, attempting to rally the troops at the 33rd Rifle Regiment headquarters, was wounded by a French shell and evacuated. With Colonel Breith, commander of the 5th Panzer Brigade, out of contact, command fell to Colonel Boyneburg of the 4th Rifle Brigade. Around 14:00, Hoepner relayed orders to cease the offensive, although he did not call off the efforts of the 3rd Panzer Division in the Ernage area and began planning a new attack with the addition of the 35th and 20th Infantry Divisions.

The German command, initially overly optimistic, now swung to pessimism. The 6th Army denied the XVI Corps's request to resume the attack the following morning, opting instead for a full-scale army assault planned for May 17th. This delay was partly due to logistical challenges and difficulties in locating and neutralizing French artillery.

The war diary of the 4th Panzer Division starkly highlighted the day's failures. By 11:07, radio contact with the 5th Panzer Brigade was lost, and reports indicated heavy tank losses, making it untenable to remain under fire. Consequently, at 12:00, the division instructed its armor to fall back to starting positions. An hour later, the 4th Rifle Brigade also began withdrawing, leading Boyneburg to order a re-engagement. Stever, having moved forward to encourage the troops, returned wounded by 14:00. By 15:00, it was reported that the Panzer Brigade staff was stranded along the railroad line, with the 4th Rifle Brigade suffering heavy losses and little prospect of success. Breith, wounded and having spent hours under artillery fire, eventually returned to division headquarters. By 20:00, the XVI Corps informed the 4th Panzer Division that the renewed attack was scheduled for May 17th, but without their participation. Earlier, Hauptmann Jungenfeld had attempted a rescue for Breith, but his tank was hit four times and forced to retreat, leaving his men relieved to withdraw.

In a final effort, several German medium tanks crossed the anti-tank obstacle near a large factory targeted by their artillery. Supported by tank fire, the infantry began advancing, but French anti-tank guns quickly engaged the tanks, causing them to abandon their infantry support. The infantry, attempting a desperate charge, managed only to advance a few hundred meters near a railroad yard before being forced to retreat as night fell.

The 3rd Panzer Division faced a distinct set of challenges. Unlike other units, it had only deployed a portion of its tanks, and one of its three rifle battalions remained relatively unengaged. Throughout the afternoon, the division contended with reports from the adjacent 18th Infantry Division about potential French armored counterattacks targeting its right flank. In response, at 13:00, 88 mm Flak units and tanks from the 5th Panzer Regiment were dispatched to the Perbais area as a precaution. By 15:55, air reconnaissance identified tanks and infantry along the railroad line between Ernage and Chastre, although enemy fighters hindered observation. At 16:48, the 3rd Panzer Brigade reported heavy enemy artillery fire.

By 18:00, elements of the 3rd Rifle Brigade started to withdraw from Perbais, leading to a deployment of tanks to curb the retreat. However, at 18:20, the 3rd Panzer Brigade encountered intense fire while breaching the anti-tank obstacle northwest of Ernage, along with a counterattack from enemy armor. Simultaneously, the 18th Infantry Division reported enemy armor attacks near Corbais. At 20:00, analysis of a captured enemy map suggested a ripe opportunity for a breakthrough. However, this was in conflict with orders from the 6th Army, and the idea was abandoned. For the most part, the division's tanks remained on standby around Orbais.

In the afternoon, the 3rd Panzer's infantry began withdrawing from Perbais under French artillery pressure and reports of advancing French armor. Yet, the situation evolved rapidly. Around 18:00, two companies from the III Battalion of the 3rd Rifle Regiment, supported by a group of tanks, advanced westwards from Ernage towards Chastre. Despite stiff French resistance and alleged sightings of a few Hotchkiss tanks (possibly from the 3rd Light Mechanized Division), the Germans reached their original objectives west of Noirmont. However, they soon faced a counter-attack from French tanks and infantry on their open flank, prompting reinforcements from the 6th Panzer Regiment, including a Panzer III and five Panzer Is.

Luftwaffe reconnaissance alerted the Germans to the French armor's presence. The ensuing engagement reportedly saw the Germans destroy six French tanks and scatter the Moroccan infantry. A German machine gun company advanced two kilometers, capturing equipment but eventually running out of ammunition. French fire then resumed, with two tanks destroying the Panzer III and three Panzer Is. Following this setback, the III Battalion halted before the French defenses in the Cortil-Noirmont area. At 20:54, orders from the XVI Corps and the brigade to halt the attack and withdraw behind the railroad line were received.

Hoepner finally instructed the 3rd Panzer's forward units to maintain their positions, but by then, nearly all of the 3rd Rifle Regiment and its supporting tanks had retreated. Both the I and II Battalions were exhausted and had not been resupplied for 36 hours. Any fleeting chance of penetrating the French defenses had seemingly vanished.

Battle of Ernage

For the Moroccan Division, the afternoon was marked by intense combat, particularly on its northern flank. The most vulnerable point was on the left at Ernage, where the 1st Battalion of the 7th Moroccan Regiment faced encirclement. They lost communication with the neighboring 110th Infantry Regiment around midday when enemy forces breached the railroad line between Ernage and Perbais. By 12:30, the 1st Battalion made a strategic retreat to the 2nd Battalion's headquarters at Cortil-Noirmont. Despite being heavily outnumbered in Ernage, the 7th Moroccan Regiment continued to resist until 18:00, with only 12 men, including the wounded commanding officer, eventually surrendering after exhausting all their resources.

General Albert Mellier initially planned a counterattack with the La Font brigade's tanks and the 3rd Battalion of the 7th Moroccans. However, learning that the tanks were unavailable, he directed the 3rd Battalion to bolster the defense behind Ernage. The battalion's movement was impeded by Ju 87 attacks, though a fighter aircraft managed to down two of the attackers. Around 14:00, the reserve forces reestablished contact with the 110th Infantry at Villeroux, but the situation remained precarious. The headquarters of the 7th Moroccan Regiment and its artillery support began retreating towards St. Gery, only to be rallied by Mellier, who arrived on his motorcycle amidst gunfire. His intervention, along with the divisional artillery, halted their withdrawal. By 16:00, the remaining companies of the 1st Battalion of the 7th Moroccans had fought their way back, extending the front towards Chastre and stabilizing the situation. The 3rd Battalion was positioned at Les Communes, where German artillery, guided by an observation balloon, inflicted casualties including wounding the battalion commander. The 1st Battalion of the 2nd Moroccan Regiment also endured heavy losses, with signs of panic among the troops. Mellier reassured them of an impending counter-attack and ordered them to hold their positions.

Powerful air attacks followed by tank and infantry assaults hit around 13:00, delaying the French counterattack. Two French companies on the railroad line were overwhelmed, but the enemy advance was stalled at the sunken road a few hundred meters back. The 5th Company at Cortil-Couvent reported abandoned heavy weapons, and the First Company of the 1st Battalion, 2nd Moroccan Regiment retreated to the stop-line in the evening, where the last of the ammunition was distributed.

Mellier's ordered counter-attack, led by Jean Ragaine's 35th Tank Battalion and Captain Saut's 3rd Battalion of the 2nd Moroccan Regiment, commenced at 11:30. The assault was launched from reserve positions, violating the immediate counter-attack directive against Panzer incursions set by Aymes's Operations Order No. 4. The formation included a mix of Moroccan infantry and Renault tanks, with machine guns and anti-tank guns distributed among the companies. A special detachment was assigned to protect the counter-attack formation's northern flank.

The attackers assembled by 14:30 and reached the stop-line around 16:30. The procession's length from the rear eliminated any element of surprise. Once in position, they faced heavy bombing, with claims of 80 bombers involved. Despite one tank being overturned and artillery support disrupted, the attack pressed on. However, German air assaults effectively separated the French tanks and infantry, breaching French tactical doctrine. The combined arms fire from the Germans halted the attack. With little artillery support and the French command tank disabled in a minefield, the Moroccan infantry took cover, and the tanks, caught off guard by German anti-tank defenses, made no progress. By 18:30, the counter-attack had ceased.

Amidst the unfolding chaos of battle, the French First Army, against all odds, had managed to maintain its positions. However, the unexpected breakthrough by German forces at Sedan, to the south of the First Army, posed a significant threat to its flank and rear. Consequently, resources including tanks from the 2nd Light Mechanized Division, most reconnaissance battalions, and even some infantry reserves were redirected to reinforce the increasingly vulnerable right flank. In response to this precarious situation, General Billotte alerted the First Army of the potential need to retreat. By around 20:00, the army was instructed to commence a phased withdrawal towards the Franco-Belgian border, using Wavre as a pivot point. Meanwhile, the IV Corps provided a defensive shield, repelling German tank advances.

At 14:00, the IV Corps was erroneously informed that Perbais and Chastre had fallen, leading to the assumption that communication between the 7th Moroccan Regiment and the 110th Infantry was severed. As the battle reached its peak, the IV Corps was ordered at 15:00 to start retreating on its right flank. Concurrently, the 3rd Battalion of the 7th Moroccan Regiment, which had been in reserve, was engaged at Cortil-Noirmont to reestablish contact with the 110th Infantry Regiment. At 16:00, a counterattack involving the 35th Tank Battalion and the 3rd Battalion of the 2nd Moroccan Regiment was initiated. Despite heavy infantry losses and limited tank survival, Aymes was incorrectly informed that the primary defensive position had been resecured.

By 18:00, new German assaults targeted the 7th Moroccan Regiment, with a few Panzer tanks penetrating as far as St. Gery, where they were halted by elements of the divisional reconnaissance battalion. Simultaneously, the regiments of the 15th Motorized Infantry Division received orders for a night retreat, successfully repelling an armored attack on Beuzet with artillery and anti-tank fire at 18:30.

At 20:00, the Moroccan Division commenced its withdrawal, while the 7th Moroccan Regiment successfully counterattacked one last German offensive. German infantry near Gembloux also began their retreat. Throughout the night, both sides disengaged, with the Germans withdrawing to avoid the enemy in front of them, and the French to evade the threat to their right rear, thereby facilitating the Moroccan Division's disengagement.

Surrender

The Belgian Army, stretched thinly from Cadzand in the north to Menen along the Leie River, and extending west from Menin to Bruges, found itself without any reserves. Dominated by the Luftwaffe, the skies offered no reprieve, as the Belgians faced constant air attacks on all significant targets, leading to substantial casualties. With no natural barriers left between them and the German forces, and most railway networks to Dunkirk destroyed, retreat seemed an impossible option. Only three roads remained viable – Bruges–Torhout–Diksmuide, Bruges–Gistel–Nieupoort, and Bruges–Ostend–Nieuwpoort – but using these routes for retreat risked significant losses due to German air superiority. Essential utilities like water, gas, and electricity were disrupted, and canals were drained to serve as emergency supply dumps. The Belgians were confined to a small area of just 1,700 km2, packed with both military personnel and about 3 million civilians.

In this dire situation, King Leopold III deemed further resistance futile. On the evening of May 27, he sought an armistice. Winston Churchill, upon learning of this, conveyed his disapproval in a message, interpreting the King's decision as a sign of surrender and a potential separate peace with Germany. He noted that the constitutional Belgian Government had relocated abroad to dissociate from such a stance. Churchill emphasized the large number of Belgians of military age in France and the resources available to continue the fight, contrasting it with the King's decision, which he saw as divisive and surrendering to Hitler.

Meanwhile, the Royal Navy evacuated the General Headquarters at Middelkerke and Sint-Andries, east of Bruges, during the night. King Leopold III and Queen Mother Elisabeth remained in Belgium, facing five years of captivity. Despite advice from his government to establish a government-in-exile, Leopold stated, "I have decided to stay. The cause of the Allies is lost." The Belgian surrender officially took effect at 04:00 on May 28. This decision was met with recriminations from the British and French, who felt betrayed, claiming the Belgians had given no prior warning of their dire situation. However, this criticism was somewhat unfounded, as the Allies had been aware since May 25 of Belgium's impending collapse.

The British response, led by Churchill, was officially restrained, influenced by Sir Roger Keyes' strong defense of the Belgian campaign presented to the British cabinet on May 28. The French and Belgian ministers criticized Leopold's actions as treacherous, unaware that his agreement with Hitler was an unconditional surrender as Commander-in-Chief of the Belgian Armed Forces, not an arrangement to form a collaborative government.

Battle of France

In the dramatic early days of May 1940, Germany mustered a colossal force to execute its ambitious military strategies. The Heer, Luftwaffe, Kriegsmarine, and Waffen-SS collectively rallied over 5.5 million men, gearing up for a massive offensive. Among them, the Heer stood out with 3 million soldiers, strategically positioned in Poland, Denmark, and Norway, ready to launch a full-scale assault. This formidable army was organized into 157 divisions, with 135 designated for the offensive, including a formidable reserve of 42 divisions.

As the spring of 1940 unfurled, Germany's military might was on full display. They deployed a staggering 2,439 tanks and 7,378 guns, a testament to their preparedness. However, beneath this veneer of strength, challenges lurked. Nearly half of the army comprised men over 40, and training was often hastily conducted over mere weeks. The army's reliance on motorized vehicles was limited; only 10% were motorized, starkly contrasting with the more equipped French and fully motorized British Expeditionary Forces. Horse-drawn vehicles were still a mainstay in German logistics.

Despite these limitations, Germany's strategy was nuanced and dynamic. Army Group A, under Gerd von Rundstedt, included over 45 divisions, with a focus on a breakthrough via the Ardennes—a tactic later termed "Sichelschnitt" or "sickle cut" by Winston Churchill. This group was a blend of armored and infantry divisions, uniquely positioned for a critical push. Meanwhile, Army Group B, led by Fedor von Bock, and comprising nearly

30 divisions, aimed to engage Allied forces in the Low Countries, creating strategic diversions. Lastly, Army Group C, under Wilhelm Ritter von Leeb, held 18 divisions, ready to counter any flanking maneuvers from the east.

A key to German success was their advanced communications network. Radios in tanks facilitated swift, coordinated maneuvers, outpacing Allied forces often reliant on slower, more traditional communication methods. This technological edge allowed German forces to efficiently concentrate firepower, negating the French advantage in heavy weaponry. The integration of air and ground forces was another innovation, with specialized units facilitating rapid support from Luftwaffe dive-bombers, further enhancing their tactical flexibility.

The German army demonstrated a masterful blend of combined arms operations. These highly mobile offensive formations, consisting of adeptly trained artillery, infantry, engineering, and tank units, were seamlessly integrated into the formidable Panzer divisions. A key to their operational success was wireless communication, connecting these diverse elements and allowing them to operate in unison at a rapid pace, often outmaneuvering Allied forces. The Panzer divisions were versatile, capable of reconnaissance, engaging the enemy, defending strategic points, and exploiting weaknesses with precision. They adeptly captured territories, setting up crucial footholds for further advances, with infantry and artillery swiftly moving in to secure these gains.

Despite facing opponents with superior tank firepower, the German tanks, often including the lighter Panzer I and II due to shortages, ingeniously avoided direct tank confrontations. Instead, they drew Allied tanks into traps set by their potent anti-tank guns. This strategic maneuvering preserved their tank forces for subsequent phases of the offensive, with units carrying enough supplies to sustain three to four days of operations. The Panzers were ably supported by motorized and infantry divisions, forming a cohesive and formidable force.

German tank battalions were ideally equipped with Panzer III and IV tanks, but often had to rely on lighter models due to equipment shortages. Unlike the heavier French Char B1, German tanks were less powerful in armament and armor but surpassed in speed and mechanical reliability. Despite being outnumbered in artillery and tanks, the Germans held advantages, notably in their Panzer crews. Each member had a specific role, allowing for efficient operation, unlike the smaller crewed French tanks where the commander was overburdened with multiple tasks.

The Luftwaffe, supporting Army Group B with a vast array of combat and transport aircraft, was a force to be reckoned with. This experienced, well-equipped, and well-trained air force significantly outnumbered the combined Allied aircraft. The Luftwaffe's capabilities were diverse, ranging from close support with dive-bombers to strategic bombing, showcasing its adaptability to various mission requirements. This flexibility contrasted with the more limited roles of Allied air forces. The Luftwaffe's doctrine was not solely focused on close support, with less than 15% of its aircraft in 1939 designed for this role, reflecting its broader strategic purpose.

The German military held a significant edge in anti-aircraft capabilities, boasting a formidable array of Fliegerabwehrkanone (Flak) guns. Their arsenal included 2,600 heavy 88 mm Flak guns and an impressive 6,700 light 37 mm and 20 mm Flak guns. These figures reflect not just the battlefield deployment but also the defense systems across Germany and training units. The versatility of the 88 mm Flak, with its capacity for both high-angle and direct fire, made it an effective weapon against enemy tanks. The Luftwaffe and army units jointly managed a substantial number of these guns, strategically distributed among heavy and light batteries and companies.

On the Allied side, France had invested significantly in its military since World War I, leading to a massive armed force of 5 million by the outbreak of World War II. However, only about 2.24 million were actively deployed in northern army units. The British contribution escalated from 897,000 to

1.65 million troops over the same period, while the Dutch and Belgian forces added another 1.05 million combined.

The French Army, with its 117 divisions, formed the backbone of the northern defense, supplemented by British, Belgian, Dutch, and Polish divisions. The Allies had a substantial artillery advantage, fielding around 14,000 guns, 45% more than the Germans. Notably, the French Army was more motorized, though the Belgians, British, and Dutch had fewer tanks. Despite this, the French tank force outnumbered the German tanks.

However, the French military faced significant challenges. Officers were often unprepared, and logistical issues plagued the mobilization process, leading to shortages of essential supplies and chaotic conditions. The newly formed mechanized divisions lacked thorough training, and many units were understaffed and ill-equipped. A glaring deficiency was the absence of adequate anti-aircraft and mobile anti-tank artillery, along with limited wireless communication capabilities.

French tactical deployment and operational strategy lagged behind the Germans, especially in utilizing armored units. Despite having more tanks, the French distributed them mainly for infantry support, limiting their potential for concentrated armored assaults. Most French tanks, except the heavy ones, lacked reliable wireless communication, impeding their maneuverability and coordination compared to their German counterparts. Additionally, the majority of French military personnel were trained for static defense, with little preparation for mobile warfare, resulting in a mismatch of tactics and execution when compared to the more agile German armored units.

The French Army in World War II was strategically divided into three primary groups. The 2nd and 3rd Army Groups were tasked with defending the Maginot Line in the east. Meanwhile, the 1st Army Group, led by General Gaston Billotte, was positioned on the western flank, ready to advance into the Low Countries. The Seventh Army, positioned near the coast and bolstered by a mechanized light division (Division Légère Mécanique, DLM), was set to move towards the Netherlands through Antwerp. South of the Seventh Army, the British Expeditionary Force (BEF)'s motorized divisions were poised to advance to the Dyle Line, flanking the Belgian army. The First Army, enhanced by two DLMs and with an armored division (Division Cuirassée, DCR) in reserve, was responsible for defending the Gembloux Gap. The French Ninth Army was further south, covering the sector from Namur to north of Sedan.

Lord Gort, the BEF commander, anticipated a few weeks to prepare for the German advance, but the Germans arrived in just four days. The Second Army, expected to form a defensive hinge, was faced with confronting Germany's elite armored divisions at Sedan. However, it was deprioritized in terms of manpower and resources, leaving it vulnerable. Despite warnings from Belgian and French intelligence about German movements through the Ardennes, French military leadership, under Gamelin, largely dismissed these as inconsistent with their strategic planning.

In terms of air power, the French Armée de l'Air, along with RAF Fighter and Bomber Commands, fielded a substantial number of aircraft, including models like the Hawker Hurricane, Curtiss Hawk 75, and Dewoitine D.520, which were competitive against the German Messerschmitt Bf 109. However, many of these aircraft, including the D.520s, were in limited supply. The Allies had more fighter aircraft overall, but the French aviation industry struggled with spare parts shortages, rendering many aircraft unserviceable. Despite these challenges, the Armée de l'Air performed admirably, achieving a favorable kill ratio in air-to-air combat.

The French Army's anti-aircraft capabilities included a range of guns from 13 mm machine guns for civilian defense to 90 mm guns, although some older models faced issues like barrel wear. The BEF was equipped with advanced QF 3.7-inch heavy anti-aircraft guns and Bofors 40 mm light anti-aircraft guns.

The Belgian and Dutch forces also had a mix of heavy and light anti-aircraft artillery, including some outdated models repurposed for anti-aircraft use.

The strategy for delaying Army Group A's advance involved Belgian motorized infantry and French mechanized cavalry divisions (DLC, Divisions Légères de Cavalerie) moving into the Ardennes. Key resistance was offered by the Belgian 1st Chasseurs Ardennais and 1st Cavalry Division, supported by engineers and the French 5th DLC. Although the Belgian forces managed to temporarily halt the 1st Panzer Division, their rapid withdrawal and the French forces' delayed arrival undermined the effectiveness of these efforts. German engineers faced little resistance in dismantling the Belgian barriers, and the French forces, caught off guard by the sheer number of German tanks and lacking sufficient anti-tank capabilities, quickly retreated behind the Meuse River.

The German advance through the Ardennes was slowed not by resistance but by logistical challenges. Panzergruppe Kleist, with over 41,000 vehicles, was constrained by the limited road network, creating massive traffic jams. Despite early French aerial reconnaissance identifying the movement of German armored convoys, these reports were initially dismissed as secondary to the main attack in Belgium. Only later, when photographic reconnaissance confirmed the presence of tanks and bridging equipment, did the scale of the German advance become apparent. Yet, despite these sitting targets, French bomber attacks were focused on northern Belgium, resulting in substantial losses and reducing their bomber force significantly within two days.

By May 11, Gamelin had ordered reserve divisions to reinforce the Meuse sector. However, due to threats from the Luftwaffe, these movements were restricted to nighttime, slowing down the reinforcements. The French command, underestimating the speed of the German buildup, felt no urgency. Their confidence lay in their strong fortifications, artillery superiority, and the expectation of slow German river crossings. However, the French units in the area were of questionable capability, particularly lacking in anti-aircraft and anti-tank artillery.

When the German advance forces reached the Meuse on the afternoon of May 12, they initially did not have a significant numerical advantage. Each of the three armies in Army Group A aimed to establish bridgeheads at Sedan, Monthermé, and Dinant. Despite the German artillery having less ammunition than the French, the French forces' overconfidence and tactical misjudgments played into the hands of the advancing Germans.

Battle of Sedan

In the tense hours leading up to the Battle of Sedan, General Heinz Guderian faced a critical dilemma. His innovative strategy, reliant on swift Panzer divisions, was hamstrung by a severe lack of artillery support. Numerous batteries, vital to his plan, were trapped in the congested Ardennes. This left Guderian with no choice but to place his bets on the aerial might of the Luftwaffe.

At the heart of this aerial strategy was a groundbreaking concept developed in collaboration with II. Fliegerkorps: the rolling raid. Eschewing the traditional approach of a single, overwhelming strike, this plan called for continuous, targeted attacks by smaller Luftwaffe formations throughout the day. This relentless assault aimed to not only neutralize the French artillery but also to shatter enemy morale and deliver precise blows to key targets like bunkers.

However, a sudden twist emerged. Unbeknownst to Guderian, his superior, von Kleist, had overruled this meticulously planned approach, advocating instead for a singular, massive assault. Guderian's objections fell on deaf ears, yet in a dramatic turn of events, Loerzer, the commander tasked with executing the air strategy, sided with Guderian. The rolling raids proceeded as originally planned, a decision later justified by the tardiness of an official order from higher command.

As dusk fell on May 12th, Guderian's forces seized Sedan, encountering surprisingly little resistance. With the city under their control, Guderian faced a pivotal decision. He could either secure his gains against potential counterattacks, advance towards Paris, or make a bold dash to the Channel. Inspired by the words of Walther Wenck, "Hit with your fists, don't feel with your fingers!", Guderian chose the most audacious option: a swift strike towards the Channel.

The early hours of May 13th saw Guderian's Panzer divisions maneuvering into position for this daring move. The 10th Panzer Division positioned itself upstream, the 2nd downstream, and the 1st in the center, ready to attack across the strategic points of the Sedan-Meuse loop. Guderian, facing an artillery shortage and a numerical disadvantage against the French, knew the success of this pivotal moment hinged on the Luftwaffe's effectiveness as a substitute for traditional artillery support. Despite the challenges, Guderian's decision to rely on air power and the audacity of his strategy marked a defining moment in the early stages of the Blitzkrieg.

In an unprecedented display of aerial power, Luftflotte 3 and Luftflotte 2, under Albert Kesselring, unleashed an aerial bombardment of staggering intensity. This operation marked the Luftwaffe's most severe assault during World War II. The air offensive saw two dedicated Sturzkampfgeschwader (dive bomber wings) execute a total of 300 sorties against French fortifications, with Sturzkampfgeschwader 77 alone undertaking 201 missions. Overall, an astounding 3,940 sorties were flown, with nine Kampfgeschwader (Bomber Wing) units participating, often in Gruppe (group) strength.

The assault was meticulously planned to last eight hours, from 08:00 to 16:00. Commanders Loerzer and Richthofen committed two Stuka units to this critical operation. Their Ju 87s conducted numerous missions against the bunkers at Sedan, with Loerzer's units completing around 180 missions and Richthofen's managing 90. This relentless aerial campaign included 900 missions by II. Fliegerkorps and 360 by VIII. Fliegerkorps, targeting strategic points along the Meuse front.

The primary target was the Marfee heights, strategically located to the southwest of Sedan. This area was key, housing fortified artillery positions and overlooking essential approaches. Despite a two-hour delay, the Luftwaffe's effort was formidable. The attacks, executed in Gruppe strength, were aimed at the enemy's most fortified lines. German fighters played a crucial role, disrupting enemy communications and movements, severing landlines, and strafing fortifications.

Sturzkampfgeschwader 77 initiated the assault on the morning of May 13. Within a mere five hours, an overwhelming 500 Ju 87 sorties had been completed, showcasing the Luftwaffe's might and precision.

The psychological impact of this aerial onslaught on the French defenders was profound. By the time German ground forces commenced their assault, the backbone of the French defense – the gunners – had largely abandoned their posts. Remarkably, the Luftwaffe sustained minimal losses, with only six aircraft downed, including three Ju 87s.

The French 55th Infantry Division, caught off-guard by this ferocious attack, suffered significantly, not just in terms of physical damage, but also psychological trauma. The haunting siren of the Ju 87 dive-bombers left an indelible mark on the French soldiers. Post-war analysis revealed that despite the intensity of the bombardment, direct hits had not destroyed any bunkers, and French casualties stood at just 56. Yet, the indirect effects were devastating – communication lines were decimated, and the division's defensive capabilities were severely impaired.

This psychological toll precipitated the "panic of Bulson." On the evening of May 13, a misinterpreted report suggested German tanks were nearing the village of Bulson. This misinformation spread rapidly through the ranks of the French 55th Infantry Division, leading to a mass desertion of their positions, despite the first German tank crossing the Meuse only 12 hours later. By the time the error was rectified, much of the division's personnel had abandoned their equipment.

The pivotal ground offensive was spearheaded by the 1st Panzer Division, with crucial support from the elite Infantry Regiment Großdeutschland and the adept Sturmpionier-Battalion 43 (43rd Assault Engineer Battalion). This arrangement was necessary as the 1st Panzer Division only had one rifle regiment at its disposal. The Großdeutschland Regiment, later attached to the 1st Panzer for the duration of the campaign, played a significant role in breaching the defenses on Hill 247, a strategic position overseeing Gaulier. To their astonishment, they found that the Luftwaffe's bombardment had not neutralized the enemy bunkers as expected.

The regiment's initial attempt to cross the river at Pont Neuf bridge using rubber assault boats was thwarted by intense enemy small arms fire, forcing a temporary retreat. Reconnaissance identified an active enemy Bunker, No. 211, which posed a significant threat to any crossing attempts. Despite the failure of an infantry gun platoon to neutralize it, the situation changed when an 8.8 cm FlaK gun, renowned for its versatility, was brought in and successfully destroyed the bunker. However, the crossing was still impeded by unforeseen machine gun fire from another position, which was eventually neutralized by the 2nd Battalion, enabling the regiment to cross the river.

Throughout that day, the regiment made significant inroads into the French defenses, with the 2nd Battalion's 6th, 7th, and 8th Companies methodically neutralizing each bunker they encountered. By 20:00, they had captured the strategically important Hill 247, penetrating 8 kilometers into enemy territory.

On Hill 301, located further west, the First Rifle Regiment under Colonel Hermann Balck also achieved notable success. Assisted by two platoons from the 34th Assault Engineer Battalion, they managed to disable several bunker positions. The regiment's westward advance allowed them to support the 2nd Panzer Division, which was engaged in combat near Donchery. The First Rifle Regiment's incursion into the 2nd Panzer's operational area proved advantageous, as they eliminated several bunkers on the eastern flank, facilitating the 2nd Panzer's advance and severing the Donchery-Sedan road. Their use of flamethrower teams proved particularly effective in subduing bunkers whose occupants were slow to surrender.

The last bunker capitulated at 22:40 on May 13, marking a significant milestone. By this time, elements of both the 1st and 2nd Panzer Divisions had successfully forged their way across the Meuse river, a testament to the effectiveness of their coordinated ground assault.

The 2nd Panzer Division faced a daunting challenge in the Battle of Sedan. Hindered by the grueling trek through the Ardennes, which involved navigating nearly 250 kilometers of congested roads, the division was significantly delayed in reaching Donchery. By the time of their arrival, the 1st and 10th Panzer Divisions had already commenced their attacks across the Meuse, alerting the enemy defenses to the imminent threat.

Assigned to cross at the far western end of the Sedan sector along the Donchery axis, the 2nd Panzer Division had to traverse 3 kilometers of open terrain under intense fire to reach the bridgehead. This perilous advance exposed them to heavy artillery fire from Donchery and the Bellevue Castle's 75mm artillery casemates, positioned to the east of the town. Several tanks, tasked with dragging boats across the river, were destroyed in the process. The French had concentrated the majority of their 174 artillery pieces in this sector, mainly in bunkers along the southern bank of the Meuse-Donchery area, with additional support from the 102nd Infantry Division's batteries from Charleville to the northwest.

Compounding the challenge, the 2nd Panzer Division had relinquished its heavy howitzers to the 1st Panzer, leaving it with only 24 guns, which didn't reach the battlefield until 17:00. Moreover, these guns were hampered by an ammunition shortage, having only a few shells each due to the logistical backlog in the Ardennes.

All initial attempts by the 2nd Panzer to land on the Meuse's southern bank were unsuccessful. However, the situation improved when the 1st Panzer Division managed to cross the river at the central sector. After crossing, the 1st Panzer moved to attack the eastern flank of the French forces at Donchery. This maneuver allowed some units to clear the Meuse bend. The Assault Engineers and 1st Panzer effectively neutralized the guns at Bellevue Castle and cleared the bunker positions along the Meuse from the rear, alleviating the artillery fire that had been pounding the 2nd Panzer Division's eastern flank.

With the threat from the right flank mitigated, the units on the 2nd Panzer's left flank successfully crossed the river and infiltrated the French positions opposite Donchery around 20:00. Despite this, heavy French fire from bunkers on the southern side of the Meuse continued unabated. It wasn't until 22:20, under the cover of darkness, that the Germans were able to commence regular ferrying operations.

Similar to its counterpart, the 2nd Panzer Division, the 10th Panzer Division found itself in a challenging position, having allocated its heavy artillery batteries to support adjacent units. This left the division with a mere 24 light 105 mm howitzers, and even these were hampered by a shortage of ammunition. Further complicating matters, the Luftwaffe's focus was primarily on aiding the 1st Panzer Division in the central sector, resulting in negligible air support for the 10th Panzer. Consequently, the French artillery and machine gun emplacements in the Wadelincourt area remained largely intact and unchallenged.

Additionally, the presence of the newly deployed 71st Infantry Division and the French X Corps in the Remilly-Aillicourt area significantly hindered the

10th Panzer Division's progress. The division had to approach the Meuse River across a vulnerable and exposed stretch of flat terrain, approximately 600–800 meters in length.

Near Bazeilles, engineers and assault infantry were preparing for a river crossing at Wadelincourt, located about 2 kilometers south of Sedan. However, a devastating artillery barrage from French positions destroyed most of their rubber boats, leaving only 15 out of the original 96 intact. This setback forced a revision of the assault plan, originally involving both the 69th and 89th Infantry Regiments. The significant loss of boats meant that only the 86th Infantry Regiment could proceed with the crossing, with the 69th Regiment relegated to a reserve role to provide subsequent reinforcements.

Throughout the Meuse front, the 10th Panzer Division's assaults met with failure. A notable exception was a daring and improvised operation by an 11-man team from the 2nd Company, Panzerpionier-Bataillon 49 (49th Panzer Engineer Battalion), attached to the 1st Battalion, 86th Infantry Regiment. Led by Feldwebel Walter Rubarth, this small but determined group, operating independently and without support, managed to neutralize seven bunker positions, creating a critical breach in the French defenses. This action paved the way for follow-up units from the 1st Battalion of the 86th Rifle Regiment to cross the river by 21:00 and overrun the remaining bunkers on Hill 246, a key position in the French defensive line. By day's end, the 10th Panzer Division had not only secured a substantial bridgehead but also achieved its strategic objective.

In the central sector at Gaulier, the German forces initiated a crucial phase of their operation by ferrying 3.7 cm Pak 36 light infantry field artillery across the Meuse to bolster their infantry on the other side. By the early hours of May 14th, a pontoon bridge was in place, enabling the passage of Sd.Kfz. 222, Sd.Kfz. 232, and Sd.Kfz. 264 armored cars into the established bridgeheads. Contrary to French reports of German tanks crossing at this time, the first Panzer tanks only made their way across at 07:20 on May 14th. Prior to this, the bridge had been primarily used by a variety of vehicles, but not tanks.

The success at Sedan and the expansion of the bridgeheads caused considerable alarm for the French. General Gaston-Henri Billotte, commanding the First French Army Group, and General Marcel Têtu, commander of the Allied Tactical Air Forces, recognized the strategic importance of these crossings and urged for a concentrated air attack to destroy the bridges, viewing them as pivotal to the outcome of the battle.

Despite these efforts, the air attacks faced significant challenges. RAF's No. 103 Squadron and No. 150 Squadron of the Advanced Air Striking Force flew 10 early morning sorties with minimal losses. However, a larger operation in the afternoon saw 71 RAF bombers, escorted by Allied fighters, encounter stiff resistance from German fighters, which outnumbered the Allied escorts three to one. This resulted in substantial losses for the RAF wings, with a high casualty rate among the dispatched bombers and the loss of several Hawker Hurricanes.

The French Air Forces, under Commandant Marcel Têtu, provided limited support, with their sorties reduced due to heavy losses in previous days. French bomber groups had been significantly weakened, with many squadrons operating at reduced capacity. These forces were redirected to Sedan on May 14th but suffered additional losses, further diminishing their capabilities.

The air battle over Sedan was fierce. The Allied bombers struggled against strong German air defenses, including fighter wings Jagdgeschwader 26 and 27, and the formidable Jagdgeschwader 53. The Germans had also amassed a formidable array of anti-aircraft guns, making the skies above the Meuse extremely perilous for Allied pilots. Despite flying numerous sorties, the Allies suffered heavy losses without achieving significant success in destroying the bridges.

For the Germans, particularly General Guderian, the Luftwaffe's effectiveness in fending off Allied bombers was a relief, ensuring the preservation of their crucial supply lines across the Meuse. By the end of the day, a substantial number of tanks, including those of the 2nd Panzer Division which had to utilize the 1st Panzer Division's bridge due to their own bridge's unavailability, had crossed the Meuse. The decisive German victory in this air battle was a critical factor in their success at Sedan, allowing them to maintain momentum in their advance.

General Huntziger, leading the French Second Army, remained seemingly unfazed by the German capture of Sedan and the crumbling of French defenses under the Luftwaffe's assault. He relied on substantial French reserves, particularly the X Corps, to re-establish stability at the front. Huntziger's forces were indeed formidable, with the 10th Panzer Division, left to guard the bridgehead by Guderian's westward move, facing a significant array of French military might. This included the XXI Corps under Flavigny, which boasted the 3rd Armoured Division, 3rd Motorised Infantry Division, 5th Light Cavalry Division, and the 1st Cavalry Brigade. Additional support came from the 2nd Light Cavalry Division, 3rd Tank Division, elements of the 71st Infantry Division, 205th Infantry Regiment, and the 4th Tank Battalion, along with nearly 300 tanks including 138 main battle tanks like the Hotchkiss and Char B1-Bis.

The French tanks, with their superior armor and armament, theoretically outclassed the German Panzers. The Panzer IV's 30 mm armor paled in comparison to the 45 mm of the Hotchkiss and 60 mm of the Char B1. The Char B1's 47 mm and 75 mm guns also had a firepower advantage. However, these French tanks had their shortcomings, notably in endurance and speed, which were not conducive to rapid maneuvers.

On May 14th, General Lafontaine moved the 55th Infantry Division's command post closer to the frontline. The French had somewhat anticipated a German breach at Sedan and had positioned the X Corps for a potential counter-attack, aiming to strike at the German bridgeheads across the Meuse. Despite these plans and the conviction of General Charles Huntziger that the French could hold their positions, the German delay in getting their armor across the bridge from the early hours till 07:30 could have been exploited by the French.

The French did initiate plans for a night counter-attack with armor, but various factors, including delayed troop movements, hesitant command decisions, and the chaos ensuing from the "panic of Bulson," delayed any potential offensive until the morning of May 14th. Colonel Poncelet, the commander of X Corps' artillery, even after reluctantly ordering a retreat, saw his artillery battalions abandon their heavy equipment, contributing to the disarray and eventual collapse of the 55th Infantry Division and the partial collapse of the 71st Infantry Division.

During May 13-14, the German forces were exposed to potential counter-attacks. A decisive French assault with their armored units at this juncture could have significantly impeded Guderian's breakout from the Meuse bridgeheads, possibly altering the campaign's trajectory. However, the French command, deeply entrenched in defensive tactics and stationed far from the frontline, lacked an accurate and timely understanding of the battlefield dynamics. Misinformed intelligence, suggesting premature German tank crossings, further muddled their response.

The pivotal race to Bulson ridge, a strategic high ground, commenced at 16:00 on May 13th. By the morning of May 14th, French armored units were advancing towards the ridge, aiming to reclaim the terrain vacated by the 55th Infantry Division and, crucially, to eliminate the German bridgeheads at the Meuse. However, the situation had evolved since the previous day, with the odds increasingly favoring the Germans.

The French X Corps' plan involved a two-pronged attack: the 213th Infantry Regiment and the 7th Tank Battalion would strike on the left flank, while the 205th Infantry Regiment and the 4th Tank Battalion would hit the right flank. Unfortunately, the right flank force was delayed, leading the 213th Infantry and the 7th Tank Battalion to proceed alone. They expected to reach a position between Chéhéry and Bulson within a couple of hours, but it took them 17 hours after the initial order before the leading French tanks arrived at the Bulson ridge, only to find that the Germans had just beaten them there.

General Lafontaine, responsible for this French counter-attack, exhibited significant hesitancy over the 24-hour period starting from the afternoon of May 13th. He was preoccupied with reconnoitering the area, managing the retreat of French infantry and artillery from the 55th and 71st Divisions, and seeking orders from his superior, General Gransard. This delay in decision-making and the issuance of orders meant that by the time the French were ready to move on the morning of May 14th, the Germans had already fortified their positions at the bridgehead, and their infantry was advancing towards Bulson. Lafontaine's hesitance, contrasted with the German principle of Auftragstaktik (Mission Command), which encouraged initiative and rapid decision-making, resulted in a missed opportunity for a critical counter-attack.

The French had a golden opportunity to repel the Germans and regain control over the Meuse bridgeheads. The 1st Panzer Division, hampered by logistical issues and exhausted from their rapid advance, was vulnerable. A swift French counter-attack by just a few infantry regiments and tank battalions could have created a crisis for the Germans. Even a limited success in holding Bulson could have facilitated a stronger defensive position, with reinforcements from the Second French Army and XXI Corps' armored divisions.

However, the French were hindered by their defensive-oriented tank doctrine. The FCM 36 tanks, primarily designed for infantry support, lacked the speed and offensive capability required for a rapid counter-attack. Consequently, it took the French armor nearly an hour and fifteen minutes to cover the final

2 kilometers to the ridge. In contrast, the lead elements of the 1st and 2nd Panzer Divisions, despite prioritizing the faster but less heavily armed and armored Panzer Is and Panzer IIs, reached the ridge just before the French.

Battle of Bulson

As the Battle of Hannut raged in Belgium, similar clashes unfolded on the southern face of Bulson ridge. Kirchner, leading the 1st Panzer Division, faced numerous tactical setbacks. The 3.7 cm PaK 36 anti-tank guns and Panzer IIIs under his command proved ineffective against the more robustly armored French tanks, with their shells bouncing off harmlessly. The German tanks, in contrast, suffered rapid knockouts. Faced with the necessity to hold the French at the ridge, Kirchner was compelled to deploy his tanks piecemeal – a tactic that Guderian disliked, but saw as the only option under the circumstances.

The German tanks, however, had an edge in their mobility and superior radio communication, allowing them to quickly reposition and coordinate their defense and attacks. This agility enabled the Panzer IIIs and IVs to outmaneuver the French tanks, attacking them from the rear where they were more vulnerable, especially between the chassis and turret.

The French artillery, camouflaged within the wooded areas, posed a signif-icant threat, proving to be more effective than the tanks themselves. One German Panzer company was nearly decimated by this artillery, retreating with only one combat-ready tank. This surviving tank was then cleverly maneuvered back and forth to simulate the presence of multiple tanks. The 2nd Panzer Company was redirected from Gaulier, near Sedan, to assist and successfully delayed the French armored advance. The late arrival of the Großdeutschland Infantry Regiment proved pivotal, as they managed to neutralize the French anti-tank defenses and entrenched infantry.

On Bulson's left side, the Germans engaged 13 French tanks supported by infantry near Chéhéry. Kirchner quickly ordered the setup of two anti-tank platoons at Connage. Despite the 37 mm guns' efforts, the French armor outflanked the position by moving west, while their infantry advanced from the southeast. The arrival of the 43rd Assault Engineer Battalion and elements of the 2nd Panzer Regiment turned the tide, pushing the French back towards Chémery-sur-Bar.

By 10:45, Lafontaine ordered a retreat, and Guderian's forces received reinforcements in the form of heavy artillery from the Großdeutschland Regiment. With the arrival of 88 mm guns and heavier Panzer III and IV tanks, the French 7th Tank Battalion was decimated and the 213th Infantry Regiment severely weakened. Out of 40 French tanks, only 10 remained operational, with the 7th Tank Battalion losing 10 of its 13 tanks in the day's battles. Delays in the deployment of the 205th Infantry Regiment and 4th Tank Battalion meant they arrived too late to influence the battle's outcome.

The 1st Panzer Division's moment of triumph in Chemery was briefly marred by a friendly fire incident when the Luftwaffe mistakenly bombed the area, causing a few casualties. Despite this mishap, the Germans had successfully held their ground, fending off the French counter-attack and maintaining control over the strategic Bulson ridge.

Battle of Stonne

The German High Command, cautious after the victory at Sedan and Bulson, wanted to hold off any further exploitation until the infantry divisions caught up with the Panzer divisions. Guderian, however, saw this as a potentially grave mistake that could squander their hard-earned gains and give the French time to regroup and strengthen their formidable armored units. Defying the High Command and even Hitler himself, Guderian resolved to push towards the Channel, leaving the 10th Panzer Division and the Infantry Regiment Großdeutschland to secure the Sedan bridgehead. Meanwhile, the 1st and 2nd Panzer Divisions were ordered to advance northwest, exploiting the largely undefended French rear.

While the Sedan bridgeheads weren't entirely secure and French forces were gathering to the south, Guderian preferred an aggressive defense over a passive one, especially in the absence of suitable anti-tank weapons. This strategy proved effective as the 1st and 2nd Panzer Divisions encountered and overcame elements of the French X Corps near Chémery-sur-Bar, prompting the French Corps to retreat southward and eliminating a potential threat to the German western flank.

Guderian also revisited his initial plan to feint south towards the Maginot Line to disguise the main thrust towards the Channel. He ordered the 10th Panzer Division and the Großdeutschland Infantry Regiment to engage in the Battle of Stonne, a critical two-day conflict. Here, the Germans faced the formidable French Char B1-Bis tanks, notably one commanded by Pierre Billotte, which proved nearly impervious to German fire. The battle for Stonne was intense, with the town changing hands 17 times. The French failure to secure Stonne signified their inability to eliminate the Sedan bridgeheads effectively.

The French offensive at Stonne was crucial, as the town's high ground provided a strategic vantage point over Sedan. The initial French attack involved both infantry and armor, but coordination issues led to the tanks outpacing their infantry support. Despite this, a German platoon managed a psychological victory by knocking out three Char B1s, causing French tank crews to retreat. Over the next 48 hours, Stonne witnessed a seesaw battle, with the Germans eventually regaining control by the evening of May 17th.

The German defense at Stonne was bolstered on the night of May 16th with the arrival of the VI Corps, including the 16th and 24th Infantry Divisions. This reinforcement was timely as the Großdeutschland Regiment had suffered significant casualties and the Panzerjägerkompanie 14 had lost half of its anti-tank guns. The battle left Stonne in ruins, with significant tank losses on both sides. By May 17th, with the support of the IV Corps, the Germans captured Stonne for the final time, cementing their control over this strategic location.

Siege of Calais

In the early hours of May 23, a dramatic scene unfolded as the 3rd RTR quickly assembled their arsenal of 21 Light Tank Mk VIs and 27 cruiser tanks in Coquelles, strategically located along the vital Calais–Boulogne road. Guided by the directives from Brownrigg and GHQ through Bailey, they sent a patrol of light tanks down the St. Omer road, only to discover the town eerily deserted, ravaged by bombardment, and aglow with the flames of burning buildings. Narrowly escaping a potential encounter with the 6th Panzer Division, which had settled for the night near Guînes, the patrol made a swift return to Coquelles by 8:00 a.m.

Meanwhile, the skies above Calais buzzed with the roar of RAF aircraft. At the crack of dawn, 6:00 a.m., the valiant pilots of 151 Squadron in their Hawker Hurricanes downed a Junkers Ju 88 bomber near Boulogne. Not to be outdone, Spitfires from 74 Squadron claimed another Ju 88 from Lehrgeschwader 1. The morning air battles raged on with 54 and 92 Squadrons clashing with Jagdgeschwader 27's Messerschmitt Bf 109s, resulting in a tally of five enemy planes for one Spitfire. The afternoon saw further dogfights, with 92 Squadron losing two Spitfires to the formidable Messerschmitt Bf 110s of Zerstörergeschwader 26 and 76.

As the Allied forces tallied their losses and gains in the sky, the German advance on the ground resumed with renewed vigor. By 8:00 a.m., German panzers had forged across the Authie. The afternoon brought encounters with French rearguards, joined by British and Belgian troops, near Desvres, Samer, and Boulogne. Despite the Luftwaffe's relative absence, the Allied air forces were relentless, launching bombing and strafing runs on the advancing German forces. In a strategic shift, Guderian released the 10th Panzer Division from its defensive position and directed the 1st Panzer

Division towards Dunkirk, aiming to cut off Allied escape routes. However, the 10th Panzer Division's advance was delayed near Amiens, giving the British reinforcements time to fortify Calais.

On the pivotal day of May 23, the German forces successfully neutralized the threats at Cambrai and Arras, paving the way for Fliegerkorps VIII, led by Generaloberst Wolfram Freiherr von Richthofen, to join the fray in support of the 10th Panzer Division at Calais. Most of the formidable Junkers Ju 87 Stuka dive-bombers, having advanced swiftly in the wake of the German frontline, were stationed around St Quentin, though Calais was at the edge of their operational range. As the German units moved forward, they also entered the range of Fighter Command aircraft based in England, prompting Richthofen to position I JG 27 (1st Wing, Fighter Group 27) at Saint-Omer for aerial protection. The skies over Calais witnessed a convergence of Luftwaffe groups, including StG 77, StG 1 led by Oberstleutnant Eberhard Baier, StG 2 under Geschwaderkommodore Oskar Dinort, and the medium bombers of Kampfgeschwader 77, commanded by Oberst Dr. Johan-Volkmar Fisser.

In the ensuing aerial battles, RAF fighters from 92 Squadron managed to down four Bf 109s, capturing three I JG 27 pilots and tragically losing one in action, while 92 Squadron suffered the loss of three Spitfires along with their pilots. To bolster the German air effort, I Jagdgeschwader 1, also stationed to the south, was summoned to provide escort for Ju 87 units targeting Calais. Operating from forward bases at Monchy-Breton, Hauptmann Wilhelm Balthasar led JG 1 in a fierce confrontation with British Spitfires, claiming two downed aircraft but at the cost of one pilot.

Meanwhile, on the ground, the 3rd RTR received a critical report from a reconnaissance patrol. Bailey, who was returning to GHQ with a light tank escort, faced a harrowing ordeal when he became separated from his escort and encountered the advanced guard of the 1st Panzer Division at a crossroads on the St. Omer road. In a grim turn of events, the driver was killed. However, the Germans were unexpectedly repelled by a Royal Army Service Corps petrol convoy that arrived just in time. Bailey, along with an injured passenger, managed to make it back to Calais around noon and informed Keller of the situation. Despite Keller's initial hesitations and reports of German tanks moving towards Calais from Marquise, he decided to dispatch the remainder of the 3rd RTR towards St. Omer at 2:15 p.m. As they approached about 1 mile southeast of Hames-Bources, they spotted the rearguard tanks and anti-tank guns of the 1st Panzer Division on the Pihen-les-Guînes road, strategically positioned to protect the division's rear as the main body advanced northeast towards Gravelines.

The 3rd Royal Tank Regiment bravely engaged German light tanks on the St. Omer road, successfully driving them back. However, the battle was not without its challenges. The German forces, equipped with heavier tanks and a robust anti-tank gun screen, managed to destroy between 7 to 12 British tanks. Following these losses, Nicholson made the tactical decision to withdraw the 3rd RTR back to Calais.

In a separate encounter, about three miles southeast of Bastion 6 in the Calais enclave, C Troop of the 1st Searchlight Regiment faced a daunting challenge. Stationed at Les Attaques, they had constructed a makeshift roadblock with a bus and a lorry, armed with Bren guns, rifles, and Boys anti-tank rifles. Despite their valiant efforts and holding out for about three hours, they were eventually overwhelmed by the advancing German forces.

Elsewhere, German tank and infantry units launched an assault on a post at Le Colombier, along the St. Omer–Calais road. However, they were caught in a deadly crossfire from other posts and the guns of the 58th Light Anti-Aircraft Regiment positioned on higher ground near Boulogne. The Germans, facing fierce resistance, were forced to retreat at around 7:00 p.m. Calais was not the primary objective of the 1st Panzer Division, but Oberst Kruger, who led the battalion engaged at Guînes, Les Attaques, and Le Colombier, had orders to seize Calais from the southeast if feasible. As night descended, the division reported Calais as being heavily fortified and ceased their attacks to continue their advance towards Gravelines and Dunkirk.

Earlier in the day, at 4:00 p.m., Schaal had directed the main force of his 10th Panzer Division, consisting of the 90th Panzer Regiment, 86th Rifle Regiment, and a battalion of medium artillery, to move towards Coquelles via the main road from Marquise. This position offered strategic observation over Calais. Simultaneously, a battlegroup based on the division's 69th Rifle Regiment was tasked with advancing from Guînes directly to central Calais.

Upon Nicholson's arrival in Calais with the 30th Infantry Brigade that afternoon, he quickly realized the dire situation. The 3rd RTR had already suffered significant losses, and the Germans were closing in on the port, severing routes to the southeast and southwest. Nicholson promptly deployed the 1st RB to defend the eastern outer ramparts of Calais and assigned the 2nd KRRC to guard the western side. The outer posts and anti-aircraft units began retreating into the town around 3:00 p.m., a movement that continued into the night. Shortly after 4:00 p.m., Nicholson received orders from the War Office to prioritize escorting a truck convoy carrying 350,000 rations to Dunkirk. However, as they prepared for this mission, the 10th Panzer Division approached from the south, bombarding Calais from the high ground.

At 11:00 p.m., the 3rd RTR dispatched a patrol comprising a Cruiser Mk III (A13) and three light tanks to scout the convoy route. They encountered roadblocks set up by the 1st Panzer Division on the road to Gravelines. Skillfully, they breached the first barricade and navigated through subsequent German positions, even managing to clear a mine-strewn bridge. However, communications problems meant that only fragmented messages reached Keller, suggesting the route was clear.

In the early hours of the next day, a force of five tanks and a composite company from the Rifle Brigade led the convoy. Near Marck, about three miles east of Calais, they outmaneuvered a German roadblock, but as daylight broke, it became evident they were at risk of encirclement, forcing them to withdraw back to Calais.

At the break of dawn on May 25, the atmosphere in Calais was charged with tension. The French coastal guns roared to life at 4:45 a.m., signaling the start of a German artillery and mortar barrage targeting the port, particularly focusing on French gun positions. This intense bombardment marked the beginning of the 10th Panzer Division's aggressive assault on the west and southwest sections of Calais's perimeter. Throughout the night, the QVR, searchlight, and anti-aircraft troops had been gradually retreating, finally completing their withdrawal to the enceinte around 8:30 a.m.

To the west, B Company of the QVR, initially positioned around Sangatte, was instructed to fall back to the enceinte's western face by 10:00 p.m. Similarly, a platoon of C Company, stationed east of Calais, also retreated, ensuring that by midday the main defensive line was firmly established along the enceinte.

The initial German assaults were largely repelled, except in the south where they managed to breach the defenses. However, a swift counter-attack by the 2nd King's Royal Rifle Corps (KRRC) and tanks from the 3rd RTR forced the attackers back. Amidst the chaos, the German bombardment extended to the harbor, where a hospital train filled with wounded awaited evacuation. In a race against time, the wounded were hurriedly loaded onto ships, along with dock workers and rear-area troops, as the vessels departed for England, some still laden with equipment.

The afternoon saw renewed German offensives on all three sides of the perimeter. The French garrison at Fort Nieulay surrendered after a heavy bombardment, while the marines at Fort Lapin and the coastal artillery units spiked their guns and retreated. The southern perimeter faced the brunt of the German incursion, and despite resistance, the defenders were unable to push the attackers back. Fifth columnists within the town exacerbated the situation by sniping at the defenders. The situation worsened as the Germans captured houses and used them to fire enfilade at the defenders.

Ammunition shortages and dwindling anti-tank gun numbers added to the defenders' plight. The Germans struggled to pinpoint British positions, and by 4:00 a.m., they had only made minimal progress. Nevertheless, by 7:00 p.m., the 10th Panzer Division reported significant losses, including a third of their equipment and personnel, and half of their tanks.

During this critical period, the Royal Navy played a crucial role, continuously delivering supplies and evacuating the wounded. A squadron of destroyers, including HMS Grafton, Greyhound, Wessex, Wolfhound, Verity, and the Polish ORP Burza, bombarded shore targets. The Ju 87 Stuka units, intensifying their efforts, targeted these naval forces. In a dramatic raid at 4:42 p.m., Wessex was sunk, and Burza was damaged. Despite their limited training in anti-shipping operations, the Stuka pilots dove from high altitudes, and as they departed, they were engaged by Spitfires from 54 Squadron, resulting in the loss of three dive-bombers.

In these dire circumstances, Wolfhound docked at Calais, and its captain reported to the Admiralty the critical situation, with Germans controlling the southern part of town. Nicholson, having received orders from the War Office for evacuation, made arrangements to embark non-combatants once unloading was complete. However, fighting troops were informed they would have to wait until May 25. With no reserves available for a counter-attack, Nicholson ordered a strategic retreat to the Marck canal and Avenue Léon Gambetta, leading the defenders to fall back to the Old Town and areas east of the outer ramparts and canals, while maintaining control of the north-south sections of the enceinte.

Command among the French forces remained divided, with Le Tellier based in the Citadel on the west side of the Old Town, and Lambertye in charge of naval artillery. Plans to demolish bridges over the canals by French engineers hadn't materialized, leaving the British without the means to execute this themselves. In a late-night message from General Edmund Ironside, Nicholson was informed that General Robert Fagalde, the French commander of the Channel Ports, had prohibited evacuation, mandating that the Calais defenders comply. With the harbor's strategic importance diminished, Nicholson was advised to choose the best defensive position, with the promise of ammunition but no reinforcements. He was also informed of the 48th Division's advance towards Calais for relief.

In the final hours of the night, the French naval gunners spiked most of their guns and headed to the docks to embark on French ships. Lambertye, despite being ill, refused evacuation and sought volunteers to remain. About fifty men from the 1,500 navy and army personnel present bravely chose to stay, fully aware that no further rescue attempts would be made. These volunteers took control of Bastion 11 on the west side, determined to hold it for the duration of the siege.

Throughout the night, Vice-Admiral James Somerville journeyed from England to meet with Nicholson. In their meeting, Nicholson expressed that with additional artillery, he could prolong the defense of Calais. They concurred that the ships docked in the port should set sail back to England. As the first light of May 25th broke, the German forces renewed their fierce bombardment, this time focusing intensely on the old town. The relentless shelling led to buildings collapsing into the streets, fires raging, fanned by high winds, and a thick blanket of smoke obscuring visibility. The situation for the defenders grew dire as the last of the 229th Anti-Tank Battery's guns were destroyed and only three tanks from the 3rd RTR remained in action. Compounding these challenges, the distribution of rations and ammunition became increasingly difficult, and with the water mains damaged, the only source of water were abandoned wells.

At 9:00 a.m., Schaal sent the mayor, André Gerschell, to negotiate Nicholson's surrender, but Nicholson firmly refused. Noon brought another offer from Schaal to surrender, even extending the deadline to 3:30 p.m. after his emissaries were delayed, but Nicholson remained steadfast in his refusal. As the day progressed, the German bombardment intensified, unrelenting even in the face of Allied naval forces attempting to counter by bombarding German gun positions.

On the eastern front, the 1st Rifle Brigade, along with units of the QVR on the outer ramparts and along the Marck and Calais canals, successfully repelled a fierce German attack. An intercepted German wireless message revealed an impending attack on the western perimeter, defended by the 2nd KRRC. In response, at 1:00 p.m., Nicholson commanded a counter-attack, assembling eleven Bren carriers and two tanks with the 1st RB for a sortie. The plan was to break out from the enceinte north of Bassin des Chasses de l'Ouest and flank the Germans from the south. Despite objections from Hoskyns, the 1st RB commander, citing the risk of weakening their defenses where the Germans were nearly breaking through, the counter-attack proceeded. However, the carriers struggled in the sandy terrain, leading to the failure of the attempt.

By approximately 3:30 p.m., the units defending the Canal de Marck were overrun, and tragically, Hoskyns was mortally wounded by a mortar bomb. Major A. W. Allan, the second-in-command of the 1st RB, took command, leading the battalion in a fighting withdrawal through the streets to the Bassin des Chasses, the Gare Maritime, and the quays. In the southeast corner, near the 1st RB positions at Quai de la Loire, a rearguard became encircled. An effort to rescue them was repelled, and their situation became even more desperate when a fifth columnist, at gunpoint, drove a van carrying some of the wounded but stopped short of safety. In the end, only about 30 of the 150 men trapped in that area managed to escape.

In a twist of fate, the Rifle Brigade and the Queen Victoria's Rifles withdrawing from the northern part of the Calais enceinte unexpectedly benefited from a German artillery error. Their own forces, specifically the II Battalion of the Rifle Regiment 69, were mistakenly shelled while assembling in a woodland east of Bastion No. 2. This error provided a brief respite for the beleaguered British troops.

During the afternoon, a German officer, accompanied by a captured French officer and a Belgian soldier, approached under a white flag to demand surrender. Nicholson, however, remained resolute in his refusal. The German offensive resumed with vigor, continuing until their commander assessed that a victory could not be secured before nightfall.

In the old town, the King's Royal Rifle Corps and additional units of the QVR valiantly defended the three bridges leading into the Old Town from the south. When the German artillery fire ceased at 6:00 p.m., panzer tanks launched an attack on the bridges. At Pont Faidherbe, two of the three attacking tanks were destroyed, forcing the remaining tank to retreat. The middle bridge, Pont Richelieu, saw its attack thwarted when the lead tank hit a mine. However, at Pont Freycinet, near the Citadel, the German forces succeeded, capturing the bridge with tanks and infantry, who then took shelter in nearby houses. This success was short-lived as they were soon counter-attacked by the 2nd KRRC. Both French and British troops held their ground at a bastion, and despite heavy losses, the French in the Citadel repelled the attacks. Nicholson, recognizing the gravity of the situation, established a joint command center with the French forces.

In another part of the battlefield, Lieutenant Colonel Keller, commander of the 3rd RTR, faced a grim situation. With his remaining tanks under intense shellfire near the Bastion de l'Estran and no longer able to contribute effectively to the defense, he ordered them to withdraw eastward through the sand dunes north of the Bassin des Chasses. Keller himself attempted to evacuate 100 wounded men from Bastion No. 1 to the dunes, but they were soon captured. Keller, riding a light tank, reached C Company of the 1st RB, suggesting a withdrawal to Dunkirk. Unfortunately, his last tanks either broke down or ran out of fuel and were subsequently destroyed. Keller and some crew members managed to reach Gavelines on foot by nightfall. The next morning, after crossing the Aa River, they contacted French troops and were eventually evacuated to Dover.

In the skies above, the RAF was actively engaged in the defense of Calais. At 10:30 a.m. GMT, 17 Squadron successfully claimed three Stukas destroyed and three damaged, along with a Do 17. Throughout the day, 605 Squadron maintained air cover, claiming four Ju 87s and a Hs 126 destroyed, and another five unconfirmed, following an engagement while escorting Bristol Blenheim on a reconnaissance mission. The large formation of Stukas, numbering 40 to 50, targeted shipping near the port. Additionally, 264 Squadron flew escort operations in the afternoon without any incidents.

On May 25th, RAF's 11 Group conducted 25 Blenheim bomber and 151 fighter sorties, resulting in the loss of two Blenheims and two fighters. In contrast, they achieved significant success against the Luftwaffe, shooting down 25 aircraft and damaging nine. RAF Bomber Command also flew 139 sorties against land targets that day. StG 2, a Luftwaffe unit, suffered the loss of four Ju 87s, with one damaged. All eight crews that were shot down were captured but later released after the French surrender.

In a tense situation, with the possibility of French Commander Fagalde changing his stance on evacuation, fifteen small naval vessels equipped to carry about 1,800 men hovered offshore near Calais. Some of these ships, driven by the urgency of the situation, sailed into Calais harbor without a formal evacuation order. One of these vessels even brought another directive for Nicholson, instructing him to persist in the fight.

At 8:00 a.m., a weary Nicholson communicated back to England, reporting the dire state of his forces: the men were exhausted, the last of the tanks had been disabled, there was a shortage of water, and reinforcements seemed unlikely to turn the tide, especially since the Germans had penetrated the northern part of the town.

The relentless resistance put up by the Calais garrison forced the German command to convene a late-night meeting on May 25th. Colonel Walther Nehring, Chief of Staff of the XIX Armee Korps, proposed to Schaal that the final assault should be delayed until May 27th, anticipating additional support from Stuka dive-bombers. However, Schaal was inclined to continue the attack, fearing that any delay might allow the British time to reinforce their positions.

The German artillery, bolstered by units from Boulogne which effectively doubled their firepower, resumed its relentless bombardment at 5:00 a.m. From 8:30 to 9:00 a.m., the old town and citadel faced a devastating assault from both artillery and up to 100 Stukas. The German infantry then launched their offensive, while the German guns, along with StG 77 and StG 2 units, continued to pound the Citadel for an additional thirty minutes. Despite this, the 2nd KRRC steadfastly defended the canal bridges against the German infantry onslaught.

Schaal received information that if Calais was not surrendered by 2:00 p.m., his division would be pulled back to allow the Luftwaffe to level the town completely. The German forces started making significant inroads around 1:30 p.m., eventually capturing Bastion 11 after the French volunteers, defending bravely, ran out of ammunition.

On the opposite side of the harbor, the 1st Rifle Brigade was engaged in a fierce battle around the Gare Maritime, facing attacks from the south and east. Major Allan, leading the 1st RB, held out in hope that the 2nd KRRC would be able to join them for a last stand in defense of the harbor. However, by 2:30 p.m., the Germans overpowered the defenses at the Gare Maritime and the Bastion de l'Estran. The remaining members of the 1st RB gathered for a final defense around Bastion No. 1, but by 3:30 p.m., they too were overwhelmed by the German forces.

The 2nd King's Royal Rifle Corps found themselves in a precarious situation as they were forced to retreat from the three bridges connecting the old and new towns of Calais. They fell back to a defensive line stretching from the harbor to the cathedral, situated between Rue Notre Dame and Rue

Maréchaux, approximately 600 yards from one of the bridges. Amidst this chaotic retreat, signs of capitulation began to emerge as troops in the Citadel started displaying white flags. German tanks successfully crossed Pont Freycinet, leading to further disarray among the British troops who lacked the means to effectively counter tank assaults.

By 4:00 p.m., the situation deteriorated rapidly, leading to the collapse of the new defensive line. The 2nd KRRC received the desperate order of "every man for himself." In this confusion, B Company, not having received the retreat orders, continued to fight as a cohesive unit, distinct from the rest of the regiment which was dispersing towards the harbor. Those in the Citadel realized around 3:00 p.m. that the German artillery had ceased firing. They soon found themselves surrounded and were informed by a French officer that Le Tellier had surrendered.

Meanwhile, the Royal Air Force was actively engaged in the skies above Calais, flying 200 sorties throughout the day. 17 Squadron, targeting Stuka dive-bombers from StG 2, claimed three Stukas, a Dornier Do 17, and a Henschel Hs 126, but suffered six fighter losses. The Fleet Air Arm dispatched Fairey Swordfish aircraft to bomb German troops near Calais, while their escorts from 54 Squadron claimed three Bf 110s and a Bf 109, albeit losing three aircraft. At noon, 605 Squadron reported the destruction of four Stukas from StG 77 and a Hs 126, with the loss of one Hurricane.

Jagdgeschwader 2 provided protection for the Ju 87s, successfully warding off attacks from 17 Squadron, resulting in no German losses while downing a Blenheim on a reconnaissance mission. I Jagdgeschwader 3 conducted fighter sweeps over Calais after noon, when the ground battle was nearing its end. They engaged a flight of Hurricanes in a dogfight over Calais, resulting in the downing of one Hurricane without any losses on their side.

Battle of Saumur

On the night of June 18th, a dramatic scene unfolded as the Wehrmacht's 1st Cavalry Division, a unique remnant of traditional cavalry amidst Germany's modernized forces, approached the river at Saumur. Their arrival, just before midnight, was marked by the presence of reconnaissance units on motorcycles with sidecars, followed by a fleet of armored cars. The first strike of the ensuing battle was claimed by a 25 mm gun operated by Cadet Hoube.

This confrontation marked the beginning of a battle that would rage until June 20th. In a strategic move, the French demolished key bridges to hinder the German advance: the Pont Napoleon at Saumur just after midnight, the Montsoreau bridge at 1:15 am, and the railway bridge to the east of Saumur was destroyed with 1,700 kilos of melinite at 3:00 am.

As dawn broke on June 19th, a moment of tense diplomacy emerged when a German staff car, carrying a German and a French officer, approached the ruined bridge at Saumur under a white flag. Mysteriously, the French forces opened fire, destroying the car and killing both officers. In retaliation, the Germans unleashed a barrage of artillery, bombarding Saumur with 2,000 shells over the next two days. This onslaught devastated numerous ancient buildings, inflicted casualties among the civilian population, and forced many to seek shelter in cellars and wine caves. The headquarters, initially cut off due to severed telephone lines and exposed to shellfire, was subsequently relocated 3 km west to the relative safety of Auberge de Marsoleau, near the airfield. Throughout the day, the battle intensified, with cadets on the island targeting any available German forces, and the 25 mm gun on the island registering nine more hits on armored vehicles.

The morning of June 20th dawned with an eerie calm. Some students from the French side ventured from the island to the north bank, only to find it deserted, leading to the assumption that the Germans had moved east or west to find alternate crossing points. Tragically, several French soldiers lost their lives on the north bank in their efforts to confront the Germans. Among them was Lt Gérard de Buffévent, who bravely fought until his death and was posthumously awarded the Légion d'Honneur for his valor.

The quiet town of Gennes, situated west of Saumur, remained untouched by the ravages of war until the afternoon of June 19th, when the tranquility was shattered by the arrival of Wehrmacht scouts. The tense atmosphere escalated when motorcyclists approached, prompting the French to blow up the suspension bridge to the north of the island, severing a crucial crossing point.

Perched on high ground, the 11th-century church of St Eusèbe offered a strategic vantage point over the area. This location was not only ideal for observation but also served as a fitting spot for one of the 25 mm guns. However, the peace of the evening was disrupted at 8 pm, as 50 German troop carriers crowded with assault troops arrived on the north bank. The onslaught began with a vicious artillery barrage that targeted both the island and Gennes, devastating the tower of St Eusèbe and igniting fires across the town.

In a daring move, the Wehrmacht attempted to storm the island using rubber boats. However, their assault was valiantly repelled by the combined efforts of the Cadets and Algerian riflemen by midnight. Amidst the chaos, an engineer, fearing that his explosives might be compromised by further bombardment, prematurely detonated the southern bridge, effectively isolating the troops on the island. This forced the evacuation of the wounded by boat under challenging conditions.

The dawn of June 20th brought renewed efforts from the Germans. Bolstered by reinforcements and additional artillery, they used rafts and boats to overpower the island's defenders, who eventually succumbed as their ammunition depleted. However, the Germans were unable to advance from the island to the strongly defended south bank of the Loire, where four units of cadets stood firm.

As the Wehrmacht continued their advance westward along the river, they identified a lightly defended gap. Despite the arrival of students who inflicted casualties, the Germans managed to establish a small foothold on the south shore.

Simultaneously, other German units pushed further west towards Angers, successfully forcing a crossing against another French defending unit and subsequently capturing the city of Angers.

Back at Gennes, as French reinforcements were en route to counter the German bridgehead, another German bridgehead emerged between Gennes and Saumur, posing a direct threat to the rear of the town. The reinforcements were swiftly redirected to address this new menace.

The cadets at Gennes, bolstered by two tanks, received orders to reclaim the bridgehead to their west. By 3 pm, the commander at Gennes reported a hard-won victory: the left bank of the Loire was back in French control, though the cost in lives was steep. The battle around Gennes resulted in between 200 and 300 German casualties, including those killed, wounded, and captured.

The atmosphere at Montsoreau, following the destruction of the bridge, was eerily quiet until the early hours of June 20th. At 5:00 am, the Germans attempted a daring crossing between Montsoreau and Saumur. Despite incurring losses, they managed to secure a foothold on the south bank at Le Petit-Puy. However, their advance towards Saumur was effectively stymied by the cadets positioned around the railway viaduct. In a strategic effort, three armored cars patrolled the river road east of Saumur, aiming to keep the area clear of additional Wehrmacht reinforcements attempting to cross the river and reinforce the assault on Saumur.

The Germans found refuge in the troglodyte houses embedded in the cliffs, making it difficult for the French to completely eliminate their presence.

Meanwhile, the Aunis farm, situated 1,800 meters inland from the Loire River and cliffs, served as the headquarters for troop leader Captain de St-Blanquat. The farm was strategically positioned to block any potential German breakout from the gap between the railway bridge at Saumur and Montsoreau. As the Wehrmacht landed on the south side of the river, the French quickly dug trenches to fortify the farm. The Germans, recognizing the farm's strategic importance, unleashed artillery fire from the north side of the river, aided by a spotter plane.

Outlying student units bravely attacked the Wehrmacht mortar positions, which were bombarding the farm, causing it to catch fire. The students suffered casualties in their valiant efforts. Reinforcements from the French military infantry officer students of St Maixent, initially headed towards Gennes, were redirected to bolster the eastern sector. Backed by five Hotchkiss tanks of the reserve, they launched a counterattack to alleviate the pressure on Aunis. However, the German artillery shifted focus to the advancing French, disabling two tanks and forcing the remaining three to retreat. The infantry students, though, managed to reach and reinforce the besieged farm.

The fighting raged for six hours, with the farm enduring relentless artillery, mortar, and machine-gun fire. Multiple German assaults were repelled, but at 1:00 pm, with the farm's cellar filled with wounded, a second barn ablaze, and facing the risk of encirclement, the French decided to withdraw southwards. The Wehrmacht ultimately took control of the farm in the late afternoon, and in a moment of wartime humanity, both the Germans and their French prisoners attended to the wounded and collected the dead from both sides in the fields surrounding the farm.

Among the fallen French soldiers was the organist and composer Jehan

Alain. Assigned to scout the German advance near Saumur, Alain heroically engaged a group of Wehrmacht soldiers at Le Petit-Puy. In a brave stand, he abandoned his motorcycle and confronted the enemy with his carbine, killing 16 before being fatally wounded. For his extraordinary bravery, he was posthumously awarded the Croix de Guerre.

To the east, the Wehrmacht also managed to cross the river towards Tours and were advancing south, circling behind Saumur. Despite a failed demolition attempt, the bridge at Port-Boulet, which remained intact, was fiercely defended until its capture at midnight on June 20/21. The German commander, recognizing the tenacity of the French resistance at Saumur and the heavy losses being incurred, ultimately decided to bypass the town rather than continue the direct assault.

On June 19th, a national armistice was agreed upon between the warring nations, but it wasn't until the afternoon of June 20th that Germany specified the details for the armistice signing: the French delegation was to cross into German territory at Tours by 5 pm. Meanwhile, the situation on the ground at Saumur was reaching a critical point. By 9:00 pm on June 20th, with both Tours to the east and Angers to the west under German control, Colonel Michon made the difficult decision to withdraw the cadets from Saumur. Despite their exhaustion, those who could muster the strength retreated south, many on bicycles, converging south of Fontevraud Abbey, the final resting place of English royalty including Henry II, Eleanor of Aquitaine, and Richard the Lionheart.

The Battle of Saumur, coinciding with the 125th anniversary of the Battle of Waterloo, was symbolically named "La Haie Sainte" (The Sacred Line) in homage to the farm La Haye Sainte at the heart of the Waterloo battlefield.

Amid the chaos, there were alarming reports of German subterfuge. At Gennes, two cadets were shot by German officers disguised as Belgian civilian refugees; one of the imposters later died and was found wearing army dog tags. In Montsoreau, a deserted house with a map detailing the defenders' positions was discovered, along with two men in civilian clothes carrying signaling equipment on the south bank.

The rationale behind the battle's intensity, despite the imminent armistice, remains a subject of speculation. The students, forming the moral backbone of the defense, likely chose to fight as an act of honor, unwilling to accept the disgrace of mere retreat. Supported by other units, they displayed numerous acts of extraordinary bravery, fully aware that they were outnumbered and outgunned with the war's end only hours away. The courage of these French students did not go unnoticed, with many Wehrmacht officers commending their bravery. To the French public, the cadets' resistance planted the seeds for the restoration of national honor. Charles de Gaulle, having made his famous appeal on June 18th, regarded the action by the cadets as the first act of resistance in a nation ready to rebuild.

Max Hastings, in his detailed account of the battle in "All Hell Let Loose," affectionately refers to Colonel Michon as "an old war horse," highlighting his crucial role in the events at Saumur.

Italian Invasion of France

In the roaring 1920s, Italy's Prime Minister, Benito Mussolini, passionately advocated for imperial expansion. He believed Italy needed more space for its growing population and that other nations should support this endeavor. Mussolini's vision was ambitious: he aimed to establish Italian dominance from Gibraltar to the Strait of Hormuz, echoing the ancient Roman Empire's control in the Balkans and Mediterranean. The plan included turning Albania into a protectorate, annexing Dalmatia, and exerting economic and military influence over Yugoslavia and Greece. Mussolini also sought to foster patron-client relationships with Austria, Hungary, Romania, and Bulgaria, extending Italy's influence in Europe.

By 1935, Mussolini's ambitions led Italy into the Second Italo-Ethiopian War, a late 19th-century-style colonial campaign. The conflict fueled dreams of raising an Ethiopian army to aid in further conquests. This aggression marked a shift in Italian foreign policy and exposed the weaknesses of Britain and France, creating an opportunity for Mussolini to pursue his imperial goals.

The Spanish Civil War in 1936 saw significant Italian involvement, tipping the scales in favor of Francisco Franco's Nationalist forces. Mussolini's involvement was part of a broader strategy to create a warrior culture and place Italy on a war footing. The war's aftermath improved German-Italian relations, leading to the Berlin-Rome Axis formation in October 1936. This alliance, driven by mutual interests and policies, increasingly tied Italy to

Germany, with Mussolini falling under Adolf Hitler's influence.

In 1938, following the Munich Agreement, Italy demanded concessions from France, including control over certain African territories and Mediterranean ports, and preservation of Italian culture in Corsica. The French, seeing through these demands as veiled territorial ambitions for Nice, Corsica, Tunisia, and Djibouti, refused. Mussolini's grand scheme encompassed not just territorial expansion but a cultural and political reshaping of Europe, with Italy at the forefront, challenging the established powers and reshaping the continent's dynamics.

In 1939, Italian leader Benito Mussolini expressed a strong belief that Italy's national sovereignty was tied to its access to global oceans and major shipping lanes. On February 4, 1939, during a secretive meeting of the Grand Council, he made a speech likening Italy to a prisoner in the Mediterranean, trapped by British-held territories like Cyprus, Gibraltar, Malta, and Egypt (which controlled the Suez Canal). He envisioned these as the bars and guards of Italy's maritime prison.

Mussolini was adamant that Italy's independence hinged on breaking British dominance in these regions. He proposed that by conquering Italian North Africa and Italian East Africa, and by neutralizing British bases in Cyprus, Gibraltar, Malta, and Egypt, Italy could shatter this 'Mediterranean prison'. This would pave the way for Italian expansion either towards the Indian Ocean through Sudan and Abyssinia or towards the Atlantic through French North Africa.

Italy's expansionist ambitions included plans, formulated as early as September 1938, to invade Albania. By April 7, 1939, Italian forces had landed in Albania, quickly occupying most of the country. Albania was seen as crucial for Italy's 'living space' to mitigate overpopulation and as a strategic base for further Balkan conflicts.

The militaristic alliance between Italy and Germany was formalized in the Pact of Steel on May 22, 1939. Contrary to the Italian assumption that war with Britain and France would not be imminent, this pact was essentially an agreement for a joint military venture against these nations, with no provisions for a peaceful interlude. Despite this, Italy was unprepared when Germany advanced its plans to invade Poland.

In September 1939, Britain's selective blockade against Italy began, targeting coal shipments from Germany through Rotterdam. Despite Germany's assurances to supply coal overland and Britain's offer to supply Italy's coal in exchange for armaments, Italy could not accept without jeopardizing the German alliance. In early 1940, Mussolini briefly considered, but then rejected, a deal with Britain to supply aircraft.

The coal issue became a focal point in international diplomacy in 1940. Britain strengthened its Mediterranean Fleet to enforce the blockade, refusing Italian concessions to avoid appearing weak. Germany stepped up, supplying Italy with more coal than Mussolini had initially requested, further entwining the two Axis powers as the shadow of war loomed over Europe.

On January 23, 1940, Benito Mussolini openly stated that Italy could independently engage in a war parallel to the ongoing global conflict. This statement was particularly focused on Yugoslavia, influenced by his meeting with the Croatian dissident Ante Pavelić on that day. By April's end, a conflict with Yugoslavia seemed increasingly probable.

On May 26, Mussolini revealed his intention to join Germany in the war against Britain and France, driven by the ambition to have a seat at the victor's table in post-war negotiations. However, top Italian military officials, including Marshals Pietro Badoglio and Italo Balbo, opposed this move, citing the unprepared state of the Italian military and empire. Despite these warnings, on June 5, Mussolini callously expressed his willingness to sacrifice lives just to ensure Italy's presence in post-war discussions.

In an intriguing turn of events, French intelligence was tipped off about Italy's impending declaration of war. In a clandestine meeting on the Pont Saint-Louis, French military intelligence officer Paul Paillole was informed by his Italian counterpart that war would be declared within four days, though significant action near Menton would not occur until June 19 or 20.

By mid-1940, Germany's view of Italy as a wartime ally had evolved. The imminent fall of France and the potential need to divert resources to assist Italy created a strategic dilemma. Politically and economically, Italy was more valuable as a neutral party, and its entry into the war could complicate peace talks with Britain and France.

On June 10, Italian Foreign Minister Galeazzo Ciano notified the Italian ambassadors in London and Paris about the imminent declaration of war. The actual declaration was received with alarm by the French ambassador André François-Poncet, but with stoicism by the British ambassador Percy Loraine. The declaration took effect at midnight, leading to President Franklin D. Roosevelt's remark that it was a "stab in the back" to Italy's neighbors.

Following the declaration, Mussolini addressed a crowd in Rome, justifying the war as a move to adjust maritime boundaries. His reasons for joining the war have been widely debated, with many historians agreeing that his motivations were opportunistic and imperialistic.

In preparation for war, the French had planned the evacuation of Menton, a key town near the Italian border. General René Olry ordered the evacuation on June 3, and within two nights, the town was emptied under the code name "Exécutez Mandrin". Following Italy's declaration of war, the French destroyed key transport and communication links with Italy and took a defensive stance, avoiding any offensive actions.

Furthermore, in anticipation of war, the French Ministry of the Interior had directed the arrest of Italian nationals suspected of anti-French sentiments.

After the war declaration, Italian citizens were ordered to report to local police, with a majority complying and signing a declaration of loyalty, which included a clause for potential military service. In Nice, for instance, over 5,000 Italians reported within just three days of the declaration.

In the wake of Italy declaring war in June 1940, Marshal Graziani, the army's chief of staff, headed to the front lines, accompanied by General Ubaldo Soddu, who acted as Mussolini's link to the action. Graziani's right-hand man in Rome, General Mario Roatta, was tasked with relaying Mussolini's orders, often bold and audacious, to the front. However, Graziani frequently contradicted these commands, anticipating the offensive's failure and meticulously documenting everything to shift blame if needed.

Italy's first aggressive move was a two-part air raid on Malta on June 11, marking the start of the lengthy Siege of Malta. The morning raid involved 55 bombers, but Malta's defenses reported far fewer, indicating a failure in hitting their targets. The afternoon saw another 38 aircraft. Following this, attacks extended to French targets in Tunisia and shipping along France's Mediterranean coast.

The British swiftly responded. On the night of June 11, a fleet of 36 RAF Whitley bombers flew from Yorkshire, aiming for Italy's industrial heart in Turin. Despite challenging conditions over the Alps, a few bombers reached their targets in Turin and Genoa, with the Italians mistaking them for their own planes at one point. The raid, however, caused minimal damage.

The French, initially hindering their own air force's retaliatory capacity, finally allowed operations on June 15. A mission that night by eight Wellington bombers targeting Genoa was largely unsuccessful due to weather and navigation challenges. Another sortie on June 16/17 had limited success, and soon after, the deteriorating situation in France forced the withdrawal of the British Haddock Force from Marseille, leaving behind equipment and stores.

Propaganda played its part too. British planes dropped leaflets over Rome with messages urging Italians to lay down their arms and warning of the consequences of war under Mussolini's rule.

Meanwhile, from French North Africa, the Armée de l'Air struck Italian cities, causing civilian casualties but hitting strategically insignificant targets. By June 22, over 600 aircraft were amassed in French North Africa, with General Charles Noguès eager to launch offensives against Italy or Libya, though initially denied permission.

On June 15, 1940, the 3a Squadra Aerea dispatched bombers and fighters to strike Corsica, and the following day, targeted airfields with strafing runs. The skies over southern France became a battleground as Italian bombers clashed with French fighters. Despite some losses on both sides, these skirmishes marked a significant moment in the campaign.

The Italian air raids took a more devastating turn on June 17 when bombers targeted the heart of Marseille, resulting in significant civilian casualties and damage. Subsequent attacks focused on the port city, both in daylight and at night. Meanwhile, over Tunisia, dogfights raged between Italian and French aircraft, each side claiming victories. The Italian aerial campaign also extended to bombing missions in Bizerte, Tunisia, and even attempted attacks on French naval assets.

On the ground, French ski scout troops engaged Italian forces in the Maddalena Pass on June 12. The surprise attack caused casualties and marked a shift in the Italian military stance. Italian leader Benito Mussolini, sensing a potential quick victory following the change in French government, ordered an unrealistic acceleration of offensive plans. Marshal Graziani, tasked with leading these operations, faced the challenge of rapidly shifting from defensive to offensive tactics.

In response, the Italians launched multiple operations through the Alps, including ambitious attacks through the Little Saint Bernard Pass and Maddalena Pass. One significant engagement involved the Italian bombardment of the French Fort de l'Olive from their formidable mountain fortress, Fort Chaberton, effectively silencing the French guns.

However, the French announcement of an impending ceasefire on June 17 threw Italian plans into confusion. Despite initial celebrations among Italian troops, conflicting orders created uncertainty. The high command believed the French forces were near collapse, a misjudgment that impacted their strategic decisions.

On the diplomatic front, Mussolini's meeting with Hitler in Munich revealed a stark reality. German support for Italian territorial claims hinged on demonstrable military achievements. This put pressure on Italian forces to make significant advances to legitimize their demands in the eyes of their more powerful ally.

Before Italy's entry into World War II, the British Royal Navy and French Marine Nationale had grand plans to challenge the Italian Regia Marina in the Mediterranean. The British aimed to test Italian defenses by moving their fleet towards Malta, while the French planned to strike along Italy's coastlines and islands. The Allied forces had a significant advantage in capital ships, but these plans were never fully realized due to the rapid German advance in France.

In the early days of the war, the French fleet patrolled the Aegean Sea and the French submarines set out to sea, while the Royal Navy stayed close to the African coast instead of advancing towards Malta.

On June 12, in response to a false report of German warships entering the Mediterranean, the French fleet encountered the Italian submarine Dandolo, which unsuccessfully launched torpedoes at them. The same day, the Italian submarine Alpino Bagnolini managed to sink the British cruiser HMS Calypso.

The French Navy launched Operation Vado on June 13, with a squadron of heavy cruisers and destroyers targeting Italian coastal installations. The French cruisers bombarded oil storage tanks, steel mills, and gasworks, causing significant damage but also facing fierce resistance from Italian shore batteries and an armoured train. The Italian torpedo boat Calatafimi, although damaged, bravely engaged the French ships, leading to exaggerated claims of its effectiveness in Italian propaganda.

Meanwhile, the French air force and British Fleet Air Arm conducted bombing raids on Italian aerodromes and Genoa, but these attacks inflicted minimal damage.

The Italian submarine Provana's attack on a French convoy off Oran resulted in its sinking by the French sloop La Curieuse, marking the only Italian submarine loss to the French Navy. Subsequent French naval sorties yielded no significant engagements.

The most notable action was the bombardment of the Italian port of Bardia in Libya by a combined force of British, Australian, and French ships, although it caused only minimal damage. French naval aircraft also targeted Livorno in mainland Italy, causing some destruction but limited overall impact.

A study by the Regia Marina concluded that a landing on Malta was not feasible, despite the island's lack of defenses. This assessment was confirmed in the first war-time meeting of the Italian chiefs of staff on June 25.

On June 19, 1940, General Roatta of the Italian Army mistakenly believed that the French troops, especially their mobile units, were already retreating. This misconception, coupled with an overestimation of French morale, led Italian officers to approach the impending offensive with a sense of overconfidence, even joking about interactions with French civilians.

Mussolini, eager for Italian forces to engage the enemy, pushed his generals to initiate offensive operations. By the evening of June 19, General Roatta ordered small offensive actions and full engagement with French forces. The main assault was scheduled to start no later than June 23. Mussolini's urgency intensified on June 20, driven by his desire to avoid the humiliation of Germans occupying French territories and handing them over to Italy. He pressed Marshal Badoglio to launch an immediate offensive.

Badoglio relayed this urgency to Graziani, instructing a full-scale attack along the entire front line from the Little Saint Bernard to the sea. The plan was to penetrate deep into French territory, with the air force providing heavy bombardment support. Graziani altered the initial directive, focusing the offensive towards Marseille and reducing the Maddalena Pass operation to a mere diversion. The primary targets were Albertville, via Operation M, and the town of Menton, through Operation R.

However, in a dramatic turn, Mussolini briefly halted the attack on the evening of June 20, only to reinstate it upon learning of the German army's continued advance in the Rhône valley.

Meanwhile, the Italian fort on Mont Chaberton, known to the French as the "battleship in the clouds," began targeting the French fort Ouvrage Janus. Despite the Italian fort's dominating position, the French managed to position mortars to attack it effectively. Over three days, despite challenges from the weather, the French silenced most of the fort's turrets.

On June 21, the main Italian offensive commenced. Italian forces crossed the French border, achieving initial success due to the weakened French lines, as many French troops had been redirected to confront the German invasion. The Italian Riviera force, numbering around 80,000, managed to advance 8 kilometers on the first day. However, they faced stiff resistance from approximately 38,000 French troops near the coast.

The Italian 4th Army, led by General Alfredo Guzzoni, spearheaded the primary attack during World War II's Italian offensive. The Army's Alpine Corps, bolstered by the IV Army Corps' artillery, launched its assault across a 34-40 km front from the Col de la Seigne to the Col du Mont. The focal point of this operation was the Little Saint Bernard Pass, which could have provided an easier route if not for the destruction of bridges by the French.

The French defenses in this region were formidable. The Redoute Ruinée, an old fort ruins now manned with seventy troops and machine guns, and the advance post at Seloge, posed significant obstacles. The French had a strong presence in the Tarentaise sub-sector, with 3,000 men, 350 machine guns, and 150 other guns, supported by 18 battalions and 60 guns. The Italian objective was to capture key locations including Bourg-Saint-Maurice, Les Chapieux, Séez, and Tignes, before advancing towards Beaufort and Albertville.

On June 21, the Alpine Corps' right column overcame the Seigne Pass and made progress across a glacier, but faced stiff resistance at Seloge. They managed to outflank this position by June 24, making their way up the Cormet de Roselend. However, the armistice halted their advance before completion. Meanwhile, the central column encountered resistance at the Little Saint Bernard from the Redoute Ruinée. The 101st Motorised Division "Trieste," summoned from Piacenza, broke through, but suffered heavy casualties while crossing a river and repairing a destroyed bridge.

On June 22, the Trieste's tank battalion was halted by a minefield, with several tanks getting trapped or damaged. While attempting a rear assault on the Redoute, the 65th Motorised Infantry Regiment faced French infantry and fortifications, eventually redirecting their efforts towards Séez. The Alpine Corps' left column encountered only light resistance, reaching the right bank of the Isère by June 22.

At the time of the armistice, the central column had taken Séez, but the Redoute Ruinée, now reinforced, continued to impede progress through the

Little Saint Bernard. The Alpine Army Corps failed to capture its ultimate objective, Bourg-Saint-Maurice. Respecting the armistice terms, they allowed the Redoute's garrison to depart with military honors.

South of the Alpine Army Corps, the Italian I Army Corps faced a challenging 40 km front, stretching from Mont Cenis to the Col d'Étache. Their ambitious plan involved breaking through the French fortifications at Bessans, Lanslebourg, and Sollières-Sardières, and the ouvrages overlooking Modane, before turning north towards Albertville. The 3rd Alpini Regiment's Battalions Val Cenischia and Susa, under Major Costantino Boccalatte, were attached to the Division Cagliari for this operation.

The Division Cagliari spearheaded the I Army Corps' attack with a three-pronged strategy aimed at capturing Bessans and Bramans, and then pushing along the river Arc toward Modane. The central column faced tough resistance as it descended through the Col des Lacs Giaset and approached the river Ambin. Meanwhile, the Battalion Val Cenischia encountered no opposition as it crossed the Col d'Étache and surprised the Fort de la Balme from the rear, capturing it by June 23.

Despite the Division Cagliari's progress, they were unable to fully reduce the stronger fortifications of Saint-Gobain at Villarodin and the Barrière de l'Esseillon before the armistice, although they were within striking distance of Modane.

The Susa Battalion's progress was more successful. After occupying Lanslebourg, they moved on to Termignon. However, the 3rd Battalion of the 64th Infantry Regiment encountered heavy resistance, with their route heavily mined and littered with anti-infantry and anti-tank obstacles. Additional support from the 231st Avellino Infantry Regiment and a tank battalion was dispatched, but two tankettes were destroyed by landmines, halting the advance.

The French forts, particularly the Fort de la Turra and the advanced post at Arcellins, continued to pose a significant challenge to the Italian forces. Despite surrounding Fort de la Turra, it remained active until the armistice. The Italian column, facing intense fire and hidden machine gun nests, struggled to make headway. By the time of the armistice, the Italians had not yet reached Lanslebourg, which had been occupied by Major Boccalatte's forces days earlier.

The Italian 1st Army, led by General Pietro Pintor, was spared the burden of the main attack, which was assigned to the 4th Army in the north. The 1st Army's southern front, held by the 37th Infantry Division "Modena" and the 5th Infantry Division "Cosseria", along with the 52nd Infantry Division "Torino" in reserve, launched its offensive on June 20. However, they faced strong resistance, with French artillery effectively repulsing most of their advances.

On June 21, the Italian units advancing through Val Roia succeeded in occupying Fontan. Meanwhile, the Cosseria Division, moving towards Nice, faced significant challenges. Their plan, which included coordination with Alpini troops and an amphibious landing by the San Marco Regiment, was thwarted by logistical issues such as engine failures and rough seas. The division faced intense shelling from French fortifications at Cap Martin and Mont Agel, but managed to capture Les Granges-Saint-Paul on June 22, encouraged by Mussolini's directive to advance at all costs.

Under cover of fog, the Cosseria Division bypassed Cap Martin and entered the Garavan quarter of Menton on the night of June 22/23. Despite bypassing French troops, the fighting in Menton was fierce, with the Italians capturing key positions including the Capuchin monastery of Notre-Dame de l'An-nonciade. A planned naval landing at Garavan was canceled due to adverse weather conditions.

By June 24, the Italian infantry reached the plain of Carnolès but were repelled by French artillery. Italian aircraft bombed the French barracks there, and the Fort of Pont Saint-Louis engaged in its final artillery duel. Mussolini later visited Menton, declaring it a significant success despite the high cost.

On the 1st Army's northern front, the 33rd Infantry Division "Acqui" faced challenges of its own. Initially positioned defensively, they were later ordered to advance 60 km into French territory. Hindered by bad weather, which affected their radios and slowed their progress, they reached the Maddalena Pass on June 23 but only managed to descend into the Ubaye Valley by June 24, just as the armistice was being signed. The division suffered casualties and frostbite due to harsh conditions, and their lack of artillery in the Ubaye Valley meant they could not engage French forts effectively.

On June 17, just a day after France requested an armistice with Germany, French Foreign Minister Paul Baudoin approached the Papal nuncio, Valerio Valeri, to relay a similar request to Italy. The French government, now led by Marshal Pétain, expressed its desire to work with Italy towards a lasting peace. That same day, Mussolini was informed by Hitler about France's armistice request to Germany. Mussolini promptly set off for a meeting in Munich, delegating the task of drafting Italy's demands to General Roatta, Admiral Raffaele de Courten, and Air Brigadier Egisto Perino.

The demands Italy eventually presented to France were surprisingly moderate. They relinquished claims to the Rhône valley, Corsica, Tunisia, and French Somaliland. General Roatta attributed this restraint to Mussolini's sense of fairness, not wanting to demand more than what had been conquered.

On the evening of June 21, Italian Ambassador Dino Alfieri in Berlin received the German armistice terms and forwarded them to Rome. Mussolini, noting the mild nature of these conditions, decided against making immediate territorial demands, preferring to wait for a formal peace conference. He hoped that further Italian military advances, particularly by General Gambara, might secure Nice.

The French delegation, led by General Charles Huntziger, arrived in Rome on June 23 to discuss the armistice. The first meeting was brief, with Roatta presenting Italy's terms and Huntziger requesting a recess to consult with the French government. During this break, Hitler suggested to Mussolini that Italy's demands were too modest and proposed a linkage of German and Italian occupation zones. However, Roatta convinced Mussolini that it was too late to alter the demands.

On June 24, at the Villa Incisa, General Huntziger, having received approval from his government, signed the armistice on behalf of France, with Marshal Badoglio signing for Italy. The armistice took effect just after midnight on June 25. Moments before the signing, Huntziger requested the removal of a clause regarding the repatriation of political refugees, a request to which Mussolini agreed.

The Franco-Italian Armistice stipulated a modest 50 km demilitarized zone on the French side of the border and confined Italian occupation to the areas already controlled at the time of the armistice, including the city of Menton. Italy also gained rights to use the port of Djibouti and the French section of the Addis Ababa–Djibouti railway, along with the demilitarization of key naval bases such as Toulon and Bizerte. However, Italy did not occupy the territory as far as the Rhône until after the Allied invasion of French North Africa in November 1942.

Despite the armistice terms, the Battle of the Alps is often considered a French defensive victory due to their successful resistance against the Italian offensive.

Battle of Britain

Adolf Hitler's strategic maneuvers during World War II were a complex blend of ambition and contradiction. Initially, he admired Britain and sought peace or neutrality, but his actions belied these sentiments. In a secretive May 1939 meeting, Hitler outlined a paradoxical strategy: attack Poland while hoping the Western Powers wouldn't intervene. He believed that if France fell and the Netherlands and Belgium were under control, England could be effectively blockaded and subdued.

As the war commenced, Hitler's military directives became more aggressive. "Directive No. 1" marked the beginning of Poland's invasion, while subsequent orders targeted England directly. The Luftwaffe was instructed to disrupt English imports, the armaments industry, and troop movements, with special attention given to attacking key naval units. Hitler reserved the decision for attacks on London, emphasizing the importance of avoiding weak, inconclusive strikes.

Both France and the UK responded to Germany's aggression by declaring war. Hitler's "Directive No. 6" outlined an ambitious offensive to seize territory in the Netherlands, Belgium, and northern France, establishing a strong base for air and sea operations against England. "Directive No. 9" further detailed plans for a naval blockade and widespread attacks on British shipping, warships, and industrial targets, laying the groundwork for the Battle of Britain.

By June 1940, Germany had overwhelmed Britain's continental allies. The German high command, OKW, debated the best strategy to pressure Britain into peace. The Luftwaffe, under Hermann Göring, focused on destroying the RAF to protect German industry and cut off Britain's overseas supplies. Simultaneously, Hitler weighed the option of Operation Sea Lion, a direct invasion of Britain, while also considering the Soviet Union as a potential target.

In July, Hitler issued "Directive No. 16," preparing for a possible invasion, contingent on Britain's refusal to negotiate. Despite the Luftwaffe's confidence, naval leaders like Grand Admiral Erich Raeder expressed doubts about the practicality of such an invasion. The debate within the German command structure reflected the complexity and uncertainty of their strategic position.

As August began, Hitler's "Directive No. 17" kept all options on the table. The Luftwaffe launched the Adlertag campaign, aiming to achieve air superiority over southern England as a prerequisite for any invasion. This strategy aimed to force the UK into peace negotiations by demonstrating their vulnerability to air attacks and initiating a blockade. However, significant Luftwaffe losses led to a shift in strategy, marking the beginning of an intense strategic bombing campaign independent of invasion plans.

Hitler's 1925 manifesto, "Mein Kampf," primarily detailed his deep-seated animosities, with a rare admiration for the common German soldiers of World War I and Britain, which he viewed as a potential ally against communism. By 1935, Hermann Göring, relishing Britain's rearmament, saw it as an ally-in-waiting. Göring, in 1936, offered to support the British Empire, asking in return for free rein in Eastern Europe. This sentiment was echoed in his 1937 meeting with Lord Halifax and von Ribbentrop's discussion with Churchill, where German domination was made clear.

Despite these diplomatic overtures, Hitler was frustrated by Britain's declaration of war following his invasion of Poland and the subsequent fall of

France, where he continually mulled over peace initiatives with his generals.

Churchill's rise to power in Britain saw continued advocacy for peace talks by Foreign Secretary Halifax. In May 1940, Halifax, adhering to a tradition of British diplomacy, sought a discreet channel through a Swedish businessman to initiate talks with Göring. Despite Halifax's push for negotiations, possibly involving Italy, Churchill, backed by the majority, stood firm against it. Even as peace seemed a possibility in Hitler's eyes, following an approach made to the Swedish ambassador, the British government perceived Hitler's July 19th speech to the German Parliament as more of an ultimatum than an offer for peace, leading to its rejection.

While Halifax persisted in his peace efforts until his appointment in Washington, Hitler remained interested in negotiating peace with Britain as late as January 1941.

In terms of military strategy, a 1939 Luftwaffe exercise revealed their limited capacity to significantly damage Britain's war economy. However, Joseph Schmid, head of Luftwaffe intelligence, identified Britain as Germany's most formidable adversary. The strategy pivoted towards countering the British blockade by disrupting British trade and attacking seaports, with retaliation against British cities if necessary. These plans were formalized in "Directive No. 9" after the successful conquest of the French coast, and "Directive No. 13" authorized attacks on British blockade efforts and industrial centers in response to RAF bombings.

Post-France's defeat, the OKW believed they were close to victory, anticipating that sustained pressure would compel Britain to capitulate. Jodl's strategy focused on intensifying attacks on British shipping, economic targets, and the RAF, aiming to break British morale and force a surrender. Göring's directive emphasized destroying the RAF as a precursor to crippling Britain's seaborne supplies, with an invasion being a last-resort measure.

In late 1939, Germany's military command, the OKW, evaluated the feasibility of an air and sea invasion of Britain. The Kriegsmarine (German Navy) faced the daunting challenge of the superior Royal Navy in the English Channel. Both the Kriegsmarine and the German Army agreed that control of the airspace was crucial. However, the navy argued that air superiority alone wouldn't suffice, citing a 1939 study that concluded naval superiority was also essential. The Luftwaffe (German Air Force) viewed an invasion as a last step in an already victorious campaign.

The concept of invading Britain first emerged in a meeting between Hitler and Grand Admiral Erich Raeder on May 21, 1940. Raeder highlighted the invasion's challenges, favoring a blockade strategy. By June 30, OKW Chief of Staff Jodl labeled invasion as a last-ditch effort, pending significant damage to the British economy and Luftwaffe's air superiority. Preliminary invasion plans were requested on July 2.

In Britain, Churchill used the threat of invasion to maintain high readiness, calling it "the great invasion scare." Historian Len Deighton noted Churchill's view of an invasion as highly risky and unlikely. On July 11, Hitler, agreeing with Raeder, considered invasion a last resort. The Luftwaffe estimated gaining air superiority would take two to four weeks. Surprisingly, Hitler showed little interest in the invasion details during a July 13 meeting with army chiefs, though he later ordered preparations for Operation Sea Lion on July 16.

The German Navy desired a narrow beachhead and extended troop landing period, conflicting with the Army's plans. At a July 31 meeting, the Navy proposed a postponement to the following year, but Hitler aimed for September. He planned to decide on the invasion eight to fourteen days after initiating air attacks. On August 1, he issued Directive No. 17, intensifying air and sea warfare and setting the stage for Operation Sea Lion, contingent on weather and other factors.

Regarding air strategy, the Luftwaffe, influenced by the 1935 "Conduct of the Air War" doctrine, prioritized battlefield attacks and close air support. They saw strategic bombing, especially against civilians, as strategically inefficient. However, France's defeat in 1940 opened the possibility of an independent air campaign against Britain. A Luftwaffe paper asserted air power as Germany's primary weapon against England, with the Navy and ground forces following. By 1940, the Luftwaffe planned an independent strategic offensive. Göring believed that strategic bombing could force Britain to negotiate and sought political gains for the Luftwaffe and himself, sidelining plans to support a ground invasion.

Kanalkampf

The Luftwaffe's aerial assaults on British shipping intensified dramatically with the capture of bases in France and the Low Countries. Notably, the North Sea's Grimsby fishing fleet had already faced two attacks in June. By July, losses due to air strikes along the east coast had surpassed those from naval mines. The situation worsened as attacks on minesweepers, escort vessels, and anti-invasion patrols increased, exacerbated by a shortage of light anti-aircraft guns and a focus on air defense in England's southeast.

The Admiralty, recognizing the effectiveness of prompt and accurate gunfire in reducing bombing accuracy and sometimes downing attackers, allowed ships to open fire on any aircraft perceived as a threat. This decision, however, led to unintended consequences. Inexperienced in aircraft recognition, naval crews often mistook RAF planes for enemy ones, especially when they escorted ships. The Admiralty's demand for close escorts, coupled with orders to engage unidentified aircraft within 1,500 yards, was deemed reckless by the RAF. As crews gained experience and underwent more training in aircraft recognition, these friendly fire incidents decreased.

The British power network, heavily reliant on coal from Wales, Northumberland, and Yorkshire, was another critical aspect of the war effort. Coal convoys, vital for power stations, railways, and industries, had to navigate treacherous waters filled with shoals, sandbars, shipwrecks, and minefields. These convoys, often escorted by destroyers and armed merchant trawlers, faced a perilous journey along the English coast, vulnerable to enemy aircraft from France. Despite the risks, these coal convoys were essential, as the southern ports alone required 40,000 long tons of coal weekly, and land transport couldn't meet this demand.

In the realm of communications, convoy code-names played a crucial role. Simple names like CW 9 were impractical over radio transmission, prone to miscommunication and reception issues. To address this, the RAF developed a list of unique code-names like "Bread," "Bacon," "Bosom," and "Peewit," assigned by Naval Control of Shipping as convoys formed. These names, reused every two weeks or less, helped identify convoys and facilitated the warning of air attacks. However, merchant ships were prohibited from broadcasting these codes, reserved exclusively for escorts and the Senior Officer of Escort, to maintain operational security.

The German occupation of the Channel Islands in late June 1940 set the stage for intensified Luftwaffe operations. Despite early morning mist hindering some operations on July 1st, reconnaissance missions led to the downing of two Dornier Do 215s by British defenses. Meanwhile, RAF squadrons, including Hurricanes and Spitfires, engaged in successful sorties, with Spitfires notably downing a Heinkel He 59 seaplane. The British made it clear that any aircraft near their convoys risked being fired upon, a policy underscored when they scrambled fighters to protect Convoy Jumbo from Ju 87 attacks.

The drama of convoy OA 177G unfolded on July 1st, as twenty ships, including large ocean-going vessels and local coal coasters, set sail. They faced a devastating attack by Ju 87 dive-bombers, leading to the sinking of the steamer Aeneas and damage to the Baron Ruthven. Amidst this chaos, a German E-Boat suffered a mine-induced demise.

The Luftwaffe also targeted Portland harbour on July 4th. A formidable force of Messerschmitts and Stukas launched a formidable assault, resulting in significant damage and loss of life, including the sinking of HMS Foylebank. Despite losing one Stuka and damaging a Bf 109, the Luftwaffe inflicted heavy losses on British ships.

Convoy OA 178, another target, faced peril as it navigated past Dover. German reconnaissance led to a coordinated Luftwaffe attack, resulting in the sinking of several ships, including the Dallas City and Deucalion. Hurricanes from 79 Squadron engaged in a desperate defense, with the loss of ace pilot Sergeant Henry Cartwright, highlighting the day's grim toll for the British.

These incidents prompted Churchill to urgently inquire about the Admiralty's plans for defending Channel convoys, emphasizing the severity of the situation. The Luftwaffe's successful attacks on Portland marked a dark day in British military history, leading to a demand from Churchill for increased air support over the Channel.

On July 5th, the English Channel's gloomy weather didn't deter aerial engagements. A Heinkel He 111 from the 8th Staffel of Kampfgeschwader 1 (KG 1) was downed by 65 Squadron, resulting in the loss of its entire five-member crew. That evening, 64 Squadron's reconnaissance mission near Calais ended with a Bf 109 from JG 51 shooting down a Spitfire, killing the pilot. These incidents pointed towards an impending Luftwaffe focus on the south, prompting Fighter Command to bolster its squadrons with pilots from Operational Training Units, a move agreed upon by Dowding and Keith Park of 11 Group.

The next day, July 6th, Air Vice-Marshal Trafford Leigh-Mallory of 12 Group pushed for relocating some squadrons closer to the coast. Anticipating German assaults from the Cherbourg peninsula, 609 Squadron was moved to RAF Middle Wallop, and 87 Squadron to Exeter, to safeguard Bristol, Plymouth, and the Western Approaches.

By July 7th, RAF resumed convoy patrols, focusing on CW and CE coal convoys along the southern coast. 145 Squadron successfully shot down a Do 17P reconnaissance aircraft, while 43 Squadron and 601 Squadron also downed enemy planes. Meanwhile, Luftwaffe Fighter Wings were encouraged to engage in freie jagd, or "free hunts," aggressively seeking RAF fighters without the burden of bomber protection. However, as 54 Squadron prepared to attack a lone He 111, they were ambushed by Bf 109s, resulting in two forced landings and another damaged RAF fighter.

Later that evening, as a convoy navigated past Dover, a large formation of Do 17s from KG 2 launched an offensive, sinking one ship and damaging three others. Despite radar warnings and RAF fighter scrambles, the attack proceeded unimpeded. 65 Squadron, engaged by 70 Bf 109s from JG 27, lost three Spitfires and their pilots, while managing to claim two Bf 109s, though these claims were not confirmed by Luftwaffe records. 64 Squadron managed to damage a Do 17, forcing it to crash-land at Boulogne.

Before nightfall, He 111s bombed Portland Harbour, narrowly missing the steamer British Inventor but hitting HMS Mercury, resulting in casualties. This relentless focus on ships and harbors convinced Dowding that the Luftwaffe would continue to target coastal and deep-sea convoys. He viewed convoy escort as a drain on resources, fearing it would deplete Fighter Command before a more significant confrontation. In response to the loss of seven reconnaissance aircraft in a week, the German Jagdgeschwader were ordered to provide escorts.

On July 8th, the Luftwaffe benefited from thick cloud cover, providing a shield for their bombers from RAF fighters. A convoy in the Bristol Channel was followed by a Do 17, which 92 Squadron claimed to have destroyed, though this is not corroborated by German records. Meanwhile, a large CW convoy departed from the Thames Estuary, encountering a He 111 near North Foreland. 74 Squadron's Spitfires engaged but the He 111 seemingly escaped despite being seen on fire.

The day saw significant aerial activity over the Pas de Calais. An unescorted Staffel of Do 17s, intercepted by 610 Squadron off Dover, hastily dropped their bombs, missing the convoy. In these skirmishes, a Spitfire pilot was killed, and a Bf 109 was claimed by the RAF. Later, Hurricanes from 79 Squadron were attacked north of Dover, suffering two pilot fatalities to Bf 109s. During these encounters, KG 54's Ju 88s made ineffective attacks, but 85 Squadron's Geoffrey Allard successfully downed a KG 1 He 111.

On July 9th, Kesselring deployed Zerstörergeschwader en masse for the first time against Britain. A Do 17 from KG 3 was damaged by 257 Squadron and crash-landed near Antwerp. Poor weather curtailed Luftwaffe operations, but the RAF continued to protect coastal convoys, with 609 Squadron relocating to RAF Warmwell for better coverage.

Park organized section strength patrols over six small coastal convoys. When Dover radar detected a large formation gathering behind the Pas de Calais, Park dispatched six squadrons into action. Wing Commander Victor Beamish, impatient at RAF North Weald, joined in with 151 Squadron. The RAF fighters encountered a substantial formation of German bombers and fighters. Despite some losses, the RAF managed to disrupt the bomber formations, with 43 Squadron downing three Bf 110s of ZG 26 and damaging another.

Later, Park's redeployed squadrons intercepted another German raid. 65 Squadron downed a Bf 109 from II./JG 51, and 17 Squadron Hurricanes destroyed a KG 53 He 111, with the crew perishing. In a dramatic engagement, 54 Squadron's Spitfires, led by Al Deere, forced down a He 59 floatplane on the Goodwin Sands, capturing its crew.

The day concluded with StG 77 Ju 87s, escorted by Bf 110s, attacking the Portland naval base. 609 Squadron's interception led to the death of Hauptmann Friedrich-Karl Lichtenfels, a distinguished pilot, and one of their own Spitfire pilots. A Bf 110 from 13./LG 1 was also lost, and the Empire

Daffodil freighter was damaged. Farther east, a KG 26 raid over Norwich resulted in civilian casualties and the destruction of a KG 26 He 111 by 17 Squadron.

On June 30th, Göring assigned the task of attacking shipping to Fliegerkorps II and VIII, mainly because they housed most of the Ju 87 Stuka units. Johannes Fink of KG 2 was appointed as the Channel Battle Leader. JG 51, based near KG 2 at Wissant, initially led the Jagdwaffe's operations over England, focusing on fighter sweeps over Kent. To balance bomber protection with fighter freedom, a new strategy was devised: Bf 110 Destroyer Wings provided close escort while Bf 109s roamed for tactical advantage.

Amidst thick cloud and rain, a Do 17 from 4.(F)/121, escorted by Bf 109s from I./JG 51, reconnoitered the Channel. 74 Squadron's Spitfires managed to damage the Do 17, but two Spitfires were damaged in return.

For Convoy CW 3, the Germans had enough time to analyze its composition before interception. Fink mobilized KG 2 and III./ZG 26 for close escort, with JG 51 providing high cover. During this time, a Staffel of Bf 109s shot down a 610 Squadron Spitfire. Park responded by dispatching multiple RAF squadrons. The ensuing aerial battle involved around 100 aircraft, with RAF fighters struggling to coordinate due to heavy radio traffic and Bf 109s thwarting attacks on the bombers.

A collision between a Hurricane and a Do 17 resulted in losses on both sides. The RAF's interception, despite the confusion, managed to limit the damage, with only a small sloop being sunk. The RAF fighters pursued the German aircraft back to the French coast, downing several enemy planes, including a Bf 110, a Do 17, and a couple of Bf 109s.

Meanwhile, in Falmouth, Luftwaffe bombers sank the British tanker Tascalusa. The Greek steamer Mari Chandris, damaged earlier and towed to Falmouth, caught fire due to the attack. Tascalusa was later refloated for scrapping. Additionally, the British steamer Waterloo was sunk, and the tanker Chancellor was damaged, with the Dutch salvage tug Zwarte Zee also suffering damage from bomb splinters.

On the morning of their operation, Richthofen's Fliegerkorps VIII launched a series of attacks from the Cherbourg Peninsula. At 07:00, StG 2's Ju 87s targeted shipping along the coast, sinking the British steam yacht HMS Warrior, resulting in one casualty. 501 Squadron's interception attempt was thwarted by Bf 109 escorts, losing a pilot in the process. 609 Squadron engaged the Stukas, but faced overwhelming odds and suffered the loss of two pilots without inflicting any damage on the Germans.

German reconnaissance aircraft patrolled extensively that day, with flights reaching as far north as Scotland. Over Yarmouth, Douglas Bader of 242 Squadron successfully downed a Do 17, while 85 Squadron's Peter Townsend bailed out after being hit. Spurred by the morning's success, Sperrle ordered a follow-up attack, this time with ZG 76's Bf 110s as escorts.

At 11:00 GMT, several RAF squadrons scrambled in response to a German formation, including Ju 87s from III./StG 2 escorted by around 40 Bf 110s. The Hurricanes arrived too late to prevent an attack on Portland, which resulted in minor damage and one vessel being hit.

A subsequent dogfight ensued near the Dorset coast. 87 Squadron's surprise attack from above led to the downing of a Bf 110 piloted by Oberleutnant Gerhard Kadow. In a tragic turn, Hermann Göring's nephew, Hans-Joachim Göring, and his gunner were killed when their plane crashed. Four Bf 110s from 9. Staffel and their crews were lost, along with a Ju 87 and another that was forced to land. The British steamer Kylemount was damaged off Dartmouth, and other steamers sustained damage in Portland harbour.

That evening, engine failure forced a He 59 to land off the Cornish coast, with another landing for rescue. However, British destroyers and Bristol

Blenheims intervened, leading to the loss of a He 59 and another evacuation. Nighttime raids on Rochester and Chatham resulted in 36 civilian casualties. KG 54 also played a role in these convoy operations.

On the morning of July 12th, amidst showery and overcast conditions, two large convoys, Booty and Agent, embarked on their respective journeys. Booty navigated south-west off the Essex coast near Orfordness, while Agent sailed off North Foreland in Kent. The Luftwaffe and Italian Air Force targeted Booty, prompting 17 Squadron to patrol from RAF Debden. As the squadron headed out, they were alerted to an incoming raid.

In response, 85 Squadron from Martlesham, 242 Squadron led by Douglas Bader from Coltishall, six Boulton Paul Defiants from 264 Squadron at RAF Duxford, and eleven Hurricanes from 151 Squadron at North Weald were scrambled. The German attack, led by two Do 17 Staffeln from II./KG 2 and III./KG 53, commenced at 08:48 and was met by fierce resistance from 17 Squadron. In the ensuing conflict, an He 111 and a Do 17 were shot down, resulting in the death of Staffelkapitän Hauptmann Machetzki and his crew.

Despite the tight formation and crossfire from the bombers, which damaged several Hurricanes and downed two, the RAF managed to shoot down two more He 111s and two Do 17s. Remarkably, trawlers from convoy Booty rescued German aircrew amidst the ongoing bombing.

Meanwhile, the steamer Hornchurch from convoy FS 19 was sunk, with its crew being rescued by the patrol sloop Widgeon. Another vessel, the steamer Josewyn, sustained damage west-north-west of St Catherine's Point.

Luftflotte 3, missing the opportunity to attack Convoy Agent, dispatched additional He 111s and Do 17s for reconnaissance to track shipping movements. One He 111 from KG 55 was lost to 43 Squadron Hurricanes in the afternoon, and further attempts by the Luftwaffe to locate and attack convoys were unsuccessful. That night, KG 55, led by Geschwaderkommodore Alois

Stoeckl, executed a night raid on Cardiff without incurring any losses.

During the turbulent days of mid-July, smaller convoys braved the perilous waters of the Channel under constant threat from the Luftwaffe. On July 13th, a KG 51 Ju 88 was downed by a 43 Squadron Spitfire. As convoy Booty steamed through Lyme Bay, 238 and 609 squadrons, comprising 12 Hurricanes and three Spitfires, flew overhead as aerial guards. They encountered around fifty Luftwaffe aircraft, downing two Do 17s and engaging in a dogfight with V./LG 1 Bf 110s, claiming three damaged.

The Luftwaffe continued its assaults with StG 1 escorted by JG 51, attacking a smaller convoy. 56 Squadron's Hurricanes engaged the Ju 87s, managing to damage two, but losing two of their own. 54 Squadron Spitfires, including New Zealander Colin Falkland Gray, managed to down a Bf 109. Luftwaffe losses totaled six aircraft destroyed and eight damaged, while the RAF lost four Hurricanes and a Spitfire to friendly fire. HMS Vanessa suffered damage from near-misses.

Bad weather on July 14th somewhat curtailed operations, but IV.(St)/LG 1 Ju 87s, escorted by JG 3 and JG 51, still managed to attack convoys. Only one Ju 87 and one Bf 109 were destroyed in these encounters, which were recorded by BBC reporter Charles Gardiner. HMS Esperance Bay, an armed merchant cruiser carrying £10 million in gold bullion, sustained serious damage, resulting in casualties. Turkish Navy's minelaying sloop Yuzbasi Hakki also suffered damage.

On July 15th, a Hurricane was shot down, and the Luftwaffe lost a He 111, a Ju 88, and a Do 18 seaplane. Convoy FN 223 saw the steamer Heworth damaged and grounded, with crew rescued by HMS Valorous. The Polish steamer Zbaraz was bombed, sank, but the crew survived. The Portuguese steamer Alpha was also sunk, with its crew rescued by destroyers.

July 16th was a more successful day for the RAF, with no losses and a KG 54 Ju

88 and a 5.(Nacht)/JG 1 Do 17 shot down. The following day saw a He 111 and Ju 88 downed, but the RAF lost a Spitfire with the pilot wounded. Continuous patrols, mostly over the sea, were wearing down Fighter Command, leading to the loss of experienced squadron leaders and flight commanders.

By July 18th, the Luftwaffe persisted in its attacks. Two 609 Squadron Spitfires were shot down by KG 54 Ju 88s, and a 603 Squadron Spitfire was damaged by a He 111. KG 27 lost its commander, Oberst Bernhard Georgi, to 145 Squadron Hurricanes. A 152 Squadron Spitfire and a 610 Squadron Spitfire were also damaged, and one LG 1 Ju 88 fell to anti-aircraft fire. A StG 77 Do 17 was destroyed over a convoy by 152 Squadron.

On July 19th, amidst a flurry of convoy activity with nine at sea, German reconnaissance planes scoured the shipping lanes. Early in the morning, a 4.(F)/121 Do 17 was downed by 145 Squadron. 141 Squadron, flying Boulton Paul Defiants and relatively inexperienced, had recently been equipped with Constant speed propellers but had little air practice. Despite reservations from Dowding and Park about the Defiant's effectiveness, 141 Squadron was assigned to escort a convoy that morning.

Taking advantage of a weather break, III./JG 51, led by Osterkamp, patrolled over Dover and engaged a formation of RAF Defiants. Exploiting the Defiant's vulnerability from below, the Bf 109s swiftly downed four Defiants, and another was lost while seeking cover. 111 Squadron intervened, downing a Bf 109, allowing the surviving Defiants to escape, albeit with significant damage.

The RAF's delayed response, due to late scramble orders, contributed to the Defiant's losses. The German pilots, now adept at identifying and countering Defiants, no longer viewed them as a significant threat. Churchill, informed by Dowding of the losses, acknowledged the Defiant's limitations. This day marked a severe blow to Fighter Command, with ten aircraft lost compared to the Luftwaffe's four. Hitler, emboldened by these successes, issued his final "appeal to reason" to Britain.

Elsewhere, 87 Squadron's engagement with Ju 87s was inconclusive, while 64 Squadron successfully downed a He 115 floatplane. III./KG 55 also lost a bomber to 145 Squadron. In various encounters, the RAF suffered the loss of several Hurricanes and pilots, highlighting the Luftwaffe's tactical advantages in numbers, experience, and formation tactics.

At 12:15, StG 1 targeted the destroyer HMS Beagle off Dover. Despite several near misses that damaged its systems, Beagle managed to escape without casualties. Later, at 16:00, German bombers attacked Dover harbour, resulting in significant damage to several vessels, including the destruction of the oiler War Sepoy and damages to the tug Simla and the destroyer HMS Griffin.

On the night of July 19th to 20th, a Focke-Wulf Fw 200 Kondor from KG 40 strayed too far inland and was brought down by ground defenses near Hartlepool, while another was lost over Northern Ireland. Despite discrepancies in German records, British sources confirm both incidents occurred on this night.

At dawn on July 20th, 54 Squadron's Hurricanes scrambled to confront a large German formation near the Thames Estuary, initially believed to be targeting a convoy. However, the German aircraft, having split into smaller groups, were on a mistaken mission and eluded interception. Shortly after, 56 Squadron engaged a group of Ju 88s from KG 4, successfully downing one near St Osyth.

Along the coast, several tethered light vessels, easy targets, were sunk. British radar often detected enemy raiders but struggled with timing due to poor lighting conditions. Park and Leigh-Mallory, concerned about attacks on East Coast lightships, agreed to establish aerial patrols in the area.

As Convoy Bosom navigated Lyme Bay, 238 Squadron's Hurricanes deterred three Bf 109s and later downed a Seenotflugkommando 4 He 59 ambulance, resulting in four crew fatalities. Another He 59 from Seenotflugkommando 1, shadowing Bosom, was engaged by 43 Squadron, leading to the loss of a Hurricane and its pilot, while the He 59 initially escaped. However, 601 Squadron eventually shot down the Heinkel, with its crew failing to survive due to low-altitude parachute deployment.

As Bosom approached RAF Kenley and RAF Biggin Hill sectors, Park ordered continuous patrols of 24 fighters over it, split between Spitfires and Hurricanes.

That evening, II./StG 1, escorted by about 50 Bf 109s from I./JG 27, some Bf 110s, and additional Bf 109s from I. and II./JG 51, launched an attack on Convoy Bosom. The British, forewarned by radar, prepared a robust defense. The ensuing battle saw two Ju 87s shot down and four damaged, with additional losses on the German side, including Hauptmann Riegel of I./JG 27. On the British side, losses included aircraft from 32, 615, 501, and 610 squadrons, with several pilots killed or severely wounded.

While the RAF engaged the German fighters, the Ju 87s struck Convoy Bosom, sinking the coaster Pulborough and severely damaging HMS Brazen, which eventually broke in two.

On July 21st, Park established standing patrols of twelve fighters to escort Convoy CW 7 through the Strait of Dover. During the day, 238 Squadron successfully shot down a Bf 110 and a Do 17. As the convoy passed near the Isle of Wight, it faced an attack from around 50 Luftwaffe aircraft, including Bf 109s and Bf 110s. 43 Squadron's engagement led to the downing of a Bf 109 and a Bf 110, while the Dorniers failed to inflict damage on the convoy. The day's other significant action involved the destruction of a 4.(F)/121 Do 17 by 145 Squadron.

July 23rd was relatively quiet, with only a Ju 88 from 4.(F)/121 being shot down near Yarmouth by 242 Squadron. The following day saw a minor skirmish as Spitfires from 54 Squadron intercepted Do 17s attacking a small convoy, but neither ships nor aircraft suffered losses. In the afternoon, StG 1 successfully sank the steamer Terlings and the Norwegian steamer Kollskegg.

On July 25th, Luftflotte 2 executed coordinated sweeps to wear down the RAF's standing patrols. Once the RAF was engaged with Bf 109s, larger bomber formations attacked. Despite RAF resistance, Ju 87s from 11.(Stuka)/LG 1 and III./StG 1 managed to strike at the convoy. 54 Squadron's attempt to intervene resulted in the loss of two Spitfires to Bf 109s.

Park adapted to these tactics by deploying only small fighter forces until a larger attack materialized. This strategy was tested when 64 Squadron's Spitfires and 111 Squadron's Hurricanes disrupted an assault by 30 Ju 88s and over 50 Bf 109s, successfully averting an attack on the convoy.

CW 8, consisting of 21 ships, was attacked on July 25th by Do 17s escorted by JG 26's Bf 109s. While 43 Squadron engaged JG 26 and 65 Squadron joined the fray, the RAF couldn't down any Do 17s due to their tight formation and effective cross-fire. JG 26 suffered two losses, while RAF pilots overestimated their success. JG 52, covering JG 26's retreat, lost three Bf 109s in an encounter with 610 Squadron.

Later, CW 8 endured another attack by Ju 87s off Folkestone, resulting in significant damage, including hits on HMS Boreas and Brilliant. RAF fighters, including those from 64 and 54 Squadrons, arrived but were hindered by Bf 109s, leading to the loss of a Spitfire. Despite naval gunfire damaging some Ju 87s, the E-Boats successfully struck three ships.

The events of July 26th, with E-boats sinking three ships and only eleven passing Dungeness, underscored the need for more extensive fighter protection for convoys in the Straits of Dover.

On July 27th, Fliegerkorps VIII dispatched 30 Ju 87s to target Convoy CW 8 near Portland. The Hurricanes of 238 Squadron intercepted, downing one Ju 87 before being engaged by Bf 109 escorts. A subsequent wave of Ju 87s and Ju 88s, also guarded by Bf 109s, faced resistance from 238 Squadron and 609 Squadron, which lost a Spitfire. As a result of escalating losses, the Admiralty deemed convoy traffic through the Dover Strait unsustainable and suspended it by evening. The day's air battles saw significant losses on both sides, with multiple RAF squadrons losing aircraft and pilots, and the Luftwaffe losing several planes, including from II./KG 51, StG 1, III./JG 27, and JG 52.

On July 28th, sunny and clear conditions prevailed, allowing Spitfires from 234 Squadron to engage and down a Ju 88 from II./LG 1, with only two crew members surviving. Anticipating large attacks, RAF sector controllers repositioned eight squadrons to strategic locations. A significant raid formation heading towards Dover prompted 74 Squadron and several others to intercept, with Hurricanes targeting bombers and Spitfires engaging fighters. Notably, Squadron Leader Sailor Malan of 74 Squadron clashed with the Bf 109s of I. and II./JG 51, led by Werner Mölders. This encounter resulted in multiple downed Bf 109s and damaged aircraft, including Mölders' own. 74 Squadron suffered three Spitfires lost, with two pilots wounded and one killed.

In addition to fighter engagements, Luftwaffe bombers targeted shipping, sinking HMS Codrington at Dover and HMS Wren off Aldeburgh. The loss of these destroyers prompted the Admiralty to cease using Dover as an advanced destroyer base. Throughout the day, Luftwaffe mine-laying operations continued, with KG 4 suffering damages to two Ju 88s from anti-aircraft fire. Meanwhile, Seenotflugkommando 1 and 3 lost two He 59s during rescue operations in the Channel.

On July 21st, with clear skies signaling potential German activity, the Kent Sector Operations Room was alerted of a German build-up over Calais. Two convoys in the Channel drew attention, but the RAF controllers held off. At

07:20, as Convoy CW 7 traversed the Dover Strait, 41 Squadron's Spitfires and 501 Squadron's Hurricanes were dispatched to flank the German formation of 48 Ju 87s from IV.(Stuka)/LG 1, II./StG 1, and II./StG 3, escorted by 80 Bf 109s from JG 51 and III./JG 26. Despite III./JG 26 failing to spot the RAF's initial attack, the Luftwaffe's counter-attack led to RAF losses. While 41 Squadron engaged the Bf 109s, 501 Squadron targeted the Ju 87s, successfully limiting harbor damage. The Luftwaffe lost four Stukas and suffered one damaged, with 501 Squadron unscathed. The SS Gronland was sunk, and several other vessels, including the patrol yacht Gulzar and Sandhurst, suffered damages.

III./KG 76's low-altitude bombing run, evading British radar, failed to hit its targets. The Gruppenkommandeur, Adolf Genth, tragically died hitting a balloon cable. 610 Squadron's Spitfires responded but were too late. Another convoy was targeted by KG 2, leading to a forced landing of a Dornier by Spitfires from 85 Squadron. 151 Squadron Hurricanes then engaged Bf 110s from ZG 26, with minimal losses on both sides.

On the evening of July 25th, III./StG 2's Ju 87s, led by Gruppenkommandeur Walter Enneccerus, attacked HMS Delight off Portland. Despite surviving crew members' rescue by HMS Vansittart and Broke, 19 were killed. The destroyer remained afloat until sinking later that night. This incident, combined with previous losses, led the Admiralty to withdraw destroyers from the Channel and cease daytime convoy operations.

The Luftwaffe's success in disrupting British naval operations was offset by the operational limit it placed on Bf 109s, now having to venture further into southern England. This change, directed by Hitler's Directive No. 17, necessitated conservative fuel usage by German fighters, as emphasized by Göring.

The Admiralty's suspension of convoys aimed at improving defenses. By late July, Fighter Command began deploying larger formations over convoys, reducing the vulnerability seen in smaller groups. Innovations like the Mobile

Balloon Barrage Flotilla and a Channel Guard armed with light machine-guns were introduced. The Hunt-class destroyers, more adept at anti-aircraft operations, replaced older escorts, enhancing convoy protection.

Despite these measures, the Luftwaffe still posed a threat. On August 5th, Convoy CE 8 traveled undetected at night, and Convoy CW 9 on August 7th survived a night attack by E-boats but faced Luftwaffe raids by day. The RAF's intervention, particularly by 145 Squadron, prevented further losses.

On July 30th, amidst low clouds and rain across Britain, Dowding anticipated hidden Luftwaffe attacks and ordered patrols over convoys and minesweeping units. However, the Luftwaffe's activity was minimal, with only KG 26's He 111s harassing the Scottish coast from Norwegian bases. Near Suffolk, two Bf 110s from the Erprobungsgruppe 210, trailing a convoy, were engaged by Geoffrey Allard and his wingman, resulting in one German aircraft being shot down after a lengthy pursuit.

The weather improved slightly on July 31st, but a haze lingered over southern England, hampering Luftwaffe raids. The RAF managed two interceptions, with 111 Squadron's Hurricanes damaging a Ju 88 from III./KG 76. At 16:00, RAF fighters, including 30 Spitfires and 24 Hurricanes, scrambled to Dover to counter Bf 109s attacking barrage balloons. During this engagement, led by Squadron Leader Sailor Malan of 74 Squadron, two Staffeln of JG 2 were engaged, resulting in RAF losses and the downing of a Bf 109 from 7./JG 2.

On August 1st, Dowding restored the fighter squadron establishment to pre-Battle of France levels, with 20 aircraft plus two in reserve. Fighter Command's pilot strength also grew, with 1,414 pilots in service by July's end, approaching the established figure of 1,454. Despite a perceived deficiency, operational pilot numbers remained stable. Dowding, however, expressed concerns over the dilution of pilot experience. The same day, a Henschel Hs 126 was downed by 145 Squadron, but the German rear gunner fatally shot one British pilot. I./KG 4 conducted a raid near Norfolk, targeting Boulton-Paul factories and Thorpe railway goods yards, managing to evade interception.

On August 2nd, KG 26's He 111s attacked a Scottish convoy, with one bomber crash-landing on the steamer Highlander. This aircraft was later displayed in Leith. Another He 111 was shot down, and ErpGr 210 sank the trawler Cape Finisterre. The following five days saw minimal combat casualties on both sides, marking a brief respite in the intense air battles over Britain.

On the morning of August 7, 1940, under misty conditions, Convoy CW 9 (Peewit) set sail from Southend, laden with coal. A KG 2 Do 17, while on patrol, spotted two minesweepers in the North Sea but missed the large westward-moving convoy and subsequently landed. As Peewit journeyed through the Channel, it was escorted by Hurricanes from several RAF squadrons. Despite low visibility, the convoy remained undetected until it was spotted by a German radar station near Wissant as it approached Dungeness.

That evening, the German Navy's 1st S-Boat Flotilla, under Kapitänleutnant Carl-Heinz Birnbacher, prepared to engage the convoy. Meanwhile, the British deployed Motor Torpedo Boats to scout for enemy activity. The German E-boats launched an attack around 2:00 AM on August 8, sinking SS Holme Force and damaging other vessels, including Fife Coast and Polly M. The British destroyer Bulldog arrived but struggled to effectively counter the E-boats in the darkness.

On August 8, fine weather exposed Peewit to air attacks. German reconnaissance identified 17 vessels south of Selsey Bill, and Fliegerkorps VIII dispatched Stuka dive bombers from StG 1. They sank several ships, including SS Ajax and SS Coquetdale, despite RAF intervention. Hurricanes from 601 Squadron and Spitfires from 609 and 234 Squadrons engaged too late, with 145 Squadron managing to down two Ju 87s.

Later that day, StG 2, 3, and 77, escorted by Bf 110s and Bf 109s, attacked the convoy south of the Isle of Wight. Several ships were sunk or damaged, with the RAF responding aggressively. The Luftwaffe suffered losses, including damaged and downed aircraft, while the RAF lost several fighters. Hauptmann Waldemar Plewig of II./StG 77 conducted reconnaissance, leading to another wave of Ju 87 attacks escorted by Bf 110s and Bf 109s.

III./JG 26 and II. and III./JG 51 conducted a fighter sweep before the attack, claiming multiple RAF Spitfires, with notable claims by Joachim Müncheberg and Gerhard Schöpfel. The RAF's 41, 64, and 65 Squadrons engaged, with 65 Squadron losing two Spitfires earlier than the German claims.

As Peewit's remaining ships sailed on, several British yachts and trawlers were dispatched for rescue operations but were attacked. RAF squadrons 145 and 43 engaged, suffering losses, including downed Hurricanes and pilots. The Luftwaffe lost several Stukas and Bf 109s, while RAF's 152 and 238 Squadrons attempted interceptions without success.

From August 9th to 10th, the Luftwaffe conducted limited sorties, as Operation Eagle Attack (Adlerangriff) was postponed due to poor weather. On August 11th, with clear skies predicted, German air activity intensified against RAF Groups 10, 11, and 12, as well as Channel shipping. Kesselring aimed to lure out and divide Fighter Command by deploying numerous single Staffeln, but Park largely refrained from responding with force.

The day started with Hauptmann Walter Rubensdörffer leading 17 Bf 110s from Erprobungsgruppe 210 in a strafing attack on Dover. Despite minimal damage and the RAF's intervention, including 74 Squadron under Sailor Malan, only fleeting engagements occurred, resulting in minimal losses for both sides.

A significant German formation was later detected near Cherbourg, prompting Park to scramble multiple RAF squadrons. This led to an engagement with 54 Ju 88s and 20 He 111s, escorted by a large contingent of Bf 110s and Bf 109s. The RAF squadrons, including 145, 152, 87, 213, and 238, were quickly scrambled. The RAF fighters primarily tangled with the escort, with only a few Spitfires managing to engage the bombers, who targeted Portland and Weymouth. The RAF's involvement resulted in minimal damage to the destroyers Scimitar and Skate.

JG 27's cover during the bombers' withdrawal led to RAF losses, including 16 Hurricanes and a 152 Squadron Spitfire. The Luftwaffe lost six Bf 110s, five Ju 88s, one He 111, and six Bf 109s. Both sides conducted search and rescue operations, with the RAF successfully engaging a He 59 protected by Bf 109s.

Convoy Booty was later targeted by Rubensdörffer's ErpGr 210 and 9./KG 2 Do 17s, with ZG 26 providing cover. The RAF's response led to the downing of several German aircraft. Another raid aimed at Convoys Agent and Arena saw 111 and 74 Squadrons scramble, resulting in the loss of several RAF Hurricanes and German aircraft. Poor weather eventually curtailed operations.

On August 12th, Adlertag, the Germans commenced bombardment of convoys using long-range artillery from Cap Gris Nez. Despite the stress on the coaster crews, no ships were hit. With the Luftwaffe shifting focus to inland targets, coastal convoy operations continued, though they remained at risk. The Kanalkampf saw significant losses on both sides, and had the RAF not bolstered convoy protection, the route might have become untenable.

Adlertag

In the pivotal moments of Adlertag, the tide was turning largely due to the intelligence game. While the Germans had not yet fallen significantly behind, the British were beginning to take the lead, thanks in part to their cracking of the Enigma machine. This breach, coupled with lax Luftwaffe communication discipline, opened a window into German plans for the British.

The role of Ultra intelligence in the Battle of Britain is debated. Official histories downplay its impact, but there's no denying that Ultra, particularly the Y service, provided the British with a steadily improving understanding of German military movements and strategies.

Joseph "Beppo" Schmid, head of the Luftwaffe's Military Intelligence, made crucial misjudgments during this period. In July 1940, he overestimated the might of the Luftwaffe and underestimated the RAF's strength. His major blunders included misreading the number of operational British airfields, underestimating British fighter production capabilities (believing they could only churn out 180–330 fighters a month against an actual output of 496), and wrongly assuming the RAF couldn't withstand a prolonged conflict. Schmid's assessments of British command structure and operations also missed the mark, notably omitting any mention of British radar technology.

This oversight proved costly for the Luftwaffe. The lack of focused attacks on British radar systems allowed them to continuously track and direct RAF units effectively. Additionally, German intelligence failed to accurately identify RAF airfield types, often mistaking Coastal and Bomber Command bases for Fighter Command ones. On Adlertag, most of the Luftwaffe's targeted airfields, even if destroyed, wouldn't have significantly hindered the RAF's Fighter Command, showcasing the critical impact of intelligence—or the lack thereof—in the theatre of war.

The backbone of Britain's WWII air defense was a sophisticated network of detection, command, and control, known as the "Dowding System." Named after its primary architect, Air Chief Marshal Sir H.C.T. "Stuffy" Dowding, Commander-in-Chief of RAF Fighter Command, this system was an evolution of Major General E B Ashmore's work from 1917. Central to Dowding's strategy was the use of Radio Direction Finding (RDF), or radar, a decision he himself championed. Coupled with reports from the Royal Observer Corps (ROC), radar was vital in enabling the RAF to effectively intercept enemy aircraft. To keep its true nature secret, the technology was deceptively termed RDF.

Initial warnings of incoming Luftwaffe raids were detected by Chain Home RDF stations along Britain's coasts. These stations could track enemy formations over their airfields in northern France and Belgium. As enemy aircraft moved inland, their positions were further tracked by the ROC. This combined data flowed to Fighter Command Headquarters at RAF Bentley Priory, where plots were analyzed to distinguish friend from foe.

In the operations room, members of the Women's Auxiliary Air Force (WAAF) plotted each raid's course based on telephoned information. This was supplemented with intelligence from the Y Service, which monitored enemy radio transmissions, and the Ultra decoding center at Bletchley Park, providing insights into German military disposition. On a large, gridded map table, color-coded counters represented each raid. Magnetic "rakes" moved these counters to reflect the real-time positions of enemy formations, enabling quick decision-making about potential targets.

This information was also relayed to group headquarters, where it underwent further verification. Each group's operations room, distinct from Bentley Priory's setup, displayed a map of its command area and airfields. A constant stream of updates was maintained via radio and telephone, coordinating with sector airfields, the Observer Corps, Anti-Aircraft Command, and the navy. The Duty Fighter Controller, acting on behalf of the Group GOC, managed the interception of each raid. If a telephone line failed, engineers were on standby to swiftly restore communication.

On August 13, amidst poor weather, a communication mishap led to a remarkable episode in WWII aerial combat. Luftwaffe chief Göring had postponed raids due to the weather, but this message failed to reach the Dornier Do 17 bombers of KG 2, who took off as planned at 04:50. Their intended escort from ZG 26, informed of the cancellation, did not join them. Despite efforts by Oberstleutnant Joachim Huth of ZG 26 to visually signal the cancellation to the Dorniers, KG 2's leader, Johannes Fink, chose to continue to their target, Eastchurch airfield on the Isle of Sheppey.

Ignoring Albert Kesselring's orders to abort if unescorted, Fink pressed on, risking a perilous return journey through RAF-controlled airspace without fighter protection. The British Observer Corps, hindered by low clouds, and radar operators incorrectly assessed the bombers' path, leading to an erroneous RAF response that failed to prevent the attack.

Early that morning, German aircraft activity was initially minimal, but around 05:30, large formations gathered near Amiens. By 06:10, these groups moved towards the English Channel, tracked by British radar and observers. RAF units, including several squadrons, were scrambled in response, although unaware of the Germans' specific target.

Due to the Observer Corps' error and radar misjudgment, KG 2 successfully struck Eastchurch airfield, mistakenly believing they had destroyed 10 Spitfires. In reality, Fighter Command suffered no such losses. This error led the Germans to incorrectly assume Eastchurch was a key fighter base, prompting several future but futile attacks. The raid did, however, cause significant damage to RAF Coastal Command at Eastchurch, destroying equipment and aircraft and resulting in casualties.

The RAF eventually intercepted the bombers. KG 2 lost five Dorniers and sustained heavy damage to six others. In the ensuing dogfight, two Hurricanes were downed, and notable RAF pilot Adolph Malan scored a hit on a Do 17. German losses included 11 killed and nine captured. Despite the raid's impact, RAF Eastchurch was operational again by the afternoon of the same day.

Several Luftwaffe units from Luftflotte 2, despite an order to cancel morning operations, initiated attacks on airfields and ports in southern Britain. KG 76 called off its attack on Debden, but targeted RAF Kenley and other airfields in Kent and Essex, with the exact losses and impact remaining unknown. KG 27 mostly aborted their missions, although III./KG 27 tried attacking the Bristol docks, losing one He 111 to RAF's No. 87 Squadron and causing minimal damage.

Luftflotte 3, not receiving the cancellation order, proceeded with its planned assaults under the command of Hugo Sperrle. Early in the morning, Ju 88 bombers from I./KG 54 and II./KG 54 took off to attack RAF Farnborough and RAF Odiham, respectively. Additionally, StG 77's 88 Ju 87s set out for Portland Harbour, escorted by a significant force of Bf 110s and Bf 109s from various squadrons. Despite cloud cover obscuring StG 77's target, KG 54 continued towards their objectives. RAF squadrons from Northolt, Tangmere, and Middle Wallop engaged the attackers, shooting down a handful of German aircraft. The Luftwaffe's claims of extensive RAF fighter losses were greatly exaggerated; only a few RAF fighters were actually lost or severely damaged.

Further raids planned by II./KG 54 on RAF Croydon were called off. I./KG 54, however, struck at the Fleet Air Arm base in Gosport. In a communication failure, ZG 2 arrived at a target without their intended Ju 88 escorts, leading to the loss of one Bf 110 to RAF's No. 238 Squadron.

Later, V./LG 1 Bf 110s took off ahead of a planned KG 54 raid, possibly to draw out RAF fighters. The bomber mission was cancelled, but the message failed to reach V./LG 1, resulting in their encounter with No. 601 Squadron RAF Hurricanes. The Luftwaffe lost several Bf 110s, while the RAF suffered minimal losses. Sources vary on the exact number of Bf 110 losses. The Zerstörergeschwader vastly overclaimed RAF fighter losses, contrasting with the actual total RAF fighter losses in combat for the entire day.

The green light for the Luftwaffe's operation was given at 14:00. At 15:30, a formation of 58–80 Ju 88s from I., II., and III./LG 1, with a 30-strong Bf 110 escort from V./LG 1, set off to bomb Boscombe Down and Worthy Down. RAF Andover was also a target, with 52 Ju 87s from StG 1 and StG 2 assigned to attack RAF Warmwell and Yeovil. A fighter sweep by I./JG 53 from Poole to Lyme Regis intended to draw out RAF fighters proved ineffective, merely alerting RAF defenses five minutes earlier than expected. Upon reaching the coast, the main wave of bombers from LG 1 and StG 2 was met by a formidable response of 77 RAF fighters.

The Ju 87s, escorted by II., III./JG 53, and III./ZG 76, faced stiff resistance. ZG 2 and JG 27 provided cover for LG 1. No. 10 Group RAF engaged in full force, with No. 609 Squadron RAF significantly impacting II./StG 2, shooting down six of their nine Ju 87s. StG 1 and 2, hindered by cloud cover, redirected their focus to Portland.

I./LG 1, abandoning its original target, bombed Southampton instead, where No. 238 Squadron RAF's attempt to intercept was thwarted by strong fighter escorts. The bombing caused damage to several warehouses and a cold storage plant in Southampton. Only Andover airfield was hit, primarily used for bomber operations. The Ju 88 groups incurred six losses but many more were damaged. This operation highlighted a critical intelligence failure: the Luftwaffe had not identified Southampton's crucial Spitfire factory as a primary target, mistakenly believing it to be a bomber factory. Even when the factory was later attacked, the Germans remained unaware of the extent of damage to Spitfire production.

StG 77, escorted by JG 27's Bf 109s, joined by KG 54's Ju 88s, targeted RAF airfields controlled by No. 10 Group RAF. However, StG 77 failed to locate its intended target, RAF Warmwell, dropping bombs randomly and escaping without much attention.

Erprobungsgruppe 210, assigned to attack targets near Southend, took off at 15:15, escorted by ZG 76. Cloud cover over Essex led to an interception by No. 56 Squadron RAF, with bombs eventually dropped over Canterbury. II./StG 1, targeting airfields near Rochester, returned without engaging due to target misidentification. IV./LG 1, with its Ju 87s, and JG 26 attacked RAF Detling, inflicting severe damage and casualties, including the loss of Group Captain E P Meggs–Davis and Squadron Leader J.H Lowe, along with other casualties.

Despite the success at Detling, the overall operation was not a strategic win for the Luftwaffe, as Detling was not a key Fighter Command station, leaving No. 11 Group RAF unaffected.

On the day in question, the Luftwaffe's I., II., and III./KG 55 units were active. III./KG 55 targeted Heathrow Airport, but the results and losses from this operation remain uncertain. KG 55 had already suffered significant losses the previous day, losing 13 Heinkel He 111s and their crews, suggesting their activity might have been constrained. Furthermore, on the following day, 14 August, they would lose their Wing Commander, Alois Stoeckl.

In the afternoon, a substantial force of 80 Do 17s from KG 3, escorted by multiple JG units and 60 Bf 109s from JG 26, totaling around 270 aircraft, launched an assault on Eastchurch airfield and the Short Brothers factory in Rochester. III./KG 3 split off to attack Eastchurch, while II./KG 3 focused on Rochester, inflicting notable damage on the factory producing the Short Stirling heavy bomber. The RAF responded with several squadrons, but JG 26 reported minimal impact from these British fighters. Skirmishes resulted in the loss of three JG 51 Bf 109s.

RAF Bomber Command also participated in the day's events. Despite objections from Air Officer Commanding Charles Portal about the futility of bombing Scandinavian airfields, the Air Ministry insisted on such missions. No. 82 Squadron RAF dispatched twelve Bristol Blenheims to target KG 30 airfields in Aalborg, Denmark. One aircraft, alleging fuel issues, was the sole returnee and its pilot faced a court-martial. The rest were lost to anti-aircraft fire and enemy fighters, resulting in 24 fatalities and nine captured airmen.

As night descended, marking the end of Adlertag, Luftwaffe's specialist night strike unit, Kampfgruppe 100, sent nine He 111s for a strategic bombing raid on the Supermarine Spitfire factory at Castle Bromwich, Birmingham. Despite their expertise in night navigation, only four crews accurately located their targets. The eleven 551 lb bombs dropped caused limited disruption to fighter production, with about half landing inside the compound. Damage was mainly to offices and a tool room, with a gas main also hit. Casualties were minimal as workers had sought shelter.

Another group, led by Captain Friedrich Achenbrenner, dispatched 15 He 111s from Brittany to bomb the Short Brothers factory in Belfast, Northern Ireland, resulting in the destruction of five Short Stirling aircraft. KG 27 also participated, targeting Glasgow, though their specific objective is not clear. Other bombers extended their operations across Britain, hitting cities like Bristol, Cardiff, Swansea, Liverpool, Sheffield, Norwich, Edinburgh, and Aberdeen. The damage was generally minor, with some rail disruptions and around 100 casualties. The fate of the German aircraft involved in these night raids is largely unknown, except for one German airman found in Balcombe, West Sussex, with no trace of his aircraft or fellow crew.

The Hardest Day

Beneath a brilliant morning sky, an air of tense anticipation hung over the Luftflotte 2 headquarters in Brussels. Albert Kesselring, the mastermind behind the fleet, orchestrated a daring aerial onslaught on Biggin Hill and Kenley. From Amiens, 60 Heinkel He 111s of KG 1 roared towards Biggin Hill, intent on a high-level bombardment. Meanwhile, KG 76, hailing from airfields north of Paris, set their sights on RAF Kenley, armed with a fleet of 48 menacing Dornier Do 17s and Junkers Ju 88s. Although fewer in number and lighter in bomb-load compared to the He 111s, the planners banked on a precision, low-level strike by KG 76's staffel to maximize impact.

A formidable fighter escort comprised of Jagdgeschwader 3, 26, 51, 52, 54, and Zerstörergeschwader 26, readied for a dual mission of free-hunting and close escort from their bases in Pas-de-Calais.

The British airfields, Biggin Hill and Kenley, unsuspecting of the impending storm, operated crucial sector operations rooms – nerve centers of RAF fighter coordination. The Luftwaffe, unaware of these strategic rooms, aimed to cripple the airfields' operational capabilities.

At Cormeilles-en-Vexin, 9 Staffel of KG 76, led by the astute Hauptmann Joachim Roth, received their orders. Their mission: a daring low-level raid on Kenley. Specializing in such attacks, the squadron was to stealthily navigate across the Channel, using the Brighton–London rail line as a guide to their target. Their Dorniers, armed with 20 50 kg bombs each, were uniquely modified for lower release heights, a tactical advantage against ground defenses.

This attack was a crucial piece of a larger strategy – a pincer movement designed to obliterate Kenley. High-altitude dive-bombing by Ju 88s would precede a dual assault by the Do 17s, aimed at cratering the runways and disabling defenses, setting the stage for 9 Staffel's critical finishing blow. A blend of high-altitude bombing and low-flying stealth, the plan was audacious, promising to leave Kenley in ruins.

The operation, scheduled for 09:00, faced an unexpected delay due to heavy haze, reducing visibility significantly. This lull saw sporadic encounters between RAF fighters and German reconnaissance aircraft, heightening the tension.

As KG 1's formations took off at 11:00, the bombers from KG 76 struggled with formation due to cloud cover and haze over Calais. This disarray caused significant delays, especially for 9 Staffel KG 76, altering the meticulously planned timing of the attack.

In the skies, Gerhard Schöpfel and his squadron of Bf 109s from JG 3 and III./JG 26 led the way, sweeping the Dover straits clear for the incoming bombers. The raiding force, comprising 108 bombers and 150 fighters, advanced in a staggered formation, a formidable fleet cutting across the sky towards their targets. Meanwhile, 9 Staffel's Do 17s, hugging the waves, stealthily approached from the southwest, their eyes set on Kenley, ready to strike under the radar.

In the control room at RAF Uxbridge, Keith Park, AOC of No. 11 Group RAF, stood over a map bristling with markers and lines. The radar at Dover had picked up a swarm of German aircraft assembling over Pas-de-Calais. By 12:45, the skies were teeming with what was estimated to be a colossal force of 350 planes, significantly more than the actual count. Park, with his keen strategic eye, quickly directed No. 501 Squadron's 12 Hawker Hurricanes, already airborne, to ascend to 20,000 feet above Canterbury. These Hurricanes, returning from patrol, were soon joined by eight more squadrons from various bases, including Kenley and Biggin Hill.

The skies soon buzzed with a formidable array of RAF fighters: 17 Supermarine Spitfires and 36 Hurricanes from five squadrons, poised to defend the Thames Estuary ports and the airfields north of it. Meanwhile, four more squadrons, armed with 23 Spitfires and 27 Hurricanes, took strategic positions above Kenley and Biggin Hill, ready to repel the impending attack.

Park strategically held back some forces as a reserve. Three squadrons at RAF Tangmere stood on alert for additional attacks from the south, while six others were reserved for potential follow-up raids.

As the German vanguard, led by Gerhard Schöpfel, approached the coast, they encountered 501 Squadron's Hurricanes, spiraling upwards in formation. Schöpfel and his wing swiftly engaged, resulting in a fierce but brief dogfight. Despite downing four Hurricanes, the confrontation was inconclusive, with one British pilot killed and three wounded.

The German bombers, including the Do 17s and Ju 88s of III./KG 76, braved flak over Dover, each group escorted by their respective fighter units. They cleverly avoided the main RAF fighter concentration by flying east of Canterbury. By 13:01, they had a clear path to Biggin Hill.

Unseen by radar, 9 Staffel's low-flying Dorniers, despite being fired upon by Royal Navy patrol boats, remained undetected as they crossed the coast. It was only when they were spotted by the Royal Observer Corps at Beachy Head that a warning was sent out. Wing Commander Thomas Prickman at RAF Kenley, upon seeing the low-flying Dorniers on his situation map, was momentarily puzzled about their target.

As reports flowed in about the approaching German formations, it became clear to the Observer Corps that a coordinated attack was underway. Two RAF Squadrons, already committed to countering the high-altitude raid, could not be redirected to engage 9 Staffel. At RAF Croydon, No. 111 Squadron, with its 12 Hurricanes, was the only immediate option. The controllers took swift action, ordering all available aircraft to take off, even those not fully combat-ready, to prevent them from being sitting ducks on the ground.

No. 111 Squadron scrambled into position above Kenley, hoping to intercept 9 Staffel. Simultaneously, Biggin Hill, under Group Captain Richard Grice, echoed this move, launching all its fighters. At 13:10, the German bombers were closing in on their target. Meanwhile, the BBC high-power transmitter at Hatfield, a potential German navigational beacon, was shut down, and the BBC Home Service went off the air. Guided by the railway lines, Roth, leading the Do 17s, zeroed in on Kenley, now just a stone's throw away.

Joachim Roth's skill in low-level navigation was remarkable. He led his unit within striking distance of their target – right on time and on course, undetected over enemy territory. However, as the Dorniers neared the airfield, they were met with an unexpected sight: no smoke or damage. They had anticipated an already weakened fighter station, but instead, they faced a fully operational airfield brimming with defensive fire.

The sky erupted with tracer rounds as the Dorniers' gunners engaged in a fierce battle with Bofors and British AAA defenses. Amidst the chaos, some of No. 111 Squadron's Hurricanes swooped down on the Dorniers. In the ensuing confusion, Flight Lieutenant Stanley Connors was tragically killed, either by the Dorniers or friendly fire, leading the rest of the squadron to pull away to avoid further casualties.

During the intense confrontation, every Dornier was hit. Feldwebel Johannes Petersen's plane, flying higher than the rest, caught fire but pressed on. Günter Unger, targeting a hangar, managed to release his bombs before his engine was hit. Unger's bombs successfully destroyed three hangars, but his aircraft started trailing black smoke, signaling damage. Harry Newton of 111 Squadron engaged Unger but was shot down, though not before damaging Unger's Dornier in a last act of defiance.

Meanwhile, Oberleutnant Hermann Magin's aircraft was critically hit. The quick thinking of navigator Wilhelm-Friedrich Illg saved the crew as he took control and managed an escape.

On the ground, Aircraftman D. Roberts, armed with parachute-and-cable launchers, lay in wait. He unleashed his rockets as three Dorniers approached, creating a barrier of lines and smoke. Wilhelm Raab, piloting one of the Dorniers, narrowly avoided the trap. However, Petersen's already damaged aircraft wasn't so lucky. Entangled in the cables, it crashed, killing all onboard. Oberleutnant Rudolf Lamberty, carrying Roth, also suffered hits that set his plane ablaze, eventually crash-landing in Kent. Tragically, Roth did not survive, but Lamberty did, albeit with injuries.

The raid's aftermath saw two bombers ditching into the sea, and two others crash-landing in France, with their crews rescued by Kriegsmarine vessels. Despite heavy damage to all nine Dorniers, four were lost, and two sustained crash landing damages. For his heroism, Illg was awarded the Knight's Cross of the Iron Cross.

9 Staffel's attack, though costly, was effective. They destroyed several hangars, damaged others, and put the operations room out of action,

wreaking havoc on Kenley's infrastructure. Had the bombs been released from a higher altitude, the damage might have been even more devastating. In total, KG 76 dropped nine tons of bombs, leaving Kenley severely crippled for hours. The aerial battle cost two Hurricanes, shot down by the Dorniers. In turn, 9 Staffel lost four Dorniers and sustained significant damage to others. This engagement marked a turning point, leading to the abandonment of low-level attacks after what became known as 'The Hardest Day'.

Guarding the airspace near Biggin Hill, Nos. 610, 615, and 32 Squadrons of the RAF hovered around 25,000 feet, anticipating the arrival of the high-altitude German bomber force. However, the German escort fighters, flying higher than expected, caught them off guard. The Bf 109s of JG 3, covering for KG 76's Ju 88s and Do 17s, spotted No. 615 Squadron below and swiftly descended in an ambush. Oberleutnant Lothar Keller and Leutnants Helmut Meckel and Helmut Landry each claimed a Hurricane from the unsuspecting RAF squadron.

While No. 615 Squadron faced heavy losses, they inadvertently played a crucial role by engaging the German escort fighters, allowing Squadron Leader Michael Crossley and No. 32 Squadron to focus on the KG 76 bombers unimpeded by enemy fighters.

ZG 26's Bf 110s, flying nearby, attempted to support JG 3 by intercepting Crossley's fighters but were unsuccessful. Crossley led a daring head-on assault, shooting down one Do 17 and causing damage to several others. The intensity of the RAF's attack forced the German bombers to evade, disrupting their bomb-aimers and causing them to miss their intended targets. Instead, some bombers redirected their focus to rail tracks near the airfield, while others opted not to release their bombs at all. Those who targeted the rail lines found it challenging to hit at 15,000 feet, resulting in some bombs unintentionally striking residential areas.

During Crossley's second attack run, the Bf 110s managed to intervene, leading to a confrontation where Flight Lieutenant 'Humph' Russell was shot down and injured. Soon after, No. 64 Squadron, led by Squadron Leader Donald MacDonell, joined the fray. In the ensuing confusion, several dogfights broke out, with MacDonell mistakenly engaging a Bf 110.

Over Kenley, the Ju 88s arrived to find the area shrouded in smoke, making dive-bombing impractical. The damage already inflicted on Kenley led the crews to deem further attacks unnecessary. As they contemplated their next move, they came under attack from RAF Spitfires and Hurricanes. Hannes Trautloft, leading the Bf 109 escorts, struggled to protect the Ju 88s as they shifted their focus to RAF West Malling for alternate dive-bombing runs.

Meanwhile, KG 1 had an unobstructed path to its target. The earlier engagements with KG 76 had drawn away most RAF squadrons, leaving No. 615 Squadron and its 15 Spitfires to confront KG 1. The squadron faced a formidable number of Bf 109s from JG 54, guarding the He 111s. Despite their efforts, the RAF fighters couldn't penetrate the German fighter screen, allowing the He 111s to proceed unchallenged. The absence of significant RAF opposition led some German bomber crews to speculate about the RAF's capacity to continue fighting. As the bombers neared Biggin Hill, most personnel managed to take cover, resulting in minimal damage to the airfield. KG 1 suffered only one He 111 lost and another damaged, likely due to an encounter with Spitfires from No. 65 Squadron, which had inadvertently stumbled into the fray while No. 615 Squadron and JG 54 were locked in battle.

As the German fighters commenced their retreat, they faced their most challenging phase: withdrawing under relentless RAF attacks. With dwindling fuel reserves, the German fighters' ability to protect the bombers was limited. This left damaged bombers, lagging behind the main formations, vulnerable to RAF pursuits. By 13:30, the German raiding groups were dispersing in various directions: 9 Staffel was escaping south over Beachy Head, KG 1 was finishing its bombing run while being shadowed by JG 54's Bf 109s and

Spitfires of 610 Squadron, the KG 76 Ju 88s, after targeting West Malling, were embroiled in battles with multiple RAF squadrons, and the Dorniers, heavily engaged by 32, 64, and 615 Squadrons, were trying to make their way home.

Meanwhile, RAF squadrons, including Nos. 1, 17, 54, 56, and 266, with a total of 23 Spitfires and 36 Hurricanes, were converging on the main German formations, exploiting their withdrawal.

Navigating through thickening haze, RAF controllers had to adapt. Instead of massing fighters for a concentrated attack, they spread them out to engage the Germans individually. This tactic proved effective. No. 56 Squadron quickly found and attacked Bf 110s from ZG 26, shooting down five and damaging another. Further losses to ZG 26 ensued as Nos. 54 and 501 Squadrons joined the fray, resulting in two more Bf 110s shot down and two damaged. No. 151 and No. 46 Squadrons also joined, adding to ZG 26's casualties, which by some accounts, totaled 12 destroyed and seven damaged.

No. 266 Squadron was among the last to engage, downing five Bf 109s, with additional Bf 109s suffering significant damage. The RAF's engagement resulted in several German pilot casualties. The bomber losses for the Germans were also substantial: eight destroyed and ten damaged, including losses from both KG 76 and KG 1.

The RAF wasn't spared either. No. 17 Squadron lost one Hurricane and pilot, while No. 32 Squadron and No. 65 Squadron each lost a Hurricane. No. 111 Squadron suffered losses both on the ground and in air combat, though all pilots survived. No. 501 Squadron faced heavy casualties with five Hurricanes destroyed. Nos. 601 and 602 Squadrons also suffered losses in both aircraft and pilots. No. 615 Squadron, heavily hit in the Kenley raid by 9 Staffel/KG 76, sustained severe losses.

The day's battles didn't end there. Kesselring dispatched additional Bf 109s from JG 2 and JG 27 to cover the retreating bombers. Near the Isle of Wight, these fighters clashed with RAF squadrons, resulting in further losses on both sides. II./JG 2 suffered a destroyed and a damaged Bf 109, with pilot casualties, while JG 27 lost six Bf 109s with three pilots killed and others missing or rescued.

On the afternoon of August 18, Luftflotte 3's commander Hugo Sperrle directed his dive bomber units to launch an offensive against key British targets along the southern coast. The chosen objectives included RAF Ford, RAF Thorney Island, and Gosport – all significant to the Fleet Air Arm or Coastal Command. Additionally, the radar installation at Poling, West Sussex, was marked for destruction.

However, reconnaissance limitations led to a critical misidentification. Images captured by Junkers Ju 86 aircraft were high-altitude and of poor quality, leading the Germans to erroneously classify these sites as fighter airfields. In reality, Gosport was home to a torpedo development unit, Thorney Island hosted No. 59 and No. 235 Squadrons of RAF Coastal Command, equipped with Bristol Blenheims, and Ford served as a naval air station, housing No. 829 Squadron Fleet Air Arm, which was operating Fairey Albacore aircraft at the time.

Tasked with executing these raids was Sturzkampfgeschwader 77 (StG 77), a dive bombing wing, which deployed an unprecedented force of 109 Junkers Ju 87 Stuka dive-bombers. This constituted the largest assembly of Ju 87s over Britain to that date.

The operational plan was precise: I./StG 77, with 28 Ju 87s, would target Thorney Island; II./StG 77, also comprising 28 aircraft, was assigned to Ford; and III./StG 77, with 31 Ju 87s, aimed to obliterate the Poling radar station. An additional unit, Sturzkampfgeschwader 3 (StG 3), dispatched 22 Ju 87s towards Gosport.

The dive-bombers were to be supported by a substantial force of 157 Bf 109s, including 70 from JG 27 and 32 from JG 53 as close escorts, plus 55 from JG 2 designated to sweep the Portsmouth area ahead of the main raid.

Due to the distance from their bases around Caen to the targets, the Stukas were relocated to airfields closer to the Channel coast near Cherbourg in the morning. Here, they were refueled, armed, and the crews briefed for their mission.

By 13:29, the first wave of Ju 87s was airborne, with all formations assembled and en route by 13:45, covering the 85-mile distance to their targets. Leading III./StG 77 to Poling was Major Helmut Bode, while Hauptmann Alfons Orthofer's II./StG 77 set course for Ford, and Hauptmann Herbert Meisel's III Gruppe, along with Hauptmann Walter Sigel's I./StG 3, headed respectively for Thorney Island and Gosport. Each Ju 87 carried a 550-lb bomb beneath the fuselage and four smaller 11-lb bombs under the wings.

The escorting Bf 109s were scheduled to take off later, as the slower speed and longer journey of the Ju 87s provided ample time for the fighters to catch up without expending unnecessary fuel on maintaining close proximity.

At 13:59, the Poling radar station detected the approaching German formations, estimating their strength at around 80 aircraft. Additional smaller groups, ranging from 9 to 20-plus aircraft, identified as German fighters, trailed behind the main force. The British, assessing the incoming Luftwaffe attack, estimated a total force of around 150 aircraft, significantly underestimating the actual numbers.

Responding to this threat, RAF's No. 10 and No. 11 Groups, operating from their command centers in Uxbridge and Box in Wiltshire, quickly mobilized additional squadrons to reinforce the 11 Hurricanes of No. 601 Squadron already in the air. Squadrons were dispatched from RAF Middle Wallop, RAF Exeter, RAF Warmwell, RAF Tangmere, and RAF Westhampnett. The

RAF's deployment included nine Hurricanes from No. 43 Squadron, led by Squadron Leader Frank Reginald Carey, patrolling Thorney Island; 12 Spitfires from No. 602 Squadron guarding Westhampnett; 11 Spitfires from No. 152 Squadron overseeing Portsmouth's airspace; No. 234 Squadron with 11 Spitfires covering the Isle of Wight; and No. 213 Squadron with 12 Hurricanes, moving eastward from Exeter to patrol St. Catherine's Point. Additionally, No. 609 Squadron, equipped with 12 Spitfires, remained in reserve around Middle Wallop to counter any unforeseen German maneuvers.

Tangmere, having lost all its Bristol Blenheim night fighters in a previous raid, deployed two Hurricanes from the Fighter Interception Unit (FIU) equipped with airborne radar for a field test. RAF Coastal Command also contributed, assigning No. 235 Squadron and its Bristol Blenheims to the defense effort. The RAF's defense lineup consisted of 68 Spitfires and Hurricanes, facing a daunting challenge with a ratio of one RAF fighter to every four German aircraft, and one to every two German fighters. Even with this realization, the RAF's options were limited, as other fighters were still refueling and rearming following the earlier attacks on Kenley and Biggin Hill, rendering them unavailable for immediate action.

Amidst the British scramble, Bf 109s from JG 52, conducting a pre-raid sweep, stumbled upon RAF fighters at RAF Manston caught in a vulnerable state during refueling. Twelve Bf 109s from 2 Staffel II./JG 52, led by Hauptmann Wolfgang Ewald, launched an attack. After two strafing runs, the Germans claimed to have destroyed 10 fighters and three Blenheims. However, the actual damage was less severe: only two Spitfires from No. 266 Squadron were destroyed, with six Hurricanes damaged but salvageable, and one additional Hurricane destroyed.

As the Ju 87 Stuka dive-bombers approached the English coast, they diverged towards their specific targets. By this point, approximately 15 miles off the Isle of Wight, their Bf 109 escorts had caught up and were deftly maneuvering around the dive-bombers for protection. Major Helmut Bode, leading III./StG

77, initiated an attack on Poling radar station, opting for a direct approach into the wind for precise bombing. Deviating from the usual line-astern attack formation, Bode chose to strike in groups of three to disperse the anti-aircraft fire. He led the assault with an 80-degree dive, using his machine guns to suppress enemy defenses, before releasing his bombs from 13,000 feet and pulling out at around 2,275 feet. His unit efficiently followed suit.

The attack on Poling radar station was notably effective, causing significant damage. This strike, along with the earlier destruction of Ventnor radar station, highlighted the vulnerability of Fighter Command's communication and control systems. Although emergency equipment was in place at Poling, the radar's functionality was greatly reduced, rendering the station inoperative for the remainder of August. However, the Chain Home (CH) radar network mitigated this impact, thanks to a mobile radar unit on the Isle of Wight and another installation planned near Poling, ensuring continuity of radar coverage. The damage at Kenley and Poling, though severe, were mere setbacks for Air Chief Marshal Hugh Dowding and Air Vice-Marshal Keith Park of the RAF. Avis Hearn, a Women's Auxiliary Air Force (WAAF) member who was monitoring the radar at Poling until the attack, was later recognized with the Military Medal for her bravery during the incident.

Concurrently, Alfons Orthofer's unit targeted Ford airfield. With minimal defensive armament at Ford, consisting of only six Lewis machine guns, the Ju 87s faced little resistance. Their bombs devastated the airfield, targeting hangars, buildings, and aircraft assembled for maintenance. A direct hit on the airfield's oil tanks caused a massive fire, exacerbating the damage.

Gosport was next to face the wrath of the Luftwaffe. Led by Hauptmann Walter Siegel, the Ju 87s of StG 3, encountering no air resistance, inflicted substantial damage.

Meanwhile, as the Ju 87s commenced their bombing runs, Spitfires from No. 234 Squadron RAF engaged the Bf 109 escort, about 25 strong, commanded by Hauptmann Karl-Wolfgang Redlich. Eduard Neumann, commander of I./JG 27, heard the unfolding battle but, due to poor communications, decided to let Redlich handle the situation. Redlich, an experienced squadron leader, faced fierce combat, resulting in the loss of three Bf 109s.

During the Luftwaffe's assault, three out of four Ju 87 groups successfully bombed their targets without interception. However, I./StG 77, consisting of 28 Stukas, faced an aggressive challenge from 18 Hurricanes of Nos. 43 and 601 Squadrons. The Stukas' escort, Bf 109s from II./JG 27, were positioned too far away to prevent the Hurricanes from attacking the dive-bombers before they commenced their dives. This resulted in three Ju 87s being shot down, with one Hurricane sustaining damage from return fire. The Bf 109 escorts soon found themselves embroiled in their own combat and were unable to effectively support the dive-bombers. Despite this, some Ju 87s managed to execute their bombing runs, targeting hangars and causing substantial damage, even as they observed Blenheims from No. 235 Squadron scrambling to defend their base.

The ensuing air battles over the skies of southern England involved around 300 aircraft across a 25-mile stretch from Gosport to Bognor Regis. Nos. 152 and 235 Squadrons engaged the German forces over Thorney Island, while No. 602 Squadron confronted the Ju 87s attacking Ford. However, III./JG 27 intervened, claiming the destruction of four Spitfires. Spitfires from No. 234 Squadron and Hurricanes from 213 Squadron each took down a Bf 109.

The aerial skirmishes proved costly for the Ju 87 units. I./StG 77 suffered the loss of 10 Stukas, with 17 crew members killed or mortally wounded, six injured, and five captured. II./StG 77 lost three Ju 87s, with casualties including five crew members dead and one captured. III./StG 77 also incurred losses, with two Ju 87s downed and four crew members killed. In total, StG 77 sustained 26 fatalities, six captured, and six wounded. The heavy losses curtailed the operational role of the Ju 87 in the Battle of Britain.

JG 27's Bf 109s also suffered, losing up to eight fighters, with only two pilots rescued. Although JG 27 claimed 14 RAF fighters, this figure was likely inflated, with only seven victories confirmed by the Luftwaffe. RAF casualties in these air battles included five fighters destroyed and four damaged.

In the aftermath, Ford airfield bore the brunt of the damage. Local fire brigades, despite water supply challenges, managed to extinguish the numerous fires and tended to casualties. The airfield suffered 28 fatalities and 75 injuries, with 14 aircraft destroyed and another 26 damaged. The destruction extended to hangars, canteens, and accommodation buildings.

Gosport, meanwhile, lost five aircraft and sustained damage to several buildings and two hangars, but remarkably, there were no casualties. The Ju 87 attack was precise, with all bombs hitting military targets.

Thorney Island's damage, though less severe due to the disruption caused by 43 and 601 Squadrons, included two destroyed hangars, two ruined buildings, and three destroyed aircraft. Five civilian workers were injured in the attack.

The loss of the Poling radar station posed minimal issues for the RAF. The Chain Home Low radar system remained functional, and the coverage was supplemented by six other radar stations along the coastline. Mobile units were quickly deployed nearby to provide temporary coverage until repairs at Poling were completed.

Following the morning's intense aerial engagements, a period of calm ensued as both the RAF's Nos. 10 and 11 Groups and the Luftwaffe's Luftflotte 2 and 3 took time to regroup and assess their situations. During this lull, commanders on both sides checked in with various units, seeking updates on crews and aircraft that might have landed safely in alternate locations after the skirmishes.

Amidst this quiet, two Bristol Blenheims from No. 114 Squadron RAF undertook a high-altitude bombing mission targeting Fécamp and Dieppe. The impact of these attacks appeared minimal, with no damage reported at Fécamp and the Dieppe raid seemingly going unnoticed. On their return flight, these bombers crossed paths with two Spitfires from the Photographic Reconnaissance Unit (PRU). These specially modified Spitfires, stripped of excess weight and armed with cameras and extra fuel tanks, were tasked with capturing aerial photographs of enemy ports and airfields.

As the day progressed, the Luftwaffe prepared for another round of attacks. By 17:00, British radar stations began picking up signs of German formations assembling off the Kent coast and over the Pas-de-Calais area. Luftflotte 2 shifted its focus to RAF North Weald and RAF Hornchurch. To execute this plan, 58 Do 17s from KG 2 were assigned to bomb Hornchurch, while 51 He 111s from KG 53 were directed towards North Weald. The two groups were coordinated to cross the coast simultaneously, with the He 111s setting off 15 minutes ahead of the Dorniers due to their longer journey. The bomber formations were escorted by a strong contingent of 140 Bf 109s and Bf 110s from JG 3, JG 26, JG 51, JG 54, and ZG 26.

Anticipating the incoming threat, the RAF's 11 Group at Uxbridge scrambled 13 squadrons, while 12 Group at Watnall ordered four more into the skies. This mobilization resulted in a formidable RAF response, comprising 47 Spitfires and 97 Hurricanes. Notably, ten of these RAF fighters, including nine Spitfires from No. 19 Squadron and one Hurricane from No. 151 Squadron, were equipped with 20 mm cannons.

No. 11 Group strategically positioned No. 32, 54, 56, and 501 Squadrons, a combination of 11 Spitfires and 33 Hurricanes, along the Margate–Canterbury line to engage the enemy formations first. The remaining RAF units climbed to higher altitudes, positioning themselves over or near the potentially targeted fighter airfields.

As KG 53 advanced towards North Weald from the east, navigating between

Maldon, Essex, and Rochford, they encountered stiff resistance from the RAF. No. 56 Squadron, equipped with 12 Hurricanes, engaged the approaching bombers, while No. 54 Squadron, flying 11 Spitfires, took on the escorting Bf 109s and Bf 110s. This engagement resulted in at least one Bf 110 being shot down. The British ground controllers, now aware of the enemy's line of advance, scrambled five additional squadrons – Nos. 46, 85, 151, 257, and 310, totaling 61 Hurricanes – to intercept the bombers either en route or directly over the target.

By 17:00, North Weald was partially obscured by stratocumulus clouds at an altitude of 5,000 feet, which lowered to 3,500 feet within half an hour. Realizing the difficulty of accurately bombing from 12,000 feet in such conditions, KG 53 aborted their mission at 17:40 and began to retreat, having lost only one bomber to 56 Squadron. However, their withdrawal was far from smooth. 28 Hurricanes from Nos. 46, 85, and 151 Squadrons prepared for a head-on attack, while 12 Hurricanes from 256 Squadron approached from behind.

During the ensuing combat, Pilot Officer Richard Milne of No. 151 Squadron shot down II./KG 53's Major Reinhold Tamm, resulting in the loss of the entire crew of the downed He 111. The Bf 109 escorts retaliated, downing two Hurricanes from No. 151 Squadron, with one pilot killed and another wounded. No. 257 Squadron also engaged, losing a pilot in a crash landing following a confrontation with Bf 110s. Meanwhile, No. 46 Squadron, the sole participating unit from 12 Group, joined the fray.

Shortly thereafter, No. 85 Squadron, led by Peter Townsend, launched an attack on the bombers but encountered resistance from ZG 26's Bf 110s and possibly III./JG 51's Bf 109s providing top cover. This led to intense and inconclusive dogfights. No. 1 Squadron's leader, David Pemberton, managed to down a Bf 109 from JG 3. No. 85 Squadron claimed a He 111 but lost a Hurricane, with Pilot Officer Paddy Hemmingway ejecting and surviving. Flight Lieutenant Dick Lee, a decorated veteran and ace, was reported missing after pursuing Bf 109s out to sea, and his body was never recovered.

With ammunition and fuel dwindling, few British squadrons remained in combat, including No. 54 Squadron. Its commander, Colin Falkland Gray, successfully destroyed a Bf 110.

As KG 53 withdrew, they jettisoned their bombs, resulting in about 32 bombs falling on Shoeburyness. This unplanned bombardment caused significant civilian casualties and property damage, including the destruction of houses and the death of residents in an Anderson shelter, as well as the killing of a railway signalman.

KG 53's losses in this encounter were relatively light, with only four He 111s destroyed and one damaged. The personnel losses included twelve dead, two wounded, and four captured, with an additional five crew members rescued by British ships, increasing the total number of captives to nine. The success in minimizing losses was largely attributed to the efforts of ZG 26, though this came at a cost of seven Bf 110s destroyed and six damaged.

Back in the fray, Squadron Leader Michael Crossley led No. 32 Squadron, joining forces with No. 501 Squadron to intercept KG 2 near Herne Bay. However, their 15 Hurricanes were impeded by Bf 109 escorts from II./JG 51. During the ensuing combat, George E.B. Stoney of No. 501 was shot down and killed by Austrian pilot Hauptmann Josef Foezoe. No. 501 retaliated effectively, downing two Bf 109s, including those piloted by ace Horst Tietzen and Hans-Otto Lessing, both of whom were killed. Peter Brothers of the RAF also claimed a Bf 109, resulting in the death of its 22-year-old pilot, Gerhard Mueller. In a collaborative effort, Crossley, Karol Pniak, and Alan Eckford took down another Bf 109, with its pilot Walter Blume severely wounded and captured. The tables turned when three Hurricanes, including Crossley's, were downed, though the pilots survived with injuries. Despite the RAF's efforts, the Dorniers flew unimpeded.

As the Dorniers flew over Sheerness, they faced anti-aircraft fire aimed at protecting the Chatham naval yard. The cloudy conditions over the target area disrupted the German bombing accuracy, leading some bombers to return with their payloads. Three Dorniers, however, attacked the Royal Marines barracks at Deal, Kent, before heading back across the Channel without further RAF engagement.

As night fell, the Luftwaffe initiated a series of night raids targeting various British cities and locations, including Sheffield, Leeds, Hull, and Colchester. Most bombs were scattered across rural areas, with significant damage reported only at Sealand. In Gloucestershire, a KG 27 He 111, piloted by Alfred Dreher, collided mid-air with an Avro Anson during night flying training, resulting in fatalities for all crew members involved.

Simultaneously, RAF Bomber Command launched attacks against German airfields in the Netherlands and France, achieving limited success in Vlissingen, Netherlands, where two JG 54 Bf 109s were damaged. Other RAF operations targeted industrial sites in Italy and Germany.

The aftermath of these actions was marked by considerable overclaiming from both sides. British propaganda claimed the destruction of 144 German aircraft, more than double the actual losses, while the Germans claimed they had lost only 36 aircraft, significantly less than the actual figure of 69 to 71. German claims of 147 British aircraft destroyed were also exaggerated, with the British admitting to only 23 losses, whereas the actual number was around 68. Conflicting sources report RAF losses ranging from 27 to 34 fighters destroyed and 29 aircraft lost on the ground. German pilot Siegfried Bethke suggested that aircraft downed in the Channel were often omitted from official German loss records, and severely damaged aircraft were sometimes disassembled and transported back to Germany without being recorded as losses.

Battle of Britain Day

On the night of September 15, London braced itself as the Luftwaffe unleashed its eighth consecutive night of terror. The skies darkened with the ominous silhouettes of Dornier Do 17 light bombers, initiating the assault just after midnight. The city's heart raced as two Junkers Ju 88s from the elite 51st Bomber Wing pierced through at 00:15, followed closely by a squadron of 11 Heinkel He 111s. As the clock struck 02:00, five more He 111s from the formidable Kampfgeschwader 4 roared above, raining destruction. Despite plans for a larger strike, inclement weather thwarted their efforts after the initial five aircraft had launched.

London's residential neighborhoods in Fulham, Chelsea, and Westminster bore the brunt, with about 19 lives lost and 31 wounded. A devastating blow was dealt to a Chelsea church, where a single bomb claimed 14 lives and injured 26 souls. Meanwhile, smaller Luftwaffe units struck Cardiff, Bootle in Liverpool, Leicester, and Ipswich. In Bootle, the damage was minimal, affecting only rail tracks and facilities at West Alexandra Dock.

The Luftwaffe's aggression extended to the sea as well. A Heinkel He 115 floatplane skillfully torpedoed the 5,548-ton freighter Mailsea River off Montrose, followed swiftly by the sinking of the freighter Halland. These lethal birds of prey also littered magnetic anti-shipping mines along the Thames Estuary, Bristol Channel, Liverpool Bay, Milford Haven, and off the coasts of Hartlepool, Berwick-upon-Tweed, and Aberdeen.

The RAF's night fighter defenses, still in their nascent stages, struggled against these nocturnal raids. Most fighters, bereft of radar and reliant on the pilots' keen sight, patrolled outside anti-aircraft gunfire, attempting to intercept enemy aircraft. A total of 28 sorties were flown that night, a humble beginning to what would later become a sophisticated defense system.

Simultaneously, RAF Bomber Command was active over German-occupied territories, launching 92 sorties against invasion targets in Boulogne, Calais, Ostend, Dunkirk, and Antwerp. Additional missions targeted Brussels marshalling yards, Hamm, and Krefeld. Sadly, one Armstrong Whitworth Whitley was lost to ground fire over the Netherlands, out of the 157 total sorties.

Daylight on September 15 brought the first combat engagement. A He 111 from the Long-range Reconnaissance Group 51, based near Paris, met its fate over the Channel, shot down by Hurricanes from No. 87 Squadron RAF. Despite a search by a Heinkel He 59 air-sea rescue aircraft, the crew of the downed Heinkel remained undiscovered.

The Luftwaffe continued to flex its aerial prowess with high altitude reconnaissance flights by Ju 88s. These craft boldly ventured over RAF Sealand, RAF Pembrey, RAF Woodward, Manchester, Liverpool, Birkenhead, Thames Haven, RAF Netheravon, RAF Benson, and even the Royal Navy base at Chatham Dockyard. Despite the difficulty in intercepting these high-flying intruders, none were lost on this fateful day of September 15, 1940.

The morning of the operation dawned, and at 10:10, a critical moment in the aerial warfare over Europe unfolded. Major Alois Lindmayr, the esteemed Group Commander of I./KG 76 and a Knight's Cross recipient for his valor in France, spearheaded the entire formation. The stage was set for a significant Luftwaffe offensive.

From their base at Cormeilles-en-Vexin, III./Kampfgeschwader 76 (KG 76) launched 19 Dornier Do 17 bombers. Concurrently, a mere 20 miles north, I./KG 76 took to the skies. Typically, a Group could boast 27 bombers, but intense weeks of combat had dwindled I./KG 76's strength to just eight Do 17s. This attrition meant two Groups were needed for a mission usually handled by one. The Dorniers, showing signs of wear from relentless operations, regrouped at Amiens before proceeding to Cap Gris Nez to rendezvous with their Bf 109 fighter escorts.

The Luftwaffe, battered by the relentless air war over Britain, was forced to innovate. One example was Feldwebel Rolf Heitsch, who daringly equipped his Dornier with an infantry flame thrower in its tail – a desperate but inventive measure aimed at repelling or downing pursuing fighters.

As the formation ascended, cloud cover scattered them, causing a 10-minute delay for reformation. Two bombers, unable to rejoin, returned to base.

On the British front, RAF Uxbridge's operations room was momentarily unsettled by Prime Minister Winston Churchill's visit. Despite his presence, the Women's Auxiliary Air Force (WAAF) maintained a relaxed demeanor. At 10:30, the first German aircraft set off alarms at the Dover Chain Home radar station. The Stanmore filter room swiftly identified the formation as hostile, prompting the WAAF to alert group and sector commands of over 40 enemy aircraft entering Kentish airspace.

By 11:04, Lindmayr's Dorniers reached Calais. Observing this, Wing Commander Lord Willoughby de Broke, alongside Churchill and Park, faced a tactical conundrum. Distinguishing bombers from fighters in the plots was crucial, as bombers were priority targets. De Broke had to balance early scramble to gain an advantageous attack position against the risk of fighters running low on fuel.

Park decided to deploy several squadrons from RAF Biggin Hill, aware that the raid might be a decoy. Nine squadrons were dispatched at 11:15.

No. 92 and No. 72 Squadrons RAF scrambled Spitfires from Biggin Hill, positioned over Canterbury at 25,000 feet. De Broke, sensing this was the primary attack, ordered additional squadrons from RAF Northolt, Kenley, and Debden to stand by. Shortly after, he dispatched squadrons from RAF Hornchurch, North Weald, and No. 10 Group's RAF Middle Wallop.

The strategy was clear: Nos. 72 and 92 would confront the high escort, while

No. 603 Squadron RAF targeted the close escort (JG 3). Squadrons positioned over Maidstone and Chelmsford provided further reinforcement.

Despite reservations, Park ordered the testing of Leigh-Mallory's Big Wing. If the Germans used the Thames Estuary for navigation, fighters from RAF Duxford's 12 Group could intercept them over Hornchurch. At 11:20, the order was relayed, and Duxford scrambled No. 19, 310, 302, and No. 611 Squadrons RAF. Led by Wing Commander Douglas Bader of No. 242 Squadron RAF, 56 fighters took to the skies by 11:22, poised for a pivotal aerial confrontation.

As the battle unfolded in the skies above England, the German Luftwaffe's Dornier bombers were closely guarded by a formidable array of fighter escorts. Jagdgeschwader 27 and I./Jagdgeschwader 52 led the vanguard with their Bf 109s soaring at 16,000 feet towards London. Above them, Jagdgeschwader 53 provided top cover for the bombers, while around 30 aircraft from Jagdgeschwader 3 maintained a close escort. The slow pace of the bombers, however, forced the fighters to reduce speed significantly, compromising their combat readiness.

The Dorniers crossed the English coastline at Folkestone at 11:36, but a strong headwind slowed their progress, simultaneously hastening the RAF fighters converging from the north. Meanwhile, II.Lehrgeschwader 2, another escort contingent, took off, tasked with dropping bombs ahead of the main force and then rejoining as fighters. This headwind not only delayed the Germans but also depleted the fuel of the Bf 109s more rapidly.

Park, interpreting the LG 2 raid as a major offensive, scrambled an additional six RAF squadrons while holding four in reserve. The aerial tableau soon presented around 120 Bf 109s and 25 Do 17s against a formidable force of 245 Spitfires and Hurricanes.

The RAF's strategy began to pay dividends. Squadrons from Biggin Hill, particularly 72 and 92 Squadrons, engaged the enemy over Canterbury. At an altitude of 25,000 feet, they positioned themselves advantageously above JG 53. Beyond Canterbury, they spotted KG 76 and JG 3 near Ashford. Launching a surprise attack from the sun at 11:50, they successfully struck several of JG 53's Bf 109s.

Despite the Spitfires of 92 Squadron attempting to penetrate the fighter screen to reach the Dorniers, they were obstructed. Shortly after, No. 603 Squadron joined the fray. Park's tactics had effectively disrupted the German escort, as 23 Hurricanes from Nos. 253 and 501 Squadrons launched a head-on assault at the same altitude as the bombers. Despite their experience and composure, Lindmayr's formation found itself increasingly isolated as the escorts were embroiled in dogfights across Kent, with half of the RAF fighters yet to engage.

JG 53 faced additional challenges from several RAF squadrons, including Nos. 1, 46, 249, and 605. Notably, No. 605, under Archie McKellar, broke off to launch a 12-fighter assault that inflicted damage on the bombers. Meanwhile, JG 27 suffered two losses, possibly in an encounter with No. 19 Squadron, and JG 3 claimed two RAF fighters at the cost of one of their own.

Until this point, the Bf 109s had effectively shielded the bombers from attacks. However, the RAF's strategy of engaging the Germans along their route exhausted the fighters' fuel reserves more quickly. As London's outskirts came into view, the German fighters, low on fuel, began to withdraw north of Lewisham at 12:07, marking a critical moment in the battle.

In the thick of the aerial battle, No. 504 and 257 Squadrons from North Weald joined the fray with a force of 20 Hurricanes, targeting the Dornier bombers. A dramatic moment unfolded when a German pilot, Feldwebel Robert Zehbe, experienced engine trouble, falling behind the main bomber group. His isolated Dornier became the focus of intense fighter attention. In a remarkable act of aerial combat, Ray Holmes of 504 Squadron, having exhausted his ammunition, resorted to ramming the bomber, sending it into a catastrophic dive. The Dornier disintegrated, its tail and wings breaking away, before crashing near London Victoria station. Its jettisoned bombs caused damage in the vicinity of Buckingham Palace. Zehbe, having ejected, landed near The Oval but was gravely injured by an angry mob. He was later rescued by the British Army, only to succumb to his injuries. Holmes, too, ejected from his damaged Hurricane, landing near Buckingham Palace, and survived despite injuries.

Above the target area, the Duxford Wing, led by Bader, swooped in during the German bomb-run. The Dorniers unleashed their payload on the Battersea rail lines, creating a swath of destruction along a 500-yard stretch. The bombs, while missing Clapham Junction, disrupted the railway network significantly, damaging tracks and a viaduct, and halting rail traffic. Despite the extensive damage, the rail lines were operational again within three days.

The German formation, initially strong, soon dwindled to 15 aircraft, most of which sustained damage. Six bombers were shot down, and four were struggling to return to base. The survivors, having released their bombs, rendezvoused with a covering force of Bf 109s and retreated to France. Meanwhile, LG 2, having completed its mission, withdrew after a brief encounter with a British fighter from No. 46 Squadron.

The Luftwaffe's losses were significant, with six bombers and 12 Bf 109s destroyed, amounting to a 12.5% reduction in their strength. However, the British claim of 81 aircraft, including 26 by the Duxford Wing, was exaggerated, with Zehbe's Dornier being claimed multiple times. Among the German casualties was Rolf Heitsch, whose innovative but untested flame-throwing Dornier attracted British fighters after malfunctioning. Despite the Luftwaffe's loss of a quarter of its bomber force, Fighter Command also suffered, losing 13 fighters, eight of which were claimed by JG 52. In the end, the operation was a strategic victory for the British.

By 13:00, as the German formations retreated back to France, a sense of triumph filled the air. Prime Minister Churchill was visibly pleased with the day's outcomes. At RAF stations, the Women's Auxiliary Air Force members, who had been due for a shift change, remained at their posts, the urgency of the situation overriding regular schedules. By 13:05, the RAF fighters had landed, and the ground crews sprang into action, rearming and refueling the aircraft to prepare them for any subsequent engagements. The pilots, in the meantime, were busy documenting their combat experiences and filing claims based on their recollections of the fierce aerial engagements.

Bader's Big Wing, having played a pivotal role, returned to base. Battle damages had taken their toll, reducing the operational capacity of Duxford's 56 fighters to 49 by the afternoon.

Meanwhile, the German bombers began landing in the Pas de Calais region. Two of them were so severely damaged they were deemed irreparable after crash landings, increasing the total German losses to eight Do 17s. Evidence of the day's fierce battles was visible on almost all the returning aircraft; one bomber bore 70 hits, another over 200.

In the afternoon, RAF Bomber Command called off additional attacks on invasion ports due to inadequate cloud cover. Instead, six Bristol Blenheims conducted armed reconnaissance over the North Sea, while RAF Coastal Command executed 95 sorties, encompassing anti-invasion, anti-submarine, mine-laying, and reconnaissance missions. Spitfires undertook crucial photographic reconnaissance missions along the coast from Antwerp to Cherbourg, revealing a gradual buildup of amphibious forces. All RAF Command aircraft returned safely from their missions.

As the KG 76 bombers were still landing, another wave of German attackers was already preparing to take to the skies. This next onslaught included bombers from various Kampfgeschwader units, escorted by JG 53 and Adolf Galland's Jagdgeschwader 26 (JG 26), converging over Calais.

The German bomber formation, facing the persistent headwind, struggled as they approached Dungeness. The formation included Do 17s from KG 2, He 111s from KG 53 and KG 26, and more Do 17s from KG 3. The German fighter pilots, tasked with close escort duties, found the tactic frustrating as it left them vulnerable to RAF attacks and limited their maneuverability.

The German escort was formidable, comprising five groups from JG 3, JG 53, and Jagdgeschwader 77, with LG 2 providing top cover. Galland's JG 26 and Jagdgeschwader 51 conducted fighter sweeps ahead of the bombers. Zerstörergeschwader 26, equipped with Messerschmitt Bf 110s, flew close escort for KG 26. Despite being smaller than the force that struck London on September 7, this formation had a much higher ratio of fighters to bombers.

At 13:45, British radar systems detected the incoming German raids. RAF's No. 11 Group immediately scrambled a Spitfire from RAF Hawkinge, piloted by No. 92 Squadron's Alan Wright, to gather intelligence on the enemy formation. The British radar estimates of the German force's size fell short; in reality, it comprised 475 aircraft. As the German formation crossed the French coast shortly before 14:00, Park ordered his forces to deploy the interception tactics used earlier in the day. Squadrons were positioned strategically over Sheerness, Chelmsford, Hornchurch, and RAF Kenley, ready to engage the formidable German force.

At precisely 14:00, RAF's No. 11 Group launched a formidable force of 68 fighters into the increasingly crowded skies. From Hornchurch, No. 603 and No. 222 Squadrons dispatched 20 Spitfires towards Sheerness, soaring at 20,000 feet. However, coordination issues led these squadrons to engage the enemy independently. Debden's No. 17 Squadron and No. 257 Squadron sent 20 Hurricanes towards Chelmsford at 15,000 feet, while Kenley deployed No. 501 and 605 Squadrons with 17 Hurricanes to patrol over Kenley at a relatively low altitude of 5,000 feet. North Weald wasn't far behind, sending No. 249 and 504 Squadrons to cover Hornchurch at 15,000 feet.

Only five minutes later, the German bombers, now divided into three groups, began their approach towards the English coast between Dungeness and Dover. Park, recognizing the urgency, scrambled four more RAF squadrons. The situation intensified as five groups of Bf 109s embarked on free-hunting patrols directly towards London, prompting Park to deploy an additional eight squadrons. This included Biggin Hill's No. 41 Squadron and 92 Squadron, contributing 20 Spitfires to patrol Hornchurch at 20,000 feet. At 14:10, Northolt's No. 1 (Canadian) and 229 Squadrons launched 21 Hurricanes towards Northolt, and North Weald dispatched nine Hurricanes of No. 46 Squadron to the London Docks. Additional support came from Biggin Hill with No. 72 and No. 66 Squadron, adding 20 Spitfires to the mix over Biggin Hill at 20,000 feet. Debden re-entered the fray, ordering No. 73 Squadron to Maidstone at 15,000 feet. Kenley, not to be outdone, sent No. 253 Squadron with nine Hurricanes to protect the airfield. RAF Tangmere made its first sortie, deploying Nos. 213 and 607 Squadron with 23 Hurricanes to defend Kenley and Biggin Hill. The largest contribution came from No. 12 Group's "Big Wing" from Duxford, comprising No. 19, 242, 302, 310, and 311 Squadrons, with a combination of 20 Spitfires and 27 Hurricanes heading to Hornchurch at 25,000 feet. Middle Wallop added to the numbers with No. 238 Squadron and 12 Hurricanes covering the Kenley area.

As Park initiated his third wave of defenses around 14:20, the aerial battles had already begun. No. 11 Group's No. 303 (Polish) Squadron, with its nine Hurricanes, took off towards Northolt at 20,000 feet. Tangmere's No. 602 Squadron RAF joined in with 12 Spitfires, hovering protectively over Kenley, Biggin Hill, and Gravesend. Meanwhile, No. 10 Group RAF was also called into action, with No. 609 Squadron and its 13 Spitfires climbing to 15,000 feet over Kenley, departing from Middle Wallop at 14:28.

The RAF had now amassed a force of 276 Spitfires and Hurricanes in the air, yet they were outnumbered by the German raiders two to one. Furthermore, the RAF faced the daunting challenge of contending with a ratio of three Bf 109s for every two of their fighters.

Over the skies of Romney Marsh, a fierce engagement unfolded as Nos. 41, 92, and 222 Squadrons clashed with JG 26. Despite their valiant efforts, the RAF squadrons suffered a loss to the Bf 109s. The battle's intensity escalated with the arrival of the second wave of RAF fighters, including 607 and 213 Squadrons armed with 23 Hurricanes. They launched a daring head-on assault against KG 3's Do 17s, resulting in a dramatic mid-air collision between a Hurricane and a Dornier, both aircraft plummeting to the ground. The Bf 109s, bound by strict orders to stick close to the bombers, desperately tried to disrupt the RAF's attacks. The bombers, meanwhile, maintained a tight formation, unleashing a formidable crossfire. Each time the Bf 109s peeled away to engage, they were compelled to return to the bomber stream, giving RAF fighters opportunities to attack anew. The arrival of No. 605 and No. 501 Squadron with 14 Hurricanes intensified the conflict. One Hurricane, struck by enemy fire, was piloted directly into a Dornier before the pilot ejected, leading the German bomber crews to mistakenly believe that such kamikaze-like tactics were a deliberate British strategy.

By 14:31, the German bombers had reached the Thames, drawing heavy anti-aircraft fire from British AAA defenses. This barrage forced evasive maneuvers, resulting in damage to one of the Dorniers. KG 53 also lost a He 111 in the chaotic airspace over the region.

At 14:35, in Uxbridge's operations room, Park and Churchill watched the unfolding aerial drama. Churchill, realizing the full commitment of squadrons, inquired about reserve forces, to which Park replied none were available, referring specifically to the stretched resources of 11 Group. Despite the presence of more aircraft in nearby sectors, Park had already committed all available squadrons from No. 10 and 12 Groups to defend the capital. This left only three squadrons in Norfolk and Dorset available for any subsequent Luftwaffe attack, with none in the immediate vicinity of Kent. Park was aware, however, that low cloud bases over RAF Croydon, Hornchurch, Northolt, RAF Hendon, and Biggin Hill limited the Germans to low-level strikes, rendering high-altitude attacks unlikely.

In a strategic move, possibly to create a reserve force, Park ordered 41, 213, and 605 Squadrons to return early, despite their sufficient fuel levels. At this critical juncture, the vast majority of RAF fighters, totaling 185 in 19 squadrons, were converging on London. The imminent battle loomed as one of the largest aerial engagements of the war, involving over 600 aircraft.

Near Gravesend, the German right-hand formation, composed of KG 3's Do 17s followed by KG 26's He 111s, encountered a formidable attack from 63 RAF fighters from 17, 46, 249, 257, 504, and 603 Squadrons. The Hurricanes from 249 and 504 Squadrons struck first, downing three Do 17s, including one led by Hauptmann Ernst Püttmann of KG 3. Meanwhile, the Bf 109s, assigned to escort KG 26, could only watch helplessly, restricted from abandoning their charges. Following this, No. 257 Squadron, led by Squadron Leader Robert Stanford Tuck, launched an aggressive attack on the Heinkels. The German escorts struggled to fend off the assault, allowing No. 257 to focus on the vulnerable bombers.

As 257 Squadron engaged KG 26, No. 1, 66, 72, and 229 Squadrons targeted KG 53. The Spitfires from these squadrons, after attacking, climbed above the bombers to avoid the Bf 109s. Two He 111s were forced to retreat, and another was shot down. Nine Bf 109s providing close escort for I./JG 3 claimed a Canadian Hurricane and a Spitfire from No. 66 Squadron. KG 2, in the left-hand column, faced an onslaught from 23 Hurricanes of Nos. 73, 253, and 303 Squadrons. JG 53 countered, shooting down a Hurricane from 303 Squadron and damaging five others.

At 14:31, over the Thames, the bombers encountered heavy anti-aircraft fire, causing damage to one Dornier. KG 53 lost a He 111 during this phase.

Meanwhile, Park awaited the arrival of Bader's Wing, hoping it would turn the tide. When the Duxford Wing finally arrived, it was immediately intercepted by Galland's JG 26. The Hurricanes engaged the Bf 109s while the Spitfires targeted the bombers. Although they didn't manage to launch a successful bombing attack, they distracted the Bf 109 escorts, allowing other RAF fighters easier access to the bombers. No. 310 Squadron lost two Hurricanes to JG 26 in the ensuing chaos. By 14:40, the bombers reached London, with KG 3 losing three Do 17s and two damaged, while KG 26 suffered one damaged bomber. KG 53 lost one bomber and three more turned back due to damage, with KG 2 also having one bomber forced to retreat.

The cloud cover, however, played a significant role in limiting RAF fighter controllers' accuracy. It also obscured the target area for the German bombers, who eventually focused their attack on West Ham, particularly targeting the Bromley-by-Bow gas works. The area sustained significant damage, including hits on Upton Park tube station and an electric substation, causing a blackout. KG 2, unable to locate the Surrey Commercial Docks, dropped its bombs over a broader area.

As the German bombers retreated, some groups dispersed while others maintained uneven formations, pursued by RAF fighters. With fuel running low, the Bf 109s had to return to France, leaving the bombers vulnerable. Most of the German bombers that were forced out of formation were subsequently destroyed. Four Do 17s and six He 111s were shot down over Kent. Despite the RAF's overestimation of German losses, the Luftwaffe had indeed suffered heavy casualties. KG 2 lost eight Do 17s, KG 3 lost six, and the He 111s suffered lighter losses, with only one aircraft lost and three more damaged. KG 53 lost six Heinkels. German fighter losses were also substantial, with JG 51, JG 52, JG 53, JG 77, and LG 2 all suffering casualties.

In total, the Luftwaffe lost 21 bombers and at least 12 fighters, while the RAF lost 15 fighters with 21 more damaged. German fighter losses might have been as high as 23.

From 15:00, another Luftwaffe unit, III./Kampfgeschwader 55, took off from Villacoublay, initially heading towards Southampton before diverting to target Royal Navy installations at Portland. British radar detected them as six intruders, but in reality, there were over 20 He 111s without fighter escort. Intercepted by six Spitfires from No. 152 Squadron, the bombers managed to release their ordnance, causing minor damage. One He 111 from KG 55's 9 Staffel was lost, and another from 8 Staffel was damaged.

The day's German offensive concluded with one final significant operation. At 17:40, 20 aircraft from Erprobungsgruppe 210 took off, detected off the Cherbourg peninsula as they crossed the Channel towards the Isle of Wight. By 17:50, they were near St. Catherine's Point. RAF squadrons, including Nos. 213 and 602 at Tangmere and No. 607 Squadron over Southampton, were poised for action. By 18:00, with the German operation nearing its end, British forces were fully deployed, including No. 238 Squadron from Middle Wallop patrolling the area.

The Germans aimed to strike the Spitfire factory at Woolston and reached the vicinity at 17:55. Despite facing continuous fire from Southampton's defenses, the attack missed its primary target. The bombs, however, did damage nearby residential areas and slightly affected the Southampton Harbour shipbuilding yard. German records indicate that around 10–11 tons of bombs were dropped, narrowly missing a critical blow to British fighter production. The attack resulted in nine civilian fatalities, with 10 seriously and 23 slightly injured.

Eyewitness Alexander McKee, an aviation enthusiast, observed the raid from a café in Stoneham, noting the impressive flying skills of the German pilots despite the intense barrage. He described the aircraft as possibly Dorniers or Jaguars, highlighting their efficient reformation and escape into the clouds post-attack.

Nos. 607 and 609 Squadrons engaged the German formation southwest of The Needles. RAF reports suggested a formation of 30–40 Bf 110s with 15 Do 17s, but the bomb tonnage indicated fewer bombers. The RAF claimed four Do 17s shot down. The German force, having penetrated British airspace without interception, narrowly missed inflicting critical damage on the Spitfire factory. Radar had alerted the RAF 20 minutes before the bombing, but a delay in scrambling fighters by No. 10 or 11 Group controllers allowed the Germans to carry out their raid.

Later in the evening, more interceptions occurred. No. 66 Squadron RAF intercepted two separate He 111s near London, likely on reconnaissance missions. One He 111, probably from I./Kampfgeschwader 1, was chased out to sea and last seen flying on one engine, later crash landing in France.

Throughout the afternoon, small groups of German bombers targeted London with limited impact. II./Kampfgeschwader 4 had a He 111 crash land near Eindhoven, while 6 Staffel Kampfgeschwader 30 lost one Junkers Ju 88 in France and another forced to land after combat. I. and II./Kampfgeschwader 51 each lost a Ju 88, with crews reported missing.

At night, Kampfgeschwader 27 bombed Liverpool, causing widespread damage in the city and neighbouring Birkenhead but inflicting only nine casualties. Additional damage was reported in various locations including Eastbourne, Worthing, Bournemouth, Cardiff, Avonmouth, Manchester, Warrington, Bootle, and Preston. RAF night fighters conducted 64 sorties and intercepted two bombers, but no successful engagements were claimed by either fighters or ground defenses.

In the day's aerial battles, the RAF and Luftwaffe experienced roughly equal fighter losses. However, the significant difference lay in bomber casualties. Fighter Command achieved more success in the afternoon attack, where it faced a 2:1 numerical disadvantage. The morning ratio of German fighters to bombers was 3:1, but this increased to 5:1 in the afternoon, presenting the RAF with a larger number of targets. Consequently, the more bombers Luftwaffe Marshal Albert Kesselring deployed, the higher the losses he suffered.

Kesselring found himself back at square one. Air Chief Marshal Sir Keith

Park's strategy during these engagements was a testament to his skill in aggressive defense. Unlike the chaotic air battles of August, these set-piece offensives played to Park's strengths and tactics.

Air Vice-Marshal Trafford Leigh-Mallory, commanding the RAF's No. 12 Group, claimed that his Big Wing formations had destroyed entire enemy formations upon encountering them. He even suggested that the RAF outnumbered the Luftwaffe in several clashes. In the afternoon battle, although Leigh-Mallory acknowledged that the Big Wing struggled to position itself against the bombers and faced German fighter interception, he claimed his units had shot down 105 enemy aircraft, possibly destroyed another 40, and damaged 18, all at the cost of 14 aircraft and six pilots.

These claims were greatly exaggerated. Nonetheless, the most significant contribution of the Big Wing that day was arguably psychological. German aircrews, who had been led to believe the RAF was a defeated force, were reportedly shocked upon witnessing the formidable formation of the Big Wing. For the crews of heavily hit units like KG 2 and KG 3, who had seen their aircraft destroyed in head-on collisions, the impact was particularly demoralizing.

Battle of the Espero Convoy

At the heart of this battle were three state-of-the-art Italian destroyers: Espero, Zeffiro, and Ostro. Their mission was to traverse from Taranto to Tobruk in Libya, carrying crucial 'Blackshirt' anti-tank units. These units were imperative for fortifying the Italian defenses against any potential armored onslaught from British forces advancing westward from Egypt. This operation was not just a military maneuver but a critical move in the strategic chess game of warfare.

Meanwhile, the British Mediterranean Fleet, commanded by the astute Admiral Sir Andrew Cunningham, was conducting operations in the vicinity. Sailing from Alexandria, their objective was to perform a destroyer anti-submarine sweep around Crete and simultaneously safeguard three Allied convoys. These convoys, one originating from Turkey and two from Malta, were vital for reinforcing the Allied presence in Egypt.

The plot thickened when British aircraft, operating out of Malta, detected the movement of the Italian destroyers. Reacting swiftly, Vice Admiral J. C. Tovey's 7th Cruiser Squadron received orders to intercept. What ensued was a gripping chase and a running battle to the south-west of Crete. The Italian destroyers, hindered by their heavy cargoes and challenging sea conditions, found themselves in a precarious situation.

In a dramatic turn of events, the Italian destroyer Espero, valiantly led by Capitano di vascello Enrico Baroni, was sunk. This heroic act allowed the remaining destroyers, Zeffiro and Ostro, to escape to Benghazi. Out of Espero's crew and passengers, numbering 225, the British ships managed to rescue 53, although three succumbed to their injuries later. This encounter had far-reaching implications, as the British and Australian cruisers used up a significant portion of their ammunition, forcing the postponement of the Malta convoys until they could replenish from their reserves.

The Italian supply chain to Libia Italiana (Italian Libya) was a crucial aspect of their war effort, with shipments landing at Tripoli, Benghazi, and Tobruk. These supplies had to be transported to the front lines, a task that was increasingly challenging given the naval superiority of the Allies. The Italian High Command, under Maresciallo d'Italia Pietro Badoglio, had to balance internal security with the need to maintain a steady supply line, a strategy that would determine the course of the war in this region.

Ammiraglio d'Armata Domenico Cavagnari, the Italian naval chief-of-staff, voiced his concerns on 11 April about the daunting challenge of engaging in offensive actions against adversaries who possessed a far superior capacity to replenish their losses. Cavagnari's apprehensions highlighted a grim reality: Italy could end the war without territorial gains, a diminished navy, and a weakened air force. This was a sobering prospect, as Italy was preparing to confront formidable opponents with the French fleet to the west and the British fleet to the east.

Despite Cavagnari's doubts, Benito Mussolini, the Italian dictator, harbored a different outlook. He envisaged a short war, lasting merely three months, during which time Libya had sufficient supplies for six months. This optimistic prediction by Mussolini set the stage for Italy's military strategy in the Mediterranean.

It was not until 10 June that Mussolini ordered the reinforcement of military forces in Libya for offensive operations, tasking the Regia Marina with protecting the central Mediterranean supply routes. However, this directive came at a time when the Regia Marina faced daunting odds. In 1940, the Italian navy boasted two modernized battleships and 19 cruisers. In stark contrast, the combined British and French Mediterranean fleets comprised three aircraft carriers, 11 battleships, and 23 cruisers, granting the Allies a 4-to-1 tonnage superiority. This advantage could be further bolstered by reinforcements from outside the Mediterranean.

The strategic positioning of naval forces added another layer of complexity to the situation. The British fleet was anchored at Gibraltar and Alexandria, with a notable absence of ships at Malta. The French fleet was stationed at Toulon in southern France and Bizerte in northern Tunisia. Meanwhile, the primary Italian bases were located at Naples and Taranto, with additional forces in Sicilian ports. The geographical layout presented a tactical challenge for the Italian forces, which could unite by traversing the Strait of Messina, a narrow and vulnerable passage susceptible to enemy ambush.

A critical aspect of Italy's naval strategy, or the lack thereof, was the control over naval aviation. Post-World War I, the Regia Marina had advocated for a naval air arm. However, following the establishment of the Regia Aeronautica in 1923, it lost control over naval aviation. The proponents of land-based air power favored land-based aircraft for all maritime aviation needs, except for reconnaissance, which was reluctantly accepted as a necessity for the navy. This division of responsibilities led to a neglect of naval preferences for aircraft carriers and specialized aircraft.

The Regia Aeronautica's doctrine of independent air operations paid little heed to the Regia Marina's needs. This situation stifled promising developments in air-launched torpedoes and hindered the navy's efforts in 1938 to gain control of a naval torpedo-bomber force, despite the lessons learned from British experiments with torpedo-bombers.

The 10th of June 1940 marked a pivotal moment in World War II, as Italy declared war on the United Kingdom and France. This declaration set in motion a series of events that would significantly shape the Mediterranean theatre of the war.

Pietro Badoglio, the Italian Chief of Staff, anticipated a bold move by the British forces into the Cyrenaican eastern part of Libya, spearheaded by armored units. In response, the Italian naval forces sprung into action. On 11 June, the 3a Divisione incrociatori and 7a Divisione incrociatori embarked on a patrol mission in the Strait of Sicily. The very next day, they spotted two British cruisers to the south of Crete, moving westward. In a strategic response, the 3a Divisione incrociatori, accompanied by two destroyer squadrons, set out to patrol the route to Malta. Meanwhile, the 30 Squadrone incrociatori and 80 Squadrone incrociatori were assigned to patrol the Ionian Sea, with additional destroyer squadrons navigating the waters between Sicily and Malta.

On 12 June, the conflict intensified when a 'Giovanni Berta' class Italian naval trawler met its demise off Tobruk, sunk by two British cruisers and four destroyers. In a significant counter, the Italian submarine Alpino Bagnolini successfully sank the British light cruiser Calypso to the south of Crete. Adding to the Italian efforts, from 11 June to 16 August, the specialized Gruppo 'Orata' undertook a critical mission to dredge up seven British cables from the seabed around Malta, seizing thousands of yards of cable to prevent their reconnection.

Confronted with the challenge of escorting merchant ships to Tobruk, the Italian navy made a strategic decision to employ warships and submarines for supply delivery. On 19 June, the submarine Zoea embarked on a mission to Tobruk, laden with ammunition. The following day, a destroyer squadron led by Artigliere left Augusta in Sicily for Benghazi, carrying troops and anti-tank guns. In a similar vein, on 25 June, a convoy with escorts departed Naples for Tripoli, transporting supplies and 1,727 troops. The submarine Bragadin also set sail for Libya, carrying equipment for the Tobruk airfield.

The Italian navy's tactical acumen was further demonstrated by the selection of the 'Turbine' class destroyers of the 20 Squadrone cacciatorpediniere (Espero, Zeffiro, and Ostro) for their high-speed capabilities, tasked with transporting anti-tank units. Additionally, two smaller World War I-era escort vessels, Pilo and Giuseppe Missori, carrying 52 troops and additional supplies, departed from Taranto for Tobruk.

The British navy, not to be outdone, planned an anti-submarine sweep near the Ionian island of Kythira on 27 June, with plans to proceed to Malta to form the close escort for the MF.1 and MS.2 convoys to Alexandria. However, intelligence about Italian submarines prompted a change in their route, leading them through the Kasos Strait, east of Crete, then north of the island, and onwards past Kythira to Malta. The RAF's No. 201 Group, operating Short Sunderland four-engined flying boats from Malta, was to collaborate with these naval operations in the Ionian Sea.

In a complex logistical operation, the passenger liner El Nil, along with the Knight of Malta and the interned Italian ship Rodi, which were at Malta when Italy declared war, formed the 13-knot MF.1 fast convoy as part of 'MA3.' Meanwhile, five slower ships (Zeeland, Kirkland, Masirah, Novasli, and Tweed), laden with naval stores for Alexandria, constituted the 9-knot MS.1 slow convoy, set to depart from Malta for Alexandria. The MF.1 convoy played a critical role in evacuating civilians from Malta, necessitating the deployment of virtually the entire Mediterranean Fleet in the 'MA5' operation for its protection. Additionally, the AS.1 convoy, comprising seven ships, was scheduled to sail from the Dardanelles to Egypt, with four ships joining from Thessaloniki, Piraeus, and Smyrna. This convoy, escorted by the light cruisers Capetown and Caledon of the 3rd Cruiser Squadron and the destroyers Garland, Nubian, Mohawk, and Vampire, was due to depart from Cape Helles early on 28 June.

The intricate choreography of naval maneuvers in the Mediterranean Sea during World War II reached a critical point on 30 June 1940. The strategic orchestration of the departures of various naval elements was meticulously planned to ensure that three key convoys converged at Position K, located south of Cape Matapan, approximately midway between Malta and Alexandria. This alignment of forces was a testament to the precision and complexity of naval warfare at the time.

At the heart of these movements was the 7th Cruiser Squadron, also known as Force 'C', under the adept command of Vice Admiral J. C. Tovey. This formidable squadron comprised five light cruisers of the 1st Cruiser Division, including the 'Leander' class ships Orion, Neptune, and the Australian Sydney, each armed with eight 6-inch guns. The 2nd Cruiser Division, featuring the 'Town' class ships Liverpool and Gloucester, each equipped with twelve 6-inch guns, was also part of this powerful assembly. Their mission was to navigate to the west of Crete, near Position K, ready for any eventuality.

The 1st Battle Squadron, under the command of Rear Admiral H. D. Pridham-Wippell, further bolstered the Allied presence in the region. This squadron included the battleships Royal Sovereign and Ramillies, the aircraft carrier Eagle, and the 2nd Destroyer Flotilla. They were positioned to the south-west of Crete, also near Position K, poised to intervene if the situation demanded.

On 26 June, at 18.00, the light cruisers Caledon, Garland, and Vampire departed Alexandria, aiming to rendezvous with their counterparts, Capetown, Nubian, and Mohawk, the following day while en route to the Dardanelles. At the break of dawn on 27 June, five ships of the 2nd Destroyer Flotilla set sail from Alexandria, followed by the departure of the 7th Cruiser Squadron for Position K at 11.00.

As dusk fell, the 2nd Destroyer Flotilla, comprising Voyager, Dainty, Decoy, Defender, and Ilex, was approximately 230 miles north of Alexandria. At 18.28, while southeast of Crete, the flotilla encountered the Italian submarine Console Generale Liuzzi. Following a tense and intense engagement, involving depth charge attacks and a subsequent surfacing of the damaged submarine, a dramatic rescue unfolded. The destroyers, led by Dainty, embarked on a rescue operation, picking up Italian survivors from the water. This operation, marked by acts of bravery and maritime skill, lasted over three hours, culminating in the sinking of the Console Generale Liuzzi, either by scuttling or by depth charges, depending on the source.

The next day, on 28 June, a new development occurred when the Italian destroyers of the 'Espero' convoy were spotted by a Sunderland flying boat of Malta-based No. 228 Squadron. The sighting, approximately 58 miles west of the island of Zakynthos in the Ionian Sea, indicated that the Italian ships might be heading for the island of Kythira. In response, Vice Admiral Tovey, commanding the 7th Cruiser Squadron, initiated a calculated pursuit. At 16.10, the squadron turned north to intercept the Italian ships, and by 16.40, following another sighting by a Sunderland, adjusted their course to the southwest, increasing speed to 25 knots. The cruisers, split into two divisions, the 1st Cruiser Division and the 2nd Cruiser Division, were now in a high-speed chase to engage the Italian convoy.

On the evening of their engagement, the Italian destroyers, burdened by age, heavy loads, and rough sea conditions, were struggling to maintain their high speed while heading southeast. At approximately 18:30, about 120 miles north of Tobruk, the British cruiser Liverpool caught sight of them. Mere minutes later, Liverpool opened fire from a distance of 18,000 yards. Despite the Italian destroyers' legendary speed, the British cruisers were gradually closing the gap.

Caught off guard and unable to launch torpedoes due to their deck cargoes, the Italian ships resorted to creating smoke screens and maneuvering evasively. This, coupled with the gathering darkness and their alignment with the afterglow of the setting sun, made them challenging targets. However, at 19:05, Neptune reported incoming torpedoes, prompting the British ships to change course.

The 2nd Cruiser Division, focusing their assault on Espero, and by 19:20, had significantly narrowed the distance to 14,000 yards. Meanwhile, the 1st Cruiser Division made a sharp turn to starboard, allowing them to bring all their guns to bear. It wasn't until the 15th salvo that Espero was hit. Recognizing the dire situation, Captain Baroni of Espero made a selfless decision to sacrifice his ship to allow Zeffiro and Ostro an opportunity to escape. He ordered Espero to create smoke and execute evasive maneuvers, drawing the enemy's attention as the other two ships made their escape to the southwest.

By 20:00, Espero was critically hit and immobilized. As night fell and with ammunition running low, Vice Admiral Tovey, commanding the British forces, called off the chase, redirecting his ships towards Malta. Sydney was tasked with sinking Espero. Approaching to within 6,000 yards, Sydney exchanged fire with Espero, scoring direct hits. Espero, engulfed in flames, began to sink around 20:40. Sydney launched a rescue operation, deploying boats and using ladders and chairs to bring survivors aboard. However, due to the risk of Italian submarines and the blazing Espero, the rescue was halted at 22:19, after 47 survivors were brought on board. Sydney left a cutter equipped with essentials and a signal projector for any remaining survivors.

This engagement, lasting around 2 hours and 10 minutes, saw the 7th Cruiser Squadron expend approximately 5,000 shells. A stray 120-mm Italian shell struck Liverpool, causing minimal damage. Some prisoners aboard Sydney revealed the operation's objective and the tragic fate of Captain Baroni, who was believed to have been killed in a bridge explosion. However, other survivors, including two officers, later claimed that Baroni had survived the initial explosion but chose to go down with his ship.

This battle underscored the challenges of daylight naval engagements at long range, highlighting their potential to be indecisive and excessively draining on ammunition. The British fleet at Alexandria faced a critical shortage of 6-inch shells, with only 800 remaining in stock, illustrating the tangible costs of such engagements.

Following the intense naval engagements, the 2nd Cruiser Division found itself critically low on ammunition, necessitating a return to Alexandria. This shortage of munitions, coupled with the looming threat of Italian submarines, led to the deferral of the scheduled Malta convoys. The 1st Cruiser Division, having faced ineffectual bombing, made its way back to Alexandria, arriving on 1 July. Concurrently, the AS.1 convoy, navigating through the Aegean Sea, endured attacks from Italian aircraft stationed in the Dodecanese islands from 29 June to 1 July. Despite these challenges, the convoy reached Alexandria and Port Said undamaged by 2 and 3 July. These events set the stage for the subsequent MF5 operation, which would eventually culminate in the 'Battle of Punta Stilo' on 9 July.

In a separate but significant development on 29 June, the 2nd Destroyer Flotilla encountered the Italian submarine Uebi Scebeli. Spotted on the surface 184 miles west of Crete, the submarine was forced to dive by the flotilla and subsequently subjected to depth charge attacks. These assaults compelled the submarine to resurface, allowing for the rescue of survivors. The Uebi Scebeli was then sunk by gunfire from the destroyer Dainty at 08:20. Following this action, the destroyers set course for Alexandria, arriving there around 19:00 on 30 June. The captured crew spoke of a submarine patrol line between Crete and the North African coast, prompting the dispatch of two destroyers from Alexandria to Derna for an anti-submarine mission. Although they attacked and claimed to have sunk a submerged submarine on 1 July, this claim was later disallowed after their return on 2 July. Meanwhile, the Italian destroyers Zeffiro and Ostro successfully reached Benghazi on 29 June and subsequently arrived at Tobruk, while the smaller vessels Pilo and Missori were redirected to Tripoli, also reaching Libyan shores.

On 5 July, an audacious aerial assault was launched by nine Fairey Swordfish biplane torpedo-bombers of the Fleet Air Arm's No. 813 Squadron. Flying from Sidi Barrani in western Egypt, they targeted Tobruk harbor. They were escorted by 12 fighters from the RAF's No. 33 Squadron and supported by aircraft from the RAF's No. 211 Squadron, which conducted strafing runs on the airfield, damaging eight Fiat CR.42 fighters and executing reconnaissance missions. The Swordfish bombers successfully deployed seven torpedoes in the harbor, resulting in the sinking of the destroyer Zeffiro and the merchant vessels Manzoni and Serenitas. Additionally, the destroyer Euro and the liner Liguria sustained damage. In a retaliatory move that evening, the Fleet Air Arm's No. 830 Squadron from Malta bombed the airfield at Catania in Sicily.

In another offensive action, the 3rd Cruiser Squadron, comprising Capetown and Caledon along with four destroyers, bombarded the port of Bardia at dawn on 6 July from a distance of 9,000 yards. This bombardment targeted two ships, and the squadron remained on standby to assist any aircraft damaged during the Tobruk raid. Despite counterattacks by Italian aircraft, the British ships sustained no damage. Notably, the guns salvaged from the downed destroyer Zeffiro were later repurposed to enhance the coastal defenses at Bardia. This series of engagements underscored the relentless nature of the Mediterranean conflict, with both sides employing a mix of naval and aerial strategies to assert their dominance and disrupt enemy operations.

Attack on Mers-el-Kébir

The strategic intricacies and anxieties surrounding the French fleet during the early stages of World War II offer a riveting glimpse into the complex geopolitical calculations of the time. In the aftermath of France's fall in 1940, the British War Cabinet faced a daunting scenario: the potential union of the French and German navies. Such an alliance posed a significant threat, potentially overturning the balance of naval power and jeopardizing British maritime interests, including vital Atlantic imports and communication lines across the British Empire.

In a crucial provision, Article 8, Paragraph 2 of the Armistice terms, the German government pledged not to make any claims on the French fleet during peace negotiations. A similar promise was echoed in the armistice with Italy. However, the British regarded these assurances as insufficient to guarantee the French fleet's neutrality. British Prime Minister Winston Churchill, aware of these risks, received assurances from French Admiral François Darlan on June 24th against the possibility of the French fleet joining the Axis powers. Nonetheless, Churchill insisted that the French Navy either align with the Royal Navy or be neutralized in a way that would prevent their ships from falling into enemy hands.

The situation grew more complicated when, on Italy's suggestion, the armistice terms were modified, allowing the French fleet to temporarily remain in North African ports, dangerously close to Italian forces in Libya. This development prompted the British to devise Operation Catapult, aimed at neutralizing the French fleet. This contingency plan emerged in mid-June, amidst growing signs that the French government, under Philippe Pétain, was moving towards a peace settlement with Germany, raising the alarming prospect of the French fleet's capture by the Axis.

Churchill, addressing Parliament, reiterated that the Armistice of June 22, 1940, was a betrayal of the Allied commitment not to seek separate peace deals. He questioned the reliability of such solemn assurances, pointing to the possibility of the armistice being nullified on any grounds of non-compliance.

The French fleet, largely unscathed during the Battle of France, was strategically distributed — approximately 40% in Toulon, near Marseille, another 40% in French North Africa, and the remainder in Britain, Alexandria, and the French West Indies. Although Churchill feared Axis use of the French fleet, logistical challenges such as manning, maintenance, and incompatible armaments made this unlikely. Both Churchill and Hitler perceived the fleet as a potential threat, while French leaders used it as a leverage against the Germans, deterring them from invading unoccupied France and French North Africa. The armistice's terms allowed France to crew its vessels, and Admiral Darlan had ordered the Atlantic fleet to Toulon, with instructions to scuttle the ships if the Germans attempted to seize them.

In parallel, British-French negotiations unfolded. The British urged North African French authorities to either continue the war or surrender the fleet to British control. British officials, including an admiral and the Minister of Information, Duff Cooper, visited Oran and Casablanca in late June. With French Atlantic ports under German control, the British strategic focus included keeping the German fleet out of the Mediterranean, confining the Italian fleet, and blockading French-controlled ports. The Royal Navy, wary of the risks of attacking the French fleet and potentially provoking a French declaration of war, initially hesitated. However, considering the risk of the French capital ships falling into Axis hands, and the difficulty of blockading

North African ports while maintaining Atlantic security, the decision was made to target the less fortified North African base, instead of the heavily defended Toulon.

The French naval stronghold at Mers-el-Kébir in French Algeria bristled with formidable warships under the command of the resolute Admiral Marcel-Bruno Gensoul. This impressive fleet included the venerable battleships Provence, commanded by Rear-Admiral Jacques Bouxin, and Bretagne, under Captain Le Pivain. Joining them were the more modern Force de Raid battleships Dunkerque and Strasbourg, captained by Barois and Louis Collinet, respectively. Accompanying these leviathans was the seaplane tender Commandant Teste, helmed by Captain Lemaire, a squadron of six swift destroyers—Mogador, Volta, Tigre, Lynx, Kersaint, and Le Terrible— led by Rear-Admiral Émile-Marie Lacroix, and the vigilant gunboat Rigault de Genouilly, captained by Louis Georges Emile Frossard.

Meanwhile, the British, wary of these powerful vessels falling into German hands, sent Admiral James Somerville of Force H, stationed in Gibraltar, with a critical mission. His orders were to deliver an ultimatum to the French, presenting terms that defied the German–French armistice. Somerville delegated this delicate task to Captain Cedric Holland, a French-speaking officer from the carrier HMS Ark Royal. Gensoul, taking umbrage at negotiating with a lower-ranking officer, sent his own lieutenant, Bernard Dufay, leading to a mire of delay and confusion.

As the tense negotiations dragged on, the likelihood of reaching an agreement dwindled. The French readied for combat, arming 42 aircraft for imminent take-off. In a critical turn, Admiral Darlan, a key decision-maker, was unreachable, leaving Gensoul to navigate the escalating situation. He informed the French government of two stark choices: either battle or internment, conspicuously omitting the possibility of retreating to the French West Indies—a strategy previously outlined by Darlan in case of foreign attempts to seize the fleet.

The British launched Operation Catapult, a bold move to either seize control of or destroy French naval vessels scattered across various ports, including Britain and Alexandria, Egypt. This operation sprang into action on the night of July 3rd, when British forces unexpectedly boarded French ships docked in Plymouth and Portsmouth. Among these was the world's largest submarine at the time, the Surcouf, docked in Plymouth. The French crew resisted, leading to a tragic skirmish that claimed the lives of three Royal Navy personnel and one French sailor.

The British successfully captured several French vessels, including the aged battleships Paris and Courbet, destroyers Le Triomphant and Léopard, eight torpedo boats, five submarines, and other smaller ships. Meanwhile, the French squadron in Alexandria, led by Admiral René-Émile Godfroy and including notable ships like the battleship Lorraine and the heavy cruiser Suffren, was neutralized through a local agreement.

The British assault force was formidable, featuring the battlecruiser HMS Hood, battleships HMS Valiant and Resolution, the aircraft carrier Ark Royal, and an escort of cruisers and destroyers. They enjoyed a tactical advantage, being mobile and prepared, in stark contrast to the French fleet, which was anchored in a confined harbor and caught off guard. The British battleships' 15-inch guns packed a more powerful broadside than their French counterparts.

In a pre-emptive move on July 3rd, before the termination of negotiations, British Fairey Swordfish planes from Ark Royal, escorted by Blackburn Skuas, dropped magnetic mines in the harbor exit. This operation was challenged by French Curtiss H-75 fighters, resulting in the downing of a Skua and the loss of its two-member crew, marking the only British casualties in this encounter.

Additionally, six French La Galissonnière-class cruisers stationed at Algiers were called to assist but didn't make it in time. The French naval authority at Toulon deployed two submarine groups to attack British ships, especially targeting HMS Hood. Despite these efforts, the French submarines failed to make contact and were recalled.

In a crucial moment, British Prime Minister Winston Churchill ordered the British fleet to open fire. The French battleship Provence responded swiftly, but Dunkerque and Strasbourg, their main armaments positioned forward, were disadvantaged due to their mooring positions. A direct hit on Bretagne led to a catastrophic explosion, sinking the ship with a heavy loss of life. After enduring a barrage of thirty salvoes, the French ceased fire. Although Provence suffered significant damage and Dunkerque was severely hit and grounded, the French destroyers managed to avoid sinking by running aground.

The air battle intensified with the arrival of French Morane-Saulnier M.S.406 fighters, engaging the outnumbered British Skuas. Subsequent dogfights saw additional French Curtiss fighters join the fray, leading to further skirmishes and damage to aircraft on both sides.

The French battleship Strasbourg, accompanied by three destroyers and a gunboat, narrowly escaped a minefield and fled to the open sea. They faced an aerial assault from a squadron of Swordfish bombers from the British aircraft carrier Ark Royal. Displaying remarkable resilience, the French ships managed to shoot down two of the attacking Swordfish, with the crew members later rescued by the British destroyer Wrestler. Meanwhile, a French flying boat launched a counterattack, bombing a British destroyer.

Admiral James Somerville, leading the British force, ordered his ships to give chase as the initial bombing proved ineffective. The French gunboat Rigault de Genouilly encountered the British force, including the formidable battlecruiser HMS Hood. Engaging in a daring exchange of fire with the British light cruisers Arethusa and Enterprise, Rigault de Genouilly managed to return fire before eventually withdrawing after being hit.

In another encounter, a British aircraft located the French submarines Danaé and Eurydice, guiding a British destroyer to them. Despite being depth-charged, both submarines emerged unscathed. British intelligence quickly decoded the French submarines' orders, prompting London to instruct Somerville to take action, but the submarines could not engage with the British Force H.

As the chase continued, the British battleships Valiant and Resolution lagged behind Hood. Somerville received intelligence that a French naval force from Algiers, including heavy and light cruisers and several destroyers, was converging to join Strasbourg. Realizing he would be outnumbered and in a disadvantageous position for a night battle, Somerville called off the pursuit at 8:20 p.m., just as Hood was closing in on Strasbourg. Despite a final attempt by Swordfish aircraft at 8:55 p.m., Strasbourg safely reached Toulon on July 4th. The French cruiser force from Algiers, which missed its rendezvous with Strasbourg, also arrived in Toulon the same day.

Meanwhile, during the night of July 3rd-4th, four French submarines — Ariane, Danaé, Diane, and Eurydice — patrolled off Oran, remaining vigilant until the evening of July 4th. On July 4th, the British submarine Pandora encountered and mistakenly sank the Rigault de Genouilly, believing it to be an enemy cruiser. In response, the French Air Force launched retaliatory raids on Gibraltar, including a minor night attack on July 5th, with many bombs missing their target and landing in the sea.

On July 8th, the British renewed their offensive in Operation Lever. Swordfish aircraft from Ark Royal targeted Mers-el-Kébir, striking the patrol boat Terre-Neuve, laden with depth charges, moored alongside Dunkerque. The resulting explosion from the sinking Terre-Neuve caused significant damage to Dunkerque. The same day, aircraft from the carrier Hermes attacked the Richelieu at Dakar, inflicting serious damage. In anticipation of further British attacks, the French submarines Ariane, Diane, and Eurydice were deployed off Cape Falcon, Algeria, but no subsequent British assault on Oran occurred.

Italian Invasion of Somaliland

The intricate political and military dynamics surrounding the Somaliland border in the late 1930s present a captivating historical narrative, marked by strategic deliberations and shifting alliances. Initially, the border spanned 750 miles, but after Italy's occupation of Ethiopia, nearly its entire length became adjacent to the new Italian colony, except for a 45-mile stretch bordering French Somaliland. The Hornby Report of 1936 revealed the British War Office's startling stance of non-resistance in the event of an invasion, a policy that was met with criticism and concern by Arthur Lawrence, the governor at the time. Lawrence proposed several alternatives, including demilitarization, British withdrawal, or active defense of the colony.

The British military commander, Brigadier Arthur Chater RM, posited that with modest reinforcements, the local garrison could hold off an invasion for twelve days, buying time for relief forces from India. However, this suggestion was not adopted. As tensions escalated in August 1939, the British devised evacuation plans contingent on two scenarios: aligning with the French in Djibouti if they were successful in defense, or retreating into the hills to await further developments if the French were defeated. The defense strategy hinged on cooperation with Legentilhomme, the designated commander of combined forces in wartime.

The onset of the Phoney War brought further complexities. General Wavell, apprehensive about British forces falling under French command, only consented to this arrangement if the retreat to Djibouti was necessary, granting Chater more autonomy but still requiring collaboration with the French. Chater's strategy involved holding positions at Hargeisa and Burao for delaying actions before withdrawing towards the hills. The main road from Djibouti into Somaliland, flanked by six passable hills for wheeled vehicles, became a strategic focal point, with both British and French agreeing on the need to fortify these passes to thwart Italian advances and lay groundwork for an Allied counterattack.

However, in December 1939, the British stance shifted dramatically, mandating resistance against any invasion and insisting on maintaining Berbera for as long as possible for imperial prestige. This commitment to the French, who had invested heavily in fortifying their colony, was complicated by internal disagreements within both the British and French administrations and alliances. This discord resulted in the critical passes at Jirreh and Dobo, along the border, remaining unfortified despite approval for defenses within the British colony.

In 1940, the strategic composition of the British forces in Somaliland presented a complex and multifaceted defense system. The Somaliland Camel Corps (SCC), numbering 631, were strategically positioned across five locations in the colony. Their arsenal included 29 motor vehicles, 122 horses, and 244 camels. However, they were equipped with outdated Belgian .475 caliber single-shot rifles, machine guns, and anti-tank rifles, supported by 1.4 million rounds of questionable quality ammunition.

The British government's plans in February to bolster these forces with 1,100 reinforcements were hampered by bureaucratic delays between the War Office and the Colonial Office. The first infantry battalion's arrival was postponed until May 15, and the second until July 12. Meanwhile, the garrison in French Somaliland was tasked with securing the Jirreh and Dobo passes. The British strategy largely hinged on the hope that the Italians would find French Somaliland a more appealing target.

By August, after the Armistice of Villa Incisa, the British forces in Somaliland had evolved into a diverse assembly. The garrison included the 1st Battalion Northern Rhodesia Regiment, the 2nd (Nyasaland) Battalion King's African Rifles, the 1st East African Light Battery, units from the Colony of Aden, and the SCC, now reinforced by officers and NCOs from the Southern Rhodesia Regiment. The 2nd Battalion, Black Watch, joined on August 8. This eclectic mix of troops, with varying customs and dietary needs, faced challenges due to inadequate artillery, transport, and communication equipment. Air support was limited, with only two 3-inch anti-aircraft guns available from Aden.

The British anticipated an Italian invasion targeting Berbera, due to the impracticality of defending the extensive frontier with Ethiopia and the lack of defensible positions along the coastal approach. The interior mountainous terrain was navigable by vehicles only through specific routes like the Hargeisa road and the Sheikh Pass near Burao.

Chater's defensive strategy involved stationing two battalions and mountain artillery at Tug Argan, with another battalion guarding alternate approaches and one kept in reserve. The arrival of the Black Watch allowed for strategic adjustments, with the 3/15th Punjab Regiment reinforcing Tug Argan. The Camel Corps played a crucial role in frontline defense, conducting patrols and delaying actions with the assistance of the Somali Police Force.

The Royal Air Force (RAF) in Aden comprised several squadrons, including Bristol Blenheim bombers, Gloster Gladiator fighters, and Vickers Wellesley aircraft. Notably, the RAF also included two Free French Martin Marylands and a Bristol Bombay from 216 Squadron, reflecting the multinational nature of the defense efforts.

In 1940, the Italian military, under the command of Duke Amedeo, Duke of Aosta, harbored deep suspicions regarding French military intentions in the region. This concern intensified after the replacement of General

Legentilhomme with General Germaine, leading to fears of a potential British invasion through Djibouti. Aosta, motivated by a desire to preempt British actions, proposed an ambitious plan to Mussolini on June 18, which involved occupying Djibouti and simultaneously advancing on Berbera to deter British intervention. In August, Aosta received Mussolini's approval for this invasion.

While awaiting authorization, Aosta and his deputy, General Guglielmo Nasi, conducted a thorough assessment of the opposition and campaign objectives. On July 14, they concluded that the decisive battles would likely occur in the Karim and Jerato passes. They anticipated that if the defenders held their ground, Italian forces could outflank them.

The Italian invasion force was formidable, comprising five colonial brigades, three Blackshirt battalions, five Bande units, a contingent of M11/39 medium tanks and L3/35 tankettes, several armored cars, 21 howitzer batteries, pack artillery, and air support.

Lieutenant-General Carlo de Simone, as the commander of the primary force, the Harrar Division, outlined his strategy on July 25. This division included eleven African infantry battalions, organized into three brigades, along with the Blackshirt battalions, tanks, and armored cars. The objective was to prevent the French and British forces from uniting or receiving reinforcements, thereby facilitating the occupation of British Somaliland.

Given the Assa Hills' elevation of over 4,500 feet and their parallel position to the coast about 50 miles inland, the Italians identified three viable approaches to Berbera for wheeled and tracked vehicles. The western column, under the direction of Lieutenant-General Sisto Bertoldi, was tasked with sealing off French Somaliland and then advancing eastwards along the coast road towards Berbera. Meanwhile, the eastern column, led by Brigadier-General Arturo Bertello, would move towards Odweina and Burao in the south, covering the flank of the central column and ready to link up if necessary.

De Simone, with the central column, planned to establish a base at Hargeisa and Adalek, then lead the primary assault through the Mirgo Pass towards Berbera.

On July 31, the 18th Squadron arrived at the Scelene airstrip near Dire Dawa, equipped with six Ca 133 bomber/transport aircraft, marking a significant escalation in preparations for the invasion of British Somaliland. This development led to the formation of the Western Sector Tactical Command (Comando Tattico dell Settore Aeronautica Ovest, CTSAO) on August 1, under Generale Collalti. The CTSAO initially commanded a fleet comprising 27 bombers, 23 fighters, and seven reconnaissance aircraft.

That very afternoon, a formation of three SM 81 bombers targeted shipping off Zeila, coinciding with an offensive by two waves of six Blenheim Mk Is from the 8th and 39th squadrons. These were escorted by two Blenheim IVFs from the 203 Squadron, aimed at bombing the newly discovered Italian airfield at Chinele. Despite heavy anti-aircraft fire and a counterattack from CR 42 fighters of the 410th Squadron based in Dire Dawa, the Blenheims managed to execute their mission.

The aerial engagement intensified as Captain Corrado Ricci of the 410th Squadron, flying a CR 32, managed to shoot down a Blenheim. Meanwhile, Blenheim crews observed and engaged a flight of SM 81 bombers attacking Zeila, successfully downing one of the Italian aircraft. The following day, 39 Squadron's raid on Chinele aerodrome was met by CR 42s from the 413th Squadron, leading to a forced landing by the squadron commander, Capitano Corrado Santoro, due to engine damage.

By August 3, British air reconnaissance reported approximately 400 Italian troops crossing the frontier at Biyad. With Nasi coordinating with de Simone through wireless and liaison aircraft, the Italian central column advanced towards Hargeisa and Tug Argan in the Assa Hills, while the western column progressed towards Zeila and the eastern column moved east for Odweina.

This multi-directional advance aimed to confuse the defenders and seize opportunities.

On the morning of August 4, as the central column approached Hargeisa, they were engaged in skirmishes by the Somaliland Camel Corps, aiming to delay their progress. That afternoon, three SM 81s bombed Berbera, and a Gladiator from 94 Squadron intercepted an Italian bomber from the 15th Squadron, causing casualties. Additionally, two SM 79 bombers from the 44th Group arrived at Dire Dawa, and two Gladiators from the 94 Squadron at Berbera were relocated to Laferug to be closer to Tug Argan. Despite these movements, the main defense at Berbera, including two 3-inch anti-aircraft guns, remained focused on protecting the port. Meanwhile, an attempt by 216 Squadron at Aden to bomb Dire Dawa was thwarted by a lightning storm, forcing the crew to divert to Zula.

On August 5, as the Italian invasion force took control of Hargeisa, they were supported by reconnaissance missions from Ro 37bis aircraft of the 110th Squadron and bombing raids by SM 79s on Zeila, Berbera, and Aden. The Italian air strength was bolstered by the arrival of additional SM 79s from Addis Ababa and Ca 133s from Doghabur. Meanwhile, British Blenheim bombers from 8 Squadron launched three attacks on Italian motor columns near Hargeisa, though one Blenheim was downed by a CR 32 fighter from the 410th Squadron.

The Italian eastern column, primarily comprised of Bande units, reached Odweina on August 6 and then veered northwest towards Adadle, a village near Tug Argan, instead of heading towards Burao. The Somaliland Camel Corps (SCC) and Illalo patrols, a local levy force typically engaged in police duties, executed delaying actions against the Italian advance as British and Commonwealth forces retreated towards Tug Argan. During an early morning offensive, twelve Italian light tanks were met with resistance from the SCC and Northern Rhodesia Regiment, resulting in three tanks being disabled by anti-tank rifle fire.

On August 6, Blenheim bombers from 8 and 39 squadrons continued reconnaissance and bombing missions against Italian columns. In one engagement, a Blenheim was heavily damaged by repeated attacks from CR 42 fighters, leading the Italians to claim a downed bomber. Following the capture of Hargeisa, Italian CR 32 and CR 42 fighters from Dire Dawa commenced patrols, and Ca 133s conducted bombing runs over the front.

The Italians, after regrouping in Hargeisa for two days, resumed their advance through the Karim Pass towards Tug Argan in the Assa Hills. Despite Aosta's urge for speed, Nasi proceeded cautiously due to the deteriorating road conditions and weather. As the Italian forces approached British defenses, reports of Italian medium tanks prompted the captain of HMAS Hobart to donate the ship's QF 3-pounder Hotchkiss saluting gun, along with ammunition and a crew, to the British defense.

The British defenses at Berbera were further strained when two Gladiators were destroyed in an airstrike by Italian fighters. In response, Blenheim IVFs from 203 Squadron in Aden patrolled Berbera, engaging SM 79 bombers. During these aerial encounters, one SM 79 was damaged and a crew member killed. Additionally, the Italians bombed key passes and continued reconnaissance and fighter patrols, with some aircraft damaged in landing accidents at Hargeisa.

Meanwhile, the Bertoldi column captured Zeila, effectively severing communications with French Somaliland, and began a gradual southeast advance along the coast road. Despite facing air attacks from Aden and naval bombardments, the Italians pushed back the SCC rearguards to the village of Bulhar by August 17.

As the situation intensified, General Wavell, before leaving Cairo for talks in London, ordered significant reinforcements from the Indian Army to Somaliland. However, the arrival of Major-General Reade Godwin-Austen to command the enlarged force and the decision to send anti-aircraft guns to the colony were counteracted by the rapidly evolving situation. Godwin-Austen's arrival on July 11 and subsequent command were overshadowed by the delay of reinforcements, which were ultimately redirected to Sudan.

Between August 7th and 8th, the defensive forces at Tug Argan received significant reinforcements, including the 1/2nd Punjab Regiment and the 2nd Battalion Black Watch. By August 10th, Italian commander de Simone had strategically positioned his forces near the British positions at Tug Argan, gearing up for an assault. The geography of the area played a crucial role in the unfolding events. The road from Hargeisa to Tug Argan, winding through the Kerim Pass, is flanked by the Assa hills to the south and a series of hills and dry riverbeds (tugs) to the north. This terrain, characterized by a flat stone landscape interspersed with thorn bushes, tugs, and rocky hills, posed unique challenges and opportunities for both attackers and defenders.

The British positions, named Black, Knobbly, Mill, and Observation hills, along with Castle Hill, were fortified with machine-gun posts and some barbed wire. Despite these fortifications, the defense strategy was hampered by the limited artillery support and the inability to fully cover the gap between the hills. The spacing between these hills also allowed potential paths for the attacking forces. Castle Hill, positioned behind the other hills, offered limited strategic depth for defense. The presence of camel tracks through the Mirgo Pass and the Jerato Pass in the Assa Hills further provided avenues for the numerically superior Italian forces to maneuver.

On the morning of August 9th, Italian fighters conducted a strafing run on the airfield at Berbera but encountered only a damaged Blenheim. Personnel at the base, along with the Australian cruiser Hobart anchored in the harbor, retaliated with gunfire, including machine-gun fire from the cruiser. The previously damaged Gladiator aircraft was subsequently dismantled and transported to Aden.

By August 10th, the Italian northern column had advanced to Zeila, despite facing naval bombardments and bombing raids from aircraft based in Aden. The rough terrain eventually impeded the column's progress, with vehicle tires being damaged.

From August 7th to 8th, the defenders at Tug Argan were bolstered by the arrival of the 1/2nd Punjab Regiment and the 2nd Battalion Black Watch. By August 10th, Italian commander de Simone had positioned his forces close to the British positions, preparing for an assault. The road from Hargeisa to Tug Argan, passing through the Kerim Pass and between various hills and dry riverbeds, offered a challenging terrain for both sides. The British defenses, comprising hills named Black, Knobbly, Mill, and Observation, along with Castle Hill, were fortified but had limitations due to the sparse artillery and wide gaps between the hills.

On August 10th, the Australians from the cruiser Hobart, armed with a Hotchkiss gun, joined the defense at Tug Argan. Despite its limited rate of fire and ammunition, the gun provided some support. The Italians intensified their air operations, with CR 32 and CR 42 fighters from Dire Dawa and bomber reinforcements from Addis Ababa and Doghabur. British Blenheim bombers from 8 Squadron carried out dive bombing missions against Italian positions, encountering fierce resistance from Italian fighters.

On August 11th, the Italians launched a concerted attack on the western end of the Assa Hills, successfully pushing back the 3rd Battalion, 15th Punjab Regiment, and later repelling a counter-attack. The British air force from Aden engaged in bombing missions against Italian artillery positions, facing stiff anti-aircraft and fighter opposition.

The situation escalated on August 12th with simultaneous attacks on all British positions, leading to the capture of Mill Hill by the Italians after intense resistance. The defenders of Knobbly Hill managed to repel another attack, but the Italians succeeded in cutting off a convoy carrying essential supplies.

Amidst these developments, Italian air support continued to target British positions and supply lines. On August 14th, Castle Hill and Observation Hill came under heavy bombardment, but the attack on Observation Hill was unsuccessful. Mussolini, recognizing the strategic importance of the operation, ordered a full-scale Italian assault with air support.

Despite ongoing air attacks and ground assaults, the British conducted a counter-attack towards Mirgo Pass, which initially showed promise but was eventually pushed back by Italian forces. The overwhelming Italian artillery and the fatigue of the defenders made the situation increasingly untenable. General Godwin-Austen, realizing the futility of further resistance, informed his superiors that withdrawal was the most viable option.

Wavell, who had been in London, was kept informed of the developments and relayed the decision to evacuate the colony to London. Churchill, upon hearing the news, acknowledged the necessity of the decision. The planned withdrawal aimed to save a significant portion of the force, with a strategic retreat to Barkasan and then Nasiyeh, close to Berbera. The evacuation plan involved moving civilians first, followed by troops, with the timing dictated by the challenging monsoon conditions.

On August 15th, Italian bombers from CTSAO continued their support for the ground forces, with Ca 133s targeting the area around Laferug and SM 79s bombing troops near Berbera. In a remarkable aerial encounter, six Blenheim I bombers en route from Iraq to reinforce RAF Aden engaged and shot down an SM 81. These bombers were then handed over to Aden, and their crews returned to Iraq.

On the ground, after a prolonged bombardment, Italian forces captured Observation Hill, leading to a retreat by the Northern Rhodesian Regiment from Black, Knobbly, and Castle hills. A rearguard, formed by the Black Watch, 2nd KAR, and elements of the 1/2nd Punjab Regiment, took positions at Barkasan on the road to Berbera, while other troops moved to Nasiyeh.

The CTSAO focused its efforts on the port of Berbera. Dawn air raids by SM 81 bombers were met with anti-aircraft fire, causing damage to the attacking planes. The Italians also conducted midday bombing runs and faced engagement with Martin Marylands from the Free French flight in 8 Squadron.

With the Italian forces cautiously following up on the British retreat, they attacked the Barkasan defenders on August 17th. Despite several counter-attacks and resistance by the Black Watch, the Italian forces were gradually outflanking the British defenses. The evacuation at Berbera proceeded more smoothly than anticipated, allowing for an orderly withdrawal of the rearguard units.

The Italian air operations continued with bombings of British positions, including the captured landing ground at Hargeisa and the British residency at Sheikh. However, a Blenheim from 39 Squadron was downed by ground fire during a reconnaissance mission.

On August 18th, three Blenheims from 11 Squadron attacked Italian vehicles near Laferug but were intercepted by Italian CR 32 fighters, leading to the downing of one Blenheim. The RAF's bombing missions also targeted Addis Ababa airfield, causing significant damage to Italian aircraft and facilities.

Meanwhile, the Italian forces continued their advance, eventually overcoming the second British defensive line before Berbera. As the evacuation neared completion, the cruiser Hobart stayed behind to collect stragglers and oversee the destruction of equipment and supplies. The Royal Navy successfully evacuated over 7,000 people, including front-line troops, civilians, and the sick.

Interestingly, Italian interference with the evacuation was minimal, possibly influenced by Aosta's order to Nasi to allow the British to evacuate with limited conflict, hoping for a peace agreement through Vatican mediation.

The final CTSAO raid targeted Berbera as British forces vacated the town, leaving much of it in flames and under Italian control. Mussolini subsequently annexed the colony to the Italian East Africa, expanding the Italian Empire.

Greco-Italian War

In the early months of 1939, the tension between Italy and Greece escalated dramatically, fueled by Mussolini's aggressive foreign policy. On February 4th, Mussolini delivered a significant speech to the Fascist Grand Council, accusing France and the United Kingdom of confining Italy and expressing his desire for territorial expansion. This speech marked Greece as a key adversary, intensifying the already strained relations.

The situation worsened when Italy invaded Albania in April. Greece, sensing the looming threat, ramped up its defensive measures. Meanwhile, Italy was busy enhancing Albanian infrastructure for easier military movement. Emanuele Grazzi, the new Italian ambassador to Athens, arrived with the aim of mending Italian-Greek relations. Despite his efforts and Greek leader Metaxas' willingness, Grazzi found himself hindered by the lack of clear policy instructions from Italy and often remained uninformed about his country's actual intentions towards Greece.

Tensions soared due to the anti-Greek propaganda in the Italian media and provocative actions by Italian officials. During Foreign Minister Galeazzo Ciano's visit to Albania, there were public displays supporting Albanian claims on Greek territories. The Italian Dodecanese governor shut down Greek schools, and Italian troops were overheard singing about conquering Greek lands. By August, Italian military preparations near the Greek border had intensified, and Metaxas had already put Greek forces on high alert, anticipating an imminent conflict.

Despite Britain and France's public declaration on April 13, 1939, to safeguard the independence of Greece and Romania, the British remained reluctant to fully commit to Greece. Their strategy was to keep Mussolini neutral in the anticipated conflict with Germany, viewing a Greek alliance as a potential drain on their resources. Consequently, with British support, Greek Prime Minister Metaxas extended diplomatic gestures to Italy in August. Mussolini, in a letter to Metaxas on September 12, assured him that Italian forces in Albania would retreat from the Greek border if Italy entered the war, and even proposed selling aircraft to Greece.

However, as Italy's entry into World War II loomed in May 1940, the Italian press launched an anti-Greek campaign, painting Greece as a puppet of foreign powers and criticizing its tolerance of British naval presence. After France's defeat, the relationship between Italy and Greece soured further. Claims of British naval activities in Greek waters were exaggerated but not entirely baseless, as Greece had limited its exports to Germany and allowed the British use of its merchant fleet.

Mussolini, envisioning a "parallel war" allied with but independent of Germany, aspired to conquer territories in the Balkans. His frustration grew with Germany's opposition to Italian expansion in the region and his forced cancellation of plans to invade Yugoslavia. Meanwhile, Italian military forces intensified their aggression towards Greece, attacking Greek naval vessels and harbors.

The summer of 1940 saw Ciano, the Italian Foreign Minister, aggressively advocating for the invasion of Greece, which he saw as a demonstration of his effective control over Albania. Ciano's manipulation of Mussolini, using the exaggerated tale of Daut Hoxha's death, fueled Mussolini's animosity towards Greece. This led to a coordinated press campaign in Italy and Albania against Greece, under the guise of avenging Hoxha, falsely portrayed as a martyred patriot. Despite these hostile actions and rhetoric, the intent behind them was believed to be more about intimidation than an actual precursor to war.

On August 15, 1940, coinciding with a significant Greek religious holiday, the Dormition of the Theotokos, the Italian submarine Delfino sank the Greek light cruiser Elli in Tinos harbour. This act followed Mussolini and Navy Chief Domenico Cavagnari's directive to attack neutral shipping. Cesare Maria De Vecchi, the Italian governor, escalated the situation by ordering the Delfino to attack any vessel near Tinos and Syros, suggesting an impending war. On the same day, Italian planes bombarded another Greek ship near Crete. Despite the Greek government's claim of an unknown submarine's involvement, the public was outraged, suspecting Italian responsibility. Ambassador Grazzi, who believed in Italian-Greek friendship and was unaware of Italy's aggressive shift, tried to smooth tensions, leaving Metaxas, the Greek Prime Minister, uncertain of Italy's true intentions.

This period also saw German intervention, advising Italy to focus on Britain and avoid Balkan conflicts. This advice, combined with the start of Italy's invasion of Egypt, delayed Italy's plans for Greece and Yugoslavia. However, Mussolini, feeling humiliated by Hitler's lack of consultation on foreign policy, advanced his plans to invade Greece independently.

On October 13, Mussolini informed Marshal Badoglio of Italy's impending war with Greece. Badoglio, initially under the impression that only Epirus would be targeted, was caught off guard when he learned of plans to occupy all of Greece. He noted that such an operation would require significant resources and time, but his concerns were not pressed further. King Victor Emmanuel III, instead of opposing the war, supported Mussolini, anticipating an easy victory and the prospect of adding another crown to his titles.

The Italian invasion of Greece unfolded with multiple columns advancing through different sectors. On the far right, the coastal group aimed south towards Konispol, with its ultimate goal being the capture of Igoumenitsa and then advancing towards Preveza. In the central sector, the Siena Division split into two columns heading towards Filiates, whereas the Ferrara Division, divided into four columns, targeted the main Greek defensive line at Kalpaki with the objective of seizing Ioannina. In the challenging Pindus sector, the Julia Division dispatched five columns to take Metsovo, intending to isolate Greek forces in Epirus from the eastern regions.

As the Italian offensive began, General Alexandros Papagos, previously the Chief of the Hellenic Army General Staff, was appointed as the commander-in-chief of the newly formed General Headquarters. The Army General Staff's responsibilities were transferred to Lieutenant-General Konstantinos Pallis, who was brought out of retirement for this role.

The Greek high command, reassured of Bulgarian neutrality and Turkish support in case of a Bulgarian attack, was able to focus the majority of its forces against the Italians in Albania. Substantial troop deployments were shifted from the Bulgarian front to the Albanian front, including nearly half of the forces previously stationed on the Bulgarian border (notably the 13th and 17th Divisions, and the 16th Infantry Brigade) along with the entire general reserve. This reserve consisted of the I Army Corps with its 2nd, 3rd, and 4th Infantry Divisions, as well as the Cretan 5th Infantry Division and the Cavalry Division, all redirected to confront the Italian invasion in Albania.

Battle of Elaia–Kalamas

In the Epirus sector, General Charalambos Katsimitros positioned five battalions along the border to impede the Italian advance. He established his primary defense at Kalpaki pass, manned by nine battalions, forming a convex front. Additionally, Major-General Nikolaos Lioumbas was in charge of two battalions in the coastal Thesprotia sector. The Kalamas river's swamps, particularly near Kalpaki, posed significant challenges for both armored and infantry movements. Another battalion and some artillery were initially sent to Preveza in anticipation of an Italian landing, but were quickly redirected to reinforce the coastal area when the landing did not occur.

By the night of October 29–30, the Greek forward units had retreated to the Kalpaki line. By November 1, Italian forces engaged the Greek positions. Over the next three days, the Italians prepared their assault, bombarding Greek positions with aircraft and artillery. Meanwhile, General Alexandros Papagos advised Katsimitros to prioritize protecting the Pindus passes and the flanks of Greek forces in western Macedonia, suggesting a strategic withdrawal if necessary. However, Katsimitros chose to defend his position while allocating some forces to guard the right flank along the Aoös River.

On November 1, the Italians captured Konitsa, shifting the focus of their military efforts from Africa to the Albanian front. An Italian amphibious assault on Corfu was canceled due to bad weather and the need for reinforcements in Albania.

The primary Italian assault on the Kalpaki front commenced on November 2. Despite initial gains, including capturing the Grabala heights, the Italians were repelled by Greek counterattacks. By November 8, facing stiff Greek resistance, the Italians began withdrawing to defensive positions, awaiting reinforcements.

In the coastal sector, the Italians initially made progress, pushing Greek units south of the Kalamas River. However, the poor condition of the roads hampered their advance. By November 7, the Italians had reached Margariti, marking their deepest penetration, but the situation was already turning in favor of the Greeks in other sectors.

As the Italian offensive faltered, Visconti Prasca was replaced by General Ubaldo Soddu on November 8. Soddu's assessment highlighted the strong Greek resistance in Epirus and the growing threat in western Macedonia, recommending a defensive posture until reinforcements arrived. With the Italians on the defensive, the Greek 8th Division began counterattacks, regaining lost ground. By November 13, Greek forces had reclaimed positions along the entire length of the Kalamas River. The Epirus sector was taken over by I Army Corps under Lieutenant-General Panagiotis Demestichas, with the 8th Division and the coastal sector under the independent command of Lioumbas.

The Italian 3rd Alpine Division "Julia", commanded by Mario Girotti, posed a significant threat to the Greek defense during the Greco-Italian War. Their strategic advance over the treacherous Pindus Mountains towards Metsovo was a daring move, aiming to sever the Greek forces in Epirus from those in Macedonia. Opposing them was the Greek Pindus Detachment, a modest force of 2,000 reservists from the 51st Regiment. Mobilized as late as August 29th, with one battalion (III/51) still forming by mid-October, these men were tasked with defending a vast 37-kilometer front over challenging terrain.

As the Italian offensive commenced under relentless torrential rain, the Greek positions were rapidly overwhelmed, forcing a retreat from their forward posts, particularly in the central sector. Colonel Davakis, leading the Greeks, had to deploy incoming companies immediately, leaving him without any strategic reserve.

The Greek high command, recognizing the precarious situation, scrambled to send reinforcements and restructured the command, assigning the Pindus sector to the more robust 1st Infantry Division. Despite the onset of harsh snowfall on October 29th, the relentless Italian assault continued, pushing the Greek lines back towards Samarina.

The Greeks, however, managed to stabilize their position from October 30th. Command in the Pindus sector was transferred to the 1st Division under Major-General Vasileios Vrachnos. Additional forces, including the Cavalry Division, the 5th Brigade, and a newly formed Cavalry Brigade, were positioned strategically to counter the Italian incursion, safeguarding vital mountain passes.

The Julia Division, trudging through 40 kilometers of rugged, icy terrain, captured Vovousa on November 2nd. However, they failed to secure their primary objective, Metsovo, and faced the increasing pressure of Greek reinforcements. On the same day, Colonel Davakis was critically injured near Fourka. The Italians soon realized their untenable position, lacking both manpower and supplies.

On November 3rd, the Italian spearhead found itself encircled. Requests for relief attacks and reinforcements were sent, leading to the deployment of the Bari Division. However, it failed to reach the isolated Italian troops. Notably, the local Greek civilians, including men, women, and children, played a crucial role in assisting the Greek military efforts.

Under intense Greek pressure, the Julia Division suffered devastating losses. By November 4th, the Greeks had recaptured the villages previously taken by the Italians. In less than a week, the Italian forces in this sector were pushed back to their original positions at the war's outset. By November 13th, Greek forces had successfully reclaimed the Grammos and Smolikas mountain ranges, marking a significant turn in the conflict. This setback led to the removal and recall of Visconti Prasca back to Italy, signaling a crucial Greek victory in the battle for the Pindus Mountains.

As of November 14th, the Italian military presence in Albania underwent a significant reorganization, resulting in the formation of two distinct field armies. The Ninth Army, emerging from the XXVI Corps in the Korçë sector, was a formidable force composed of five infantry and two alpine divisions, including elite Alpini troops. Additionally, it included several independent regiments, notably Blackshirt and Albanian battalions. The Eleventh Army, formerly known as the XXV Corps and positioned in the Epirus sector, comprised three infantry divisions, an armored division, a cavalry division, and various independent units.

Despite this reorganization, the Italians faced severe challenges. The troops had been engaged in continuous combat for three weeks and were showing signs of exhaustion. Compounding these difficulties was the logistical nightmare they faced: a shortage of vehicles, horses, and mules severely hampered their supply lines. The limited capacity of Albania's main ports, Valona and Durrës, further exacerbated the situation by creating a bottleneck for essential supplies and reinforcements. An airlift operation set up between Italy and Tirana consumed all of the Italian Air Force's transport capacity, previously allocated to Africa. While this airlift could move troops, it was incapable of transporting heavy equipment.

On the Greek side, the order of battle on November 14th showcased a well-organized military structure. Lieutenant-General Demestichas led the I Corps in the coastal sector, commanding the 2nd, 8th, and Cavalry Divisions, along with the Lioumbas Detachment. Lieutenant-General Papadopoulos headed the II Corps in the Pindus sector, with the 1st Infantry Division, 5th Brigade, and Cavalry Brigade under his command. In western Macedonia, Lieutenant-General Tsolakoglou's III Corps included the 9th, 10th, and 15th Infantry Divisions, with the 11th Division assembling in its rear. These latter two corps were under the strategic direction of TSDM, led by Lieutenant-General Pitsikas. Additionally, the 3rd, 4th, and 5th Infantry Divisions, along with the 16th Brigade, remained in reserve.

By November 12th, General Alexandros Papagos, the Greek commander-in-chief, had successfully deployed over 100 infantry battalions. These forces, well-acquainted with the terrain, faced fewer than fifty Italian battalions, indicating a significant numerical and strategic advantage for the Greeks in this phase of the conflict.

From the onset of November, the Greek III Corps initiated limited incursions into Albanian territory. By November 6th, they had already proposed a plan for a comprehensive offensive. However, General Alexandros Papagos, assessing the plan as overly ambitious at the time, delayed the offensive until November 14th. The primary goal of the III Corps was to seize control of the strategically vital Korçë plateau, which dominated access into Albania's interior via the Devoll river valley. The plateau was defended by Italian forces, including the 29th Piemonte, 19th Venezia, and 49th Parma divisions, and was later reinforced by the 2nd Alpine Division "Tridentina", the 53rd Infantry Division "Arezzo", and a contingent of 30–50 tanks from the Centauro Division.

To secure its rear, the III Corps left behind five battalions, attacking with twenty battalions and 37 artillery batteries. Anticipating challenges from Italian armored units, and lacking tanks or anti-tank weapons of their own, the Greeks opted for a strategy that relied on movement along mountain ridges, avoiding valley floors. The offensive commenced on the morning of November 14th without preliminary artillery bombardment, aiming for the element of surprise.

The Greek strategy proved effective, catching the Italian forces off guard and enabling them to create multiple breaches in the Italian lines between November 14th and 16th. On November 17th, the III Corps was bolstered by the addition of the 13th Division, followed by the 11th Division the next day. These, along with the 10th Division, formed the new "K" Group of Divisions or OMK, under Lieutenant-General Georgios Kosmas.

A critical moment for the Greeks occurred on November 18th when parts of the 13th Division faltered during a poorly coordinated attack, nearly leading to a retreat. The division's commander was promptly replaced by Major-General Sotirios Moutousis, who halted the retreat and stabilized the front. By November 19th–21st, the Greeks had secured the summit of Morava. The Italian forces, fearing encirclement and isolation, retreated towards the Devoll valley overnight. This led to the capture of the city of Korçë by the Greek 9th Division on November 22nd.

By November 27th, the entire Korçë plateau was under Greek control, albeit with significant casualties: 624 dead and 2,348 wounded. Meanwhile, the

Greek I and II Corps successfully expelled Italian forces from Greek territory by November 23rd. The II Corps then advanced across the border, capturing Ersekë on November 21st and Leskovik the following day. Facing mounting military setbacks, Mussolini, under pressure from Marshal Pietro Badoglio and General Roatta, reversed his early October order for demobilization on November 23rd, signaling a shift in Italy's military stance.

After the significant victory of capturing Korçë and pushing Italian forces off Greek territory, the Greek General Headquarters (GHQ) was presented with a strategic dilemma: whether to continue the offensive towards Elbasan in the Korçë sector or to shift their focus to the left flank, aiming for the port of Valona. They opted for the latter, recognizing the immense strategic value of Valona, which would leave the Italians with only Durrës as a viable entry port.

To execute this plan, the GHQ decided that TSDM (comprising III Corps and OMK) would maintain their positions on the right flank and apply continuous pressure on the Italians. Simultaneously, I Corps was tasked with advancing north along the Gjirokastër–Tepelenë–Valona axis, while II Corps would support this movement by securing the connection between I Corps and TSDM, advancing towards Berat in coordination with I Corps. To reinforce this strategy, I Corps was strengthened with the addition of the 3rd Division on November 21st, and II Corps received the 11th Division on November 27th and the Cavalry Division a day later.

Between November 24th and 30th, I Corps progressed northwards along the Drinos river in Albania, while II Corps advanced towards Frashër, capturing it in early December. Meanwhile, TSDM continued to exert pressure, with the 10th Division seizing Moscopole on November 24th and Pogradec falling to the 13th Division without opposition on November 30th.

The Greek advance triggered a crisis within the Italian military hierarchy. The fall of Pogradec and grim reports from the Italian commanders in Albania reportedly led Mussolini to contemplate a truce, mediated by Germany. However, he regained his resolve and instructed General Ugo Cavallero, who replaced Marshal Pietro Badoglio as Chief of the General Staff on December 4th, to hold firm, believing that the Greeks would exhaust their resources. Following this shift, Governor Cesare Maria De Vecchi and Admiral Cavagnari also resigned.

Key victories for the Greek forces continued: I Corps captured Delvinë on December 5th and Gjirokastër on the 8th. The Lioumbas Detachment took Sarandë (renamed Porto Edda in honor of Edda Mussolini) on December 6th. The 2nd Division overcame fierce resistance to secure the Suhë Pass between December 1st–4th, and the 8th Division, despite heavy losses, captured strategic positions near the Kakavia Pass, resulting in significant Italian casualties and the capture of prisoners, artillery, and tanks.

In the TSDM sector, Lieutenant-General Kosmas's command, essentially the 10th Division, captured Ostravicë Mountain on December 12th. III Corps, bolstered by the 17th Division since December 1st, secured the Kamia massif and Pogradec.

On December 2nd, General Papagos, accompanied by Crown Prince Paul, visited the front. Commanders Pitsikas and Tsolakoglou urged an immediate assault on the strategic Klisura Pass. However, Papagos insisted on adhering to the original plan, relegating III Corps to a more passive role—a decision later criticized as it, along with the onset of winter, immobilized the Greek right wing.

Despite the severe winter conditions, the Greek offensive persisted. I Corps, now composed of the 2nd, 3rd, and 4th Divisions (with the 8th Division and the Lioumbas Detachment in reserve), captured Himarë on December 22nd. II Corps, advancing between the Aöos and Apsos rivers, neared Klisura but couldn't secure the pass. To its right, the V Army Corps (formerly the K Group but still primarily the 10th Division) made progress up to Mount Tomorr, ensuring the connection between II and III Corps, which held their positions firmly.

In late December 1940, the Greek General Headquarters (GHQ) decided to halt major offensive operations due to increasing Italian resistance, worsening supply issues, and severe weather conditions, which were causing a high number of frostbite casualties among Greek troops. This decision, effective from January 6, 1941, meant that only local offensive operations to improve Greek lines would be conducted until the weather improved. The Italian forces, comprising eleven infantry divisions, four Alpine divisions, and the 131st Armored Division "Centauro", along with various independent units, were strengthening their positions in Albania. This buildup led General Ugo Cavallero, who assumed overall command in Albania after General Soddu's recall, to plan a counteroffensive aimed at recapturing Korçë in early February.

The key operation planned by the Greek GHQ was the capture of Klisura Pass by II Corps, supported by minor offensives from I Corps and TSDM. The attack began on January 8, with 1st Division on the left and 15th Division, followed by 11th Division, on the right. After intense fighting, especially against the Julia Division, the Greeks managed to capture the pass on January 9. This offensive forced Cavallero to deploy reserves intended for the Korçë counteroffensive, which subsequently never materialized. The Lupi di Toscana division, deployed hastily and underprepared, suffered a disastrous defeat, losing a battalion and retreating with heavy casualties.

On January 26, the Italians attempted to recapture Klisura Pass, but the reinforced II Corps, now including the 5th Division, repelled the attack and launched a counteroffensive. In the ensuing Battle of Trebeshina (February 2-12), the Greeks captured the strategic Trebeshinë massif. The success at Klisura Pass was recognized as a significant Allied victory, earning praise from British Commander Archibald Wavell.

With the growing threat of a German invasion from Bulgaria, General Alexandros Papagos initiated a final push to capture Valona as quickly as possible. The Royal Air Force (RAF) agreed to challenge the air superiority of the Regia Aeronautica and increased close support operations. Despite initial progress towards Tepelenë, Italian resistance and worsening weather halted the Greek advance before reaching Valona or Berat. The Italian defense was costly, but the looming threat of an Italian counteroffensive in the central sector prompted a Greek return to defensive positions.

By February 1941, the Greek Army faced critical shortages in artillery ammunition and other materials, with the Italians possessing ample reserves. Appeals for American aid were made, but British demands took precedence. The limited British material and air support provided thus far was insufficient to significantly alter the Greeks' precarious situation.

In response to concerns over the Bulgarian frontier, the GHQ established the Epirus Army Section (TSI) under Lieutenant-General Markos Drakos, comprising I and II Corps. Despite successes in Albania, internal disagreements among the Greek leadership over strategy regarding the anticipated German attack and the need for withdrawal in Albania led to a major reshuffling of commanders in early March. Papagos replaced the commanders of TSI, I and II Corps, and TSDM, appointing Lieutenant-General Pitsikas, Lieutenant-General Demestichas, and Major-General Georgios Bakos, respectively, with Tsolakoglou taking over TSDM.

On March 4th, 1941, the British initiated Operation Lustre, dispatching the first convoy with W Force (under Lieutenant-General Sir Henry Maitland Wilson) and essential supplies to aid Greece. Anticipating German intervention, the Italian leadership sought a significant victory against the Greek army and bolstered their forces in Albania to 28 divisions, supported by an average of 26 serviceable bombers, 150 fighters, and additional air units from Italy.

General Cavallero planned a concentrated attack on a 32 km stretch of the central front, aiming to recapture Klisura and advance towards Leskovik and Ioannina. The offensive was to be led by the VIII Army Corps, supported by the XXV Corps as a second echelon, and with the Centauro and Piemonte divisions as general reserves. The opposing Greek II Corps comprised several divisions, with additional regiments as TSI's general reserve, and the 4th Division for reinforcement. Greek II Corps continued limited offensives until March 8th to consolidate their positions.

The Italian attack, observed by Mussolini, commenced on March 9th with intense artillery and air bombardment. Despite the onslaught, the Greek 1st Division held its ground on March 9th-10th. An Italian flanking attempt on March 11th was repelled, leading to the withdrawal of the Puglie Division, replaced by the Bari Division. However, all Italian assaults up to March 15th were unsuccessful.

After a brief pause, allowing the Greeks to reinforce and reorganize their lines, the Italian offensive resumed on March 19th, focusing on Height 731. Despite daily attacks and artillery barrages until March 24th, the offensive yielded no significant results. Mussolini conceded that the offensive had failed to achieve its objectives. The Italian forces incurred over 11,800 casualties, while Greek losses amounted to 1,243 killed, 4,016 wounded, and 42 missing.

The Italian spring offensive exposed a critical shortage of arms and equipment in the Greek Army. Despite British support, Greece was nearing the end of its logistical capacity. British intelligence estimated that Greek reserves, though substantial in numbers, couldn't be mobilized due to a lack of arms and equipment. By the end of March, the Greek Army had about a month's supply of various artillery ammunition, despite recent British supplies.

In contrast, the Italians maintained reserves of men and material. The Greek defenses in Macedonia and Thrace, crucial against a potential German advance, were undermanned and underequipped due to the focus on the Albanian front. TSAM, responsible for the Metaxas Line, was particularly underpowered, while TSKM, guarding the Yugoslav border, was significantly weaker, lacking in anti-air and anti-tank weaponry, armored vehicles, and basic supplies.

By late March, 14 out of 20 Greek divisions were engaged on the Albanian front, totaling 33 regiments. Despite increased British aid in March and April, the Greek military considered it insufficient for a successful continuation of the war.

While the Greek forces faced logistical challenges, their supply lines functioned more effectively than the Italians', who struggled with inadequate logistics and supply issues. Italian General Gabriele Nasci acknowledged the Greeks' superior familiarity with mountain warfare and their ability to employ local resources and guides.

At the end of March, Italian General Mario Roatta requested German intervention to alleviate pressure on Italian formations. Prior to the German intervention in April, Greek, British, and Yugoslav officers considered a joint operation to push the Italians back to the Adriatic. General Papagos directed the Epirus Army to advance towards Vlore and Berat, while the West Macedonia Army would cut off Italian units in Elbasan and Durrës. Papagos also advised the Yugoslavs to advance towards Durrës, Kukes, and Elbasan, aiming to quickly defeat the Italians and free up forces to defend Macedonia against the looming German threat.

As the Greek army was heavily engaged on the Albanian border, Germany launched Operation Marita through Bulgaria on April 6th, opening a second front against Greece. The Greek forces, having received only a modest reinforcement from British troops based in Egypt, were significantly outnumbered and unprepared for the German onslaught. The Bulgarian defensive line, lacking adequate reinforcements, was swiftly overrun by the advancing German forces.

The German strategy effectively outflanked the static Greek units on the Albanian border. This maneuver led to the rapid surrender of the Eastern Macedonia Field Army section within just four days. Concurrently, British Empire forces commenced a strategic withdrawal. Despite temporary resistance at Thermopylae, which allowed for the preparation of evacuation ships, the Allied position quickly deteriorated. By April 27th, the Germans had captured Athens, and by April 30th, they had reached the southern coast, resulting in the capture of approximately 7,000 British troops. The conquest of Greece was finalized with the capture of Crete about a month later, leading to the occupation of Greece by German, Italian, and Bulgarian forces until late 1944.

On the Albanian front, General Papagos ordered the TSDM to initiate an attack towards Elbasan on April 6th, coordinating with Yugoslav forces. The operation commenced on April 7th, with some progress made by the 13th Division. However, the rapid collapse of the Yugoslav army under German attack led to the cancellation of this joint operation.

By April 12th, the Greek GHQ in Athens ordered a retreat from the Albanian front, but the decision came too late. The Greek commanders were aware that the retreat would likely lead to disintegration due to Italian pressure, logistical challenges, and the physical exhaustion of the Greek army. Requests to retreat before the German attack had been previously ignored. As the morale of the Greek troops, who had been fighting continuously for five months, deteriorated rapidly, units began to disband by April 15th.

General Pitsikas, recognizing signs of disintegration within I Corps, implored Papagos to allow the Greek army to surrender to the Germans to avoid complete collapse. On April 17th, TSDM was reorganized as III Army Corps under Pitsikas's command. Pressure mounted from the corps commanders and the metropolitan bishop of Ioannina, Spyridon, for Pitsikas to initiate surrender negotiations with the Germans. When he refused, General Tsolakoglou was chosen to negotiate. After a few days' delay and a misleading message from his chief of staff implying Papagos's permission, Tsolakoglou reached out to SS Obergruppenführer Sepp Dietrich, commander of the Leibstandarte SS Adolf Hitler brigade. The surrender protocol was signed by Tsolakoglou and Dietrich on April 20th. Presented with this fait accompli, Pitsikas resigned his command, marking the end of Greek resistance on the Albanian front.

Attack on the Convoy BN7

The 'Attack on the BN.7 Convoy', a crucial event in maritime history, unfolded as a gripping naval encounter in the Red Sea. This engagement, occurring on the nights of October 20th and 21st, 1940, involved a dramatic confrontation between an assertive Italian destroyer fleet and a resolute British-led alliance safeguarding the BN.7 convoy. This convoy comprised a remarkable aggregation of 32 merchant vessels, each brimming with vital supplies and personnel.

In this high-stakes clash, the Italian offensive, though ambitious, ultimately faltered. The attack's limited success was evident in the minor damage inflicted on just one merchant vessel. The British response was swift and decisive. In a pulsating chase, the British destroyer Kimberley skillfully torpedoed the Italian destroyer Francesco Nullo. The Francesco Nullo, severely crippled, met its fate on the shores of Harmil Island, off the coast of Massawa in Eritrea. However, the battle was not without its challenges for the British; the Kimberley, having engaged courageously, sustained significant damage from the relentless fire of an Italian shore battery situated on the same island. In a turn of fortune, it was towed to safety by the light cruiser Leander.

The tactical approach of the Italian forces was to split into two groups, aiming to maximize their chances of intercepting the British convoy. This strategy initially showed promise but ultimately led to the loss of cohesion against the British escorts. The outcome was costly for the Italians, as they lost a destroyer without achieving a significant military advantage. The British command stationed in Aden later critiqued the performance of the escorting vessels, except for Kimberley, for their apparent lack of aggression. This criticism highlighted the dilemma faced by the escorts: the need to protect the convoy versus engaging in a risky, aggressive chase through the misty, night-time conditions of the Red Sea.

The Italian naval forces, undeterred by this setback, continued their operations in the region. Another attempt to disrupt the Allied convoy system was made on December 3rd, although it proved unproductive. A planned sortie in January 1941 was aborted after the destroyer Daniele Manin suffered bomb damage, and a subsequent attempt on January 24th also failed to yield results.

The Red Sea, the backdrop for this naval drama, is an environment characterized by extreme temperatures and high humidity. Its shores present a diverse landscape, ranging from barren deserts to towering mountain ranges. Navigational challenges are rife in these waters, exacerbated by the presence of offshore reefs and the deceptive optical phenomena of atmospheric refraction.

This naval engagement was set against a larger strategic canvas. In May and early June of 1939, French and British military officials convened in Aden to formulate a joint strategy aimed at maintaining control over the waters surrounding Italian East Africa, anticipating Italy's entry into the war. They foresaw the possibility of Italy blocking access to the Mediterranean Sea, thereby forcing Allied maritime traffic to reroute via the Cape of Good Hope, the Indian Ocean, and ultimately through the Red Sea. The strategic importance of controlling the Gulf of Aden, the Red Sea, and the Gulf of Suez at its northern end was paramount. The preservation of the bases at Aden and Djibouti was crucial, although the prospect of withdrawing from French and British Somaliland was also considered under these complex geopolitical circumstances.

Situated strategically on the western shores of the Red Sea, the British-controlled Port Sudan was a vital maritime hub, positioned approximately 690 miles between the historical Suez in the north and the strategically significant Strait of Bab el Mandeb in the south. This port played a pivotal role in the complex geopolitical and military tapestry of the region. To the north, about 400 miles away, lay the Italian port of Massawa in Eritrea, a key location in the Axis powers' naval strategy. Further east, just 115 miles from the Strait of Bab el Mandeb, was Aden, a crucial point in the Allied maritime operations.

In this region, marked by its strategic importance and volatile political landscape, the Allies devised a meticulous plan, codenamed 'Begum', aiming to enforce a stringent blockade along the coast of Italian Somaliland and the entrance to the Red Sea. The primary objective was to choke off any reinforcements and supplies reaching the Italian forces, effectively crippling their operational capabilities. To safeguard the critical Allied merchant ships traversing the Indian Ocean and the Red Sea, the strategy necessitated the formation of escorted convoys, a move designed to provide maximum protection against enemy threats.

The Royal Navy, recognizing the gravity of the situation, established a formidable presence in the area. In April 1940, they set up the Red Sea Force under the experienced and astute leadership of Rear Admiral A. J. L. Murray. This force initially included the light cruisers Liverpool, Australian Hobart, and New Zealand Leander. By September, the Red Sea Force had expanded significantly, comprising an impressive array of naval assets including light cruisers Hobart, Leander, and Caledon, the anti-aircraft cruiser Carlisle, and a fleet of destroyers and sloops. Aden, serving as the operational base, was equipped with minesweepers, armed merchant cruisers, and trawlers, forming a formidable defensive line.

On the other side of the conflict, the Italian naval and air bases in East Africa, notably Massawa, were strategically located for launching attacks on shipping in the Red Sea and the Indian Ocean. Massawa, the homeport of the Italian Flottiglia del mar rosso, was a fortified naval stronghold, protected by numerous islands, reefs, and mined waters. The Italian naval fleet, including the scout cruisers Pantera and Leon, boasted a formidable armament. These ships, equipped with a unique eight-gun broadside, anti-aircraft guns, torpedo tubes, and mines, represented a significant threat to Allied maritime operations. The 'Sauro' class destroyers further augmented the Italian naval strength with their comprehensive armament.

However, the effectiveness of the Italian Flottiglia del mar rosso was increasingly hampered by the British blockade. The blockade led to a gradual depletion of fuel reserves and exacerbated the mechanical wear of the Italian ships.

The Italian naval base at Massawa became a focal point of submarine and aerial operations in the Red Sea. June 1940 marked a period of intense activity and significant losses for the Italian forces. Four of the eight submarines stationed at Massawa were lost in quick succession, signaling a turbulent start to Italy's maritime campaign. However, undeterred, the Regia Aeronautica initiated its operations over the Red Sea. On June 11th, a daring sortie by a Savoia-Marchetti SM.81, a robust three-engined warplane, marked the beginning of Italian aerial reconnaissance in the region.

The Italian submarine Galileo Galilei demonstrated its prowess on June 16th by sinking the Norwegian tanker James Stove, a massive vessel of 8,215 tons, near Aden. This operation, executed with precision, showcased the latent threat posed by the Italian submarines. However, the Allies were quick to respond. On June 19th, the Australian cruiser Hobart launched a daring mission. Its Supermarine Walrus, a single-engined biplane amphibian, embarked on a bombing raid targeting an Italian wireless station on Centre Peak island, signaling the Allies' resolve to counter Italian advancements.

July saw further Italian naval operations with mixed results. The BN.1

convoy, comprising six tankers and three freighters, mustered in the Gulf of Aden on July 2nd. The Italian response involved several submarines and destroyers, including Guglielmotti, Galileo Ferraris, Francesco Nullo, and the destroyers Pantera and Tigre. Despite numerous sorties and reconnaissance efforts, these missions largely failed to locate their targets, highlighting the challenges faced by the Italian navy in these vast waters.

The air war over the Red Sea intensified in September. On the 4th, Italian bombers inflicted severe damage on the merchant vessel Velko. The following day, a squadron of Savoia-Marchetti SM.79 bombers launched an assault on the BS.3A convoy. A Bristol Blenheim IVF, a twin-engined fighter, engaged the bombers but sustained damage in the skirmish. The Italian aerial aggression continued, with repeated attacks on Allied convoys, including the BN.4 and BN.5. Despite these efforts, the Italians often failed to secure decisive victories, partly due to the effective Allied air and naval defenses.

One notable success for the Italians was the torpedoing of the Greek tanker Atlas by the submarine Guglielmotti. This attack demonstrated the persistent threat posed by Italian submarines in the region. However, the Italian air force faced increasing challenges as Allied fighter planes, including Gloster Gladiators and Blenheims, began to effectively counter their bombing runs. These engagements over the Red Sea showcased a dynamic and relentless air battle, with both sides adapting tactics and countering each other's moves.

As the Italian efforts continued, individual bombing runs by SM.79 bombers targeted the BN.7 convoy later in October. These attacks, though persistent, were increasingly met with stiff resistance from Allied fighters, signifying the escalating air war over the Red Sea.

The BN.7 convoy, a grand assemblage of maritime commerce, voyaged northward through the strategically vital waters of the Red Sea. This convoy was a microcosm of international cooperation, comprising 32 merchant ships from the United Kingdom, Norway, France, Greece, and Turkey. The responsibility of escorting this vital fleet fell to a formidable team led by Commander J. Riovett-Carnac aboard the light cruiser Leander. This protective detail also included Commander J. S. M. Richardson's destroyer Kimberley, the 'Egret' class sloop Auckland, the 'Grimsby' class sloops Yarra and Indus, and the 'Hunt' class minesweepers Derby and Huntley. Together, they formed a shield of steel and resolve, safeguarding the precious cargo and lives entrusted to their care.

On the afternoon of October 19th, as the convoy was drawing near Perim, a volcanic island situated off the southwestern coast of Yemen in the Strait of Bab el Mandeb, tension suddenly escalated. An enemy aircraft, like a hawk eyeing its prey, swooped down and released four bombs in a menacing arc behind one of the merchant ships. The Leander and Auckland, vigilant and ready, responded with a barrage of anti-aircraft fire as the plane retreated to the west. Adding to the day's drama, a landing gear wheel from an Italian aircraft was later retrieved 17 miles south of the island, a stark reminder of the ever-present danger lurking in the skies.

The following morning, Italian aircraft returned to haunt the convoy, dropping four bombs in a strategic pattern around the French liner Félix Roussel, which was valiantly transporting New Zealand troops to Suez. Two bombs plunged ahead of the convoy, and two fell harmlessly behind the Félix Roussel. As dusk settled on the Red Sea, the Leander strategically positioned itself on the port beam of the convoy, guarding against any threats from the nearby Italian base at Massawa. The night was filled with tension as the convoy executed a series of zigzag maneuvers, a dance of survival on the high seas.

The Italian response was swift and calculated. On October 20th, their flotilla, comprising destroyers operating in coordinated pairs, set sail. Sezione I included the fast and agile Sauro, commanded by Capitani di Fregata Moretti degli Adimari, and the Francesco Nullo under Capitano di Corvetta Costantino Borsini. Sezione II was made up of the heavily armed yet slower Pantera and

Leone, tasked with diverting the convoy's escort before launching a torpedo attack. At 21:15, the two sections split, and by 23:21, Pantera had spotted the convoy's distant smoke. Moving to intercept with Leone trailing, they prepared for engagement.

At 02:19 on October 21st, approximately 40 miles north-north-west of Jabal al Tair island, the Leander identified two ominous plumes of smoke to the north. The Auckland, vigilant and alert, reported sighting two destroyers at a distance of 4.6 miles. The Leander, with tactical acumen, altered course to intercept, assuming the Italian ships would attempt an escape through the South Massawa Channel. The confrontation escalated when Pantera opened fire over the Yarra at the convoy, causing splinter damage to a lifeboat on the convoy commodore's ship. The Auckland immediately retaliated, forcing the Italian destroyers to separate and retreat at full speed towards Massawa, while continuing to fire their aft guns. In a dramatic turn, Pantera launched a series of torpedoes at 23:31 and 23:34. The Yarra, demonstrating remarkable agility, narrowly avoided the torpedoes by executing a swift turn towards them, combing their tracks. Observers aboard the Yarra believed that their fourth or fifth salvo had struck the leading Italian vessel.

In the tense and dark hours of October 21st, amidst the vast, unforgiving waters of the Red Sea, a dramatic and strategic naval dance unfolded. The Italian destroyers Sauro and Nullo, having received the report of the convoy's sighting from Pantera, maneuvered into a more advantageous position to launch their attack. At 01:48, Sauro, seizing an opportune moment, launched a torpedo at the light cruiser Leander, only to miss its target. Leander, quick to respond, unleashed a barrage of gunfire, but the elusive Sauro vanished into the night after a brief two-minute encounter. Sauro attempted another torpedo strike at 02:07, subsequently retreating towards Massawa.

Meanwhile, Nullo found itself in a precarious situation when its rudder jammed, causing the vessel to circle uncontrollably and lose contact with Sauro. The situation for Nullo was dire, and its commander, Borsini, made the decision to head towards the Italian batteries on Harmil Island off Massawa for assistance. Leander, ever vigilant, altered its course to the northwest to intercept enemy ships in the South Massawa Channel. In a dramatic turn, Leander engaged a ship firing red and green tracer with its formidable 6-inch guns, but the quarry soon disappeared into the increasing range and darkness.

Leander, determined to bring its full firepower to bear, altered its course westward towards the South Massawa Channel. In a remarkable stroke of naval warfare, Leander's searchlights caught Nullo in their glare at 02:20. A fierce exchange of fire ensued for about 10 minutes at a range of approximately 4,600 yards. Leander's salvoes inflicted significant damage on Nullo, disabling its gyrocompass and gunnery director. However, Nullo faded into the haze, and Leander ceased fire after expending 129 rounds of 6-inch ammunition. Nullo limped toward Harmil Island, with Leander in pursuit. In a twist of fate, Leander encountered Kimberley, another of its own, in pursuit of the same target. Leander then altered its course eastward to rejoin the convoy, leaving Kimberley to continue the chase.

Kimberley, pushing her engines to the limit, sighted smoke ahead at 03:50, signaling the presence of enemy ships. At 05:40, off Harmil Island, Kimberley and Nullo spotted each other. Borsini, mistaking Kimberley for Sauro, was taken by surprise when Kimberley opened fire at 05:53. Nullo, caught off guard, delayed its response by four minutes. Kimberley closed in, reducing the distance to 5,000 yards. Nullo, already wounded, struck a reef at 06:20, causing further damage and leaks. As Nullo rounded Harmil Island, it suffered critical hits to its engine rooms, resulting in a total loss of power. Borsini gave the order to abandon ship, attempting to run Nullo aground. Tragically, the ship was struck by a second torpedo at 06:35 and broke in two, with Borsini and his assistant remaining on board, meeting their end with the ship.

At 06:15, Harmil Island's shore batteries engaged Kimberley, causing damage and injuries. Kimberley, although adrift, managed to silence two of the guns and wound several gunners. Eventually, Kimberley regained movement, albeit at a reduced speed, and escaped further shelling. Leander, having left the convoy, increased its speed to assist Kimberley. By 08:25, Leander was near Kimberley, maintaining a vigilant stance against possible air attacks. Kimberley, having lost water in her boilers, received assistance from Leander. The wounded were transferred, and Kimberley was taken in tow by Leander around 10:00.

August marked a significant period in the British naval operations during World War II, as they successfully orchestrated the movement of four convoys under the BN series and four of the reciprocal BS convoys. The efforts were amplified in the following months, with five convoys in September and seven in October. The northbound BN convoys were a testament to the Allies' maritime logistics, involving 86 ships, while the southbound BS convoys comprised 72 ships. These efforts were crucial in maintaining the supply chain for the Allied forces.

Despite the meticulous planning by the Regia Aeronautica and the Italian naval forces, which included diligent agent reports and aerial surveillance, their attempts to disrupt these convoys met with limited success. Italian submarines and ships often struggled to locate their targets. In October, the Italians could only muster six air attacks on these convoys, and after November 4th, such attacks ceased entirely. This lack of effective engagement reflected the challenges faced by the Axis powers in countering the well-organized Allied convoy system.

During the renowned 'Attack on the BN.7 Convoy', the British forces encountered their own challenges, particularly in night combat. The flash from their own guns momentarily blinded them, providing a tactical disadvantage, in stark contrast to the Italian ships which utilized flashless cordite and had superior tracer ammunition. Despite this, the British convoy escorts, except for Kimberley, faced criticism for what was perceived as a lack of aggression.

However, this cautious approach was largely due to the inherent risks of leaving the convoy unprotected at night and under poor visibility conditions. The Italian navy, for their part, managed to execute two torpedo attacks as per their plan. However, the decision to divide their destroyers into two sections reduced their combined firepower, ultimately diminishing their effectiveness against the robust British escorts.

The aftermath of these encounters was poignant, particularly for the Italian destroyer Nullo. Of its 120-man crew, the ship's commander, Borsini, and a dedicated seaman named Vincenzo Ciaravolo, chose to stay aboard the sinking ship, leading to their tragic deaths. Remarkably, 106 crew members were rescued by sailors from the Harmil island battery. Kimberley, having played a significant role in these operations, was temporarily sidelined for repairs until the end of October and could only return to service at reduced speed until fully repaired in the spring of 1941.

Following these events, Leander continued to demonstrate its resilience and firepower. On October 21st, it engaged three aircraft, managing to repel their bombing attempt with no damage sustained. Leander and Kimberley were able to rejoin the BN.7 convoy shortly after noon. In a strategic move, Leander transferred the tow of Kimberley to Kingston, which then proceeded to Port Sudan with Kimberley the following morning. Meanwhile, the southbound BS.7 convoy, comprising 20 ships, experienced an uneventful passage and dispersed safely east of Aden on October 28th.

In a continued effort to disrupt Allied shipping, the Italian navy launched another sortie on December 3rd, which proved unfruitful. A planned sortie in January 1941 was canceled due to damage sustained by the destroyer Daniele Manin, and a subsequent sortie on January 24th also ended without success.

The night of February 2nd to 3rd, 1941, saw a renewed attempt by the Italian destroyers Pantera, Tigre, and Sauro to intercept the BN.14 convoy, which consisted of 39 merchant vessels under the protection of the cruiser Caledon, the destroyer Kingston, and the sloops Indus and Shoreham. Sauro engaged first, firing torpedoes and attempting a secondary attack before retreating. Pantera also engaged, reporting probable hits on two merchant ships, though these claims were later found to be mistaken. Tigre, however, failed to locate the convoy. Near Massawa in the South Channel, Sauro had a brief encounter with Kingston but had exhausted its torpedoes. Fearing a British ambush, the Italian ships regrouped and called for air support, managing to return to port unharmed. Local Italian press reports initially claimed success, but these were later corrected, underscoring the challenges and complexities of naval warfare in this crucial maritime theater.

Japanese Invasion of French Indochina

The intricate geopolitical landscape of the early 1940s was marked by Japan's ambitious visions, particularly their concept of the Greater East Asia Co-Prosperity Sphere. This grandiose plan envisioned an expansive coalition of Asian nations under Japanese influence, designed to counter Western imperialism. The ultimate goal was a self-sufficient bloc, free from Western dominance, where Asian countries could freely trade and share resources. This vision was not merely ideological; it had significant strategic and military implications, especially in the context of World War II.

In 1940, the Imperial Japanese Army (IJA) initiated decisive movements to expand their influence. They strategically seized southern Guangxi and Longzhou County, focusing on the critical region where the eastern branch of the Kunming–Hai Phong Railway met the border at the Friendship Pass in Pingxiang. This railway was crucial as it represented the Chinese government's last secure overland connection to the wider world, a lifeline in the face of increasing hostilities.

The global context of these events is crucial. On 10 May 1940, a significant turning point in the European theatre of World War II occurred when Germany launched an invasion of France. This offensive culminated in the French signing an armistice with Germany on 22 June, which came into effect three days later. In a swift and dramatic political shift, on 10 July, the French parliament granted full powers to Marshal Philippe Pétain, heralding the end of the Third Republic. Although the German forces occupied much of metropolitan France, the French colonies remained under the control of Pétain's Vichy government. However, opposition to this regime began to coalesce rapidly, notably with Charles de Gaulle's impassioned appeal on 18 June, which laid the groundwork for the formation of the Free France government-in-exile in London, a significant force of resistance against the Vichy regime and its policies.

The Japanese, astutely recognizing the vulnerability of France following its defeat and the looming armistice, initiated a bold and strategic move against Indochina. On 19 June, they presented an ultimatum, disguised as a request, to Governor-General Georges Catroux. This ultimatum demanded the closure of all supply routes to China and permitted the entry of a 40-man Japanese inspection team, led by General Issaku Nishihara. The Americans, privy to the true intentions behind this move through intelligence intercepts and aware of Japan's communication with their German allies, watched these developments closely.

Catroux, confronted with this Japanese demand, initially resisted, citing concerns of sovereignty infringement. His reluctance was palpable, yet the mounting pressure from Japanese military maneuvers left little room for defiance. French intelligence reported threatening positions taken by Japanese army and navy units, signaling a potential conflict for which the French government was ill-prepared. Reluctantly, on 20 June, Catroux acquiesced to the Japanese demands. This submission led to the last munitions-laden train crossing the border towards Kunming before the end of June, marking a significant moment of humiliation for the French colonial administration. Consequently, Catroux was swiftly replaced by Admiral Jean Decoux, who chose not to return to France but instead headed to London.

Meanwhile, on 22 June, even as Catroux grappled with the aftermath of his decisions, the Japanese issued a second, more aggressive demand. This time, they sought naval basing rights at Guangzhouwan and demanded the complete closure of the Chinese border by 7 July. The arrival of Issaku

Nishihara in Hanoi on 29 June further intensified the situation. By 3 July, Nishihara had escalated Japan's demands, now including air bases and the right for Japanese combat troops to transit through Indochina. These new demands were promptly relayed to the French government, underscoring the rapidly escalating stakes.

The situation took a new turn with the arrival of the new governor, Decoux, in July. Despite recognizing Indochina's vulnerability to a Japanese invasion, Decoux advised the French government to reject Japan's demands. He believed that Indochina, while unable to defend itself fully, had sufficient strength to deter a Japanese invasion. His views found support in Vichy, where General Jules-Antoine Bührer, chief of the Colonial General Staff, also advocated for resistance. The United States, still neutral at this point, had committed to providing aircraft, and there were additional resources available, such as the 4,000 Tirailleurs sénégalais stationed in Djibouti, ready to be deployed if necessary. Decoux, commanding a force of 32,000 regulars and 17,000 auxiliaries in Indochina, albeit poorly equipped.

On 30 August, a critical moment emerged as Japanese Foreign Minister Yōsuke Matsuoka and his French counterpart, Paul Baudouin, converged on a draft proposal. This agreement allowed for the temporary stationing and transit of Japanese forces in Indochina, strictly during the Sino-Japanese War. However, the advice to prolong negotiations via Tokyo-Vichy channels went unheeded, leading to direct discussions in Indochina. Thus, on 3 September, negotiations began in Hanoi between Maurice Martin, the supreme commander of Indochinese troops, and General Nishihara, representing Japan.

Amidst these tense negotiations, the French government, desperate to moderate Japan's escalating demands, sought intervention from Germany, its occupier and Japan's ally. However, the Germans remained unresponsive. Governors Decoux and Martin, feeling isolated, turned to the American and British consuls in Hanoi for support. They even reached out to the Chinese government, contemplating a joint defense against a potential Japanese invasion of Indochina.

The situation escalated on 6 September when the Japanese Twenty-Second Army, stationed in Nanning, breached the Indochinese border near the French fort at Đồng Đăng. This bold move, reminiscent of the aggressive tactics seen in the 1931 Mukden Incident, was a clear attempt by Japanese officers to push for a more assertive policy in Southern China. In response, Decoux halted negotiations. But on 18 September, the tension peaked as Nishihara issued a stern ultimatum to Decoux: Japanese troops would enter Indochina by 22:00 on 22 September, with or without French consent.

This ultimatum forced Decoux's hand. He negotiated fervently to reduce the proposed number of Japanese troops from 25,000 to 6,000, a significant concession facilitated by Nishihara's support from the Imperial General Headquarters. This negotiation was finalized mere hours before the ultimatum's deadline, on 22 September. The agreement authorized the stationing of 6,000 Japanese troops north of the Red River in Tonkin, usage of four airfields in Tonkin, and allowed for the transit of up to 25,000 troops to Yunnan and the movement of a division through Tonkin via Haiphong for operations in China.

Parallel to these diplomatic maneuvers, the Japanese military was already making assertive moves. By 5 September, the Japanese Southern Army had organized the Indochina Expeditionary Army under Major-General Takuma Nishimura. This formidable force, backed by a fleet of ships and both carrier- and land-based aircraft, lay in wait off Hainan Island. As soon as the agreement was inked, a convoy was poised to transport this expeditionary force to Tonkin.

The accord, carefully negotiated to prevent further escalation, was communicated to all relevant commands by 21:00 on 21 September, just an hour before the expiration of the Japanese ultimatum. The agreement had stipulated that Japanese troops would arrive by ship, but the Twenty-Second Army, under the leadership of Lieutenant-General Aketo Nakamura, had other plans. Demonstrating a bold disregard for protocol, Nakamura ordered his 5th Infantry Division to cross the border near Đồng Đăng at exactly 22:00, seizing the initiative.

This incursion led to a tense exchange of fire at Đồng Đăng, which rapidly escalated to other border posts. The Battle of Lạng Sơn ensued, where the French forces, stationed at the railhead, found themselves surrounded by Japanese armor. By 25 September, they were compelled to surrender. In a desperate act to prevent their 155mm cannons from falling into Japanese hands, the French commanders threw the breechblocks into a river. This act mirrored a similar scenario from the Sino-French War of 1884–1885, where equipment was discarded to prevent enemy capture. Interestingly, when the breechblocks from 1940 were retrieved, they also unearthed several chests of money lost over half a century earlier. Among the captives at Lạng Sơn was the 2nd Battalion of the 5th Foreign Infantry Regiment, which notably included 179 German and Austrian volunteers. The Japanese unsuccessfully attempted to persuade these prisoners to switch allegiances.

The French government, outraged by this blatant breach of the recent agreements, lodged a formal protest against the Japanese actions on 23 September. However, the situation continued to escalate. On the morning of 24 September, Japanese aircraft, launched from carriers in the Gulf of Tonkin, commenced aerial assaults on French coastal positions. Amidst these attacks, a French envoy was dispatched for negotiations, but French coastal defenses remained on high alert, ready to engage any Japanese landing attempts.

By 26 September, Japanese military momentum was in full swing. Troops landed at Dong Tac, south of Haiphong, and advanced towards the port. This operation was bolstered by a second landing that brought tanks ashore and additional aerial bombings of Haiphong, inflicting casualties and chaos. By early afternoon, a formidable Japanese force of approximately 4,500 troops and a dozen tanks had positioned themselves just outside Haiphong.

As the day turned into evening, the intensity of the fighting began to wane. Japan had successfully established control over strategic locations: Gia Lam Airbase outside Hanoi, the rail marshaling yard at Lao Cai on the Yunnan border, and Phu Lang Thuong along the railway from Hanoi to Lạng Sơn. Additionally, Japanese troops were strategically stationed in the port of Haiphong and in Hanoi, marking a significant expansion of their influence and control in the region.

On 5 October 1940, in a rare act of diplomatic contrition during wartime, the Japanese government issued an official apology for the incident at Lạng Sơn. Subsequently, the towns occupied by Japanese forces were handed back to French control, and all French prisoners were released, marking a brief period of reconciliation and the restoration of the status quo.

However, the broader strategic landscape was far from stable. The full–scale occupation of southern French Indochina by Japanese forces was a calculated move that unfolded over time. On 9 December 1940, a pivotal agreement was reached. This accord reaffirmed French sovereignty over its military and administrative affairs, while simultaneously granting Japanese forces the liberty to utilize Indochinese soil for their war efforts against the Allies. The Vichy government acquiesced to the stationing of around 40,000 Japanese troops. Despite this agreement, Japanese planners hesitated to deploy these troops immediately, cautious of exacerbating tensions with key Western powers, particularly the United Kingdom and the United States.

Amidst these geopolitical calculations, internal debates raged within the Japanese high command, particularly regarding the looming Soviet threat to their northern territories in Manchuria. The landscape shifted dramatically following the German invasion of the Soviet Union in late June 1941. With the Soviet forces preoccupied, the Japanese high command opted for a southern expansion strategy. This approach aimed to address Japan's growing concerns about American disapproval of their actions in China and the looming threat of an oil embargo. In preparation for a potential invasion of the Dutch East Indies, a substantial force of some 140,000 Japanese troops invaded southern French Indochina on 28 July 1941. While the French military and administrative structures were allowed to remain, they now operated under the watchful eye of Japanese supervision.

The Vietnamese perspective on these events was multifaceted and complex. The Japanese occupation stirred a sense of rebellion against Western colonial powers among the Vietnamese. Japan, as an Asian power, was initially perceived as a potential liberator from European colonial rule. However, this view was tempered by the harsh realities of Japanese wartime occupation, which included severe policies contributing to the Vietnamese famine of 1945.

As World War II progressed, the geopolitical dynamics continued to evolve. With the Allied invasion of France in 1944, Japanese suspicions grew regarding the likelihood of French authorities in Indochina assisting Allied operations. In response, in the spring of 1945, Japan decisively deposed the French authorities, imprisoning administrators and assuming direct control over Indochina. This shift in power set the stage for significant political changes. When the war drew to a close, Vietnamese nationalists, rallying under the Viet Minh banner, seized the opportunity presented by the power vacuum. In the August Revolution, they proclaimed the independence of the Democratic Republic of Vietnam. The Japanese occupation, with its complex legacies, played a critical role in strengthening the Viet Minh movement, setting the stage for the First Indochina War in 1946, a pivotal struggle against French colonial rule and the beginning of a new chapter in Vietnam's quest for independence and self-determination.

Bibliography

Atkin, Ronald. Pillar of Fire: Dunkirk 1940. Birlinn, 1990.

Auphan, Gabriel Paul, and Jacques Mordal. The French Navy in World War II. United States Naval Institute, 1959.

Bauer, Eddy. The History of World War II. Revised ed., edited by Peter Young, Orbis, 2000.

Beevor, Antony. The Second World War. Phoenix (Orion Books), 2013.

Belgian American Educational Foundation. The Belgian Campaign and the Surrender of the Belgian Army, 10–28 May 1940. 3rd ed., University of Michigan, 1941.

Bishop, Edward. Their Finest Hour: The Story of the Battle of Britain, 1940. Ballantine Books, 1968.

Bond, Brian. Britain, France, and Belgium, 1939–1940. Brassey's (UK) Riverside, N.J, 1990.

Booth, Owen. The Illustrated History of World War II. Chartwell Books, Inc., 1998.

Bragadin, Marc'Antonio. Italian Navy in World War II. 1st ed., US Naval Institute, 1957.

Carr, John C. The Defence and Fall of Greece 1940–1941. Pen and Sword, 2013.

Carswell, Richard. The Fall of France in the Second World War: History and Memory. Palgrave MacMillan, 2019.

Collier, Richard. Eagle Day: The Battle of Britain, 6 August – 15 September 1940. Pan Books, 1968.

Corum, James. The Luftwaffe: Creating the Operational Air War, 1918–1940. University Press of Kansas, 1997.

Fowler, Will. France, Holland, and Belgium 1940. Ian Allan, 2002.

Hooton, Edward R. Luftwaffe at War; Blitzkrieg in the West: Volume 2. 2007.

Jackson, Julian. The Fall of France: The Nazi Invasion of 1940. Oxford University Press, 2003.

Keegan, John. The Second World War. Penguin Books, 2005.

Mack Smith, Denis. Mussolini's Roman Empire. Longman, 1976.

Mockler, Anthony. Haile Selassie's War: The Italian-Ethiopian Campaign, 1935–1941. Random House, 1984.

O'Hara, Vincent P. Struggle for the Middle Sea: The Great Navies at War in the Mediterranean Theater, 1940–1945. 1st ed., Naval Institute Press, 2009.

Petrow, Richard. The Bitter Years; The Invasion and Occupation of Denmark and Norway, April 1940-May 1945. William Morrow & Co., 1974.

Powaski, Ronald E. Lightning War: Blitzkrieg in the West, 1940. Book Sales Inc., 2008.

Richards, Dennis. The Royal Air Force 1939–1945, Vol I: The Fight at Odds. History of the Second World War, United Kingdom Military Series. Edited by J. R. M. Butler, Her Majesty's Stationery Office, 1953.